For too long psychology studied issues independent of context, often leaving constituencies misunderstood, wrongly blamed and poorly supported. *Mea Culpa* is a brave and impressive corrective to this approach, offering new and insightful understandings of how social and religious attitudes impact every aspect of gay men's lives in Ireland. A painful yet profound contribution to the human sciences.

Martin Milton, Regents University London

In an extraordinary, moving synthesis of family trauma, clerical sex abuse, and stigmatization by the Catholic Church in Ireland, Gerard Rodgers leads readers on an emotional, sometimes tragic and sometimes hopeful journey into personal suffering to uncover the indelible imprint early experiences make on self-formation. Challenging psychiatry and psychology to heed and examine the power of social contexts over human development and embodiment, the book is a courageous exposition of how socio-historic circumstances shame and shape personal histories. Refusing to disappear with his story or to surrender it to the silence that shame so often bequeaths to those who have endured trauma, Rodgers highlights how integrating academic research with lived experience offers a pathway for self-reflection, understanding, and self-love, offering a gift of hope to readers who share his experience.

Stephanie N. Arel, Postdoctoral Fellow at the
Institute for the Bio-Cultural Study of Religion, Boston University.

D0838742

Resisting the Power of Mea Culpa

Resisting the Boers of Life

RESISTING THE POWER OF
MEA CULPA

A Story of Twentieth-Century Ireland

Gerard Rodgers

PETER LANG

Oxford • Bern • Berlin • Bruxelles • New York • Wien

Bibliographic information published by Die Deutsche Nationalbibliothek. Die Deutsche Nationalbibliothek lists this publication in the Deutsche National-bibliografie; detailed bibliographic data is available on the Internet at http://dnb.d-nb.de.

A catalogue record for this book is available from the British Library.

Library of Congress Cataloging-in-Publication Data
A CIP catalog record for this book has been applied for at the Library of Congress.

Cover image: Adam Prezewoski via Unsplash
Cover design by Brian Melville.

ISBN 978-1-78874-656-4 (print) • ISBN 978-1-78874-657-1 (ePDF)
ISBN 978-1-78874-658-8 (ePub) • ISBN 978-1-78874-659-5 (mobi)

© Peter Lang AG 2019
Published by Peter Lang Ltd, International Academic Publishers,
52 St Giles, Oxford, OX1 3LU, United Kingdom
oxford@peterlang.com, www.peterlang.com

This publication has been peer reviewed.

Printed in Germany

Resisting the Power of Mea Culpa:
A Story of Twentieth-Century Ireland

Dedication

Paul, thank you for your love and support throughout this whole process. You inspired and supported me every step of the way.

I also dedicate my second book to the remarkable strength of my recently deceased mother Anne Rodgers (1932–2014) and my older brother Eamonn (1958–2017).

Thank you to my close friends and the many others who have inspired, challenged and changed my thinking in significant ways. And to my eldest living sister Yvonne Kavanagh in Pittsburg, Kansas.

Contents

Foreword

For too long academia has studied issues independent of physical, discursive and historical context. While there may have been (and on occasion still are) advantages to such a narrow focus, this often leaves constituencies misunderstood, wrongly blamed and poorly supported. At best we have been negligent in leaving toxic and traumatic events in the shadows, at worst our facilitation and complicity is evident.

There is a need in the sciences, and in scholarship more generally, to recognize the multi-faceted nature of experience and the fact that, more often than not, it is only through an inter-disciplinary approach that we can gain a clearer understanding of experience. And within this, I am including the importance of exploring and learning from subjective experience. And that's not easy. There are limits to what individuals or even disciplines can think. We are hostage to history, to convention and to vested interests. And now in Ireland, where history is being relegated to a 'non-mandatory' status in curricula, we see the forgoing of learning through experience, rejecting methods of being accountable, open and transparent regarding how we have treated people and communities. This is what Rodgers rightly recognizes as 'a master-stroke of how power works, where working through the past is viewed as an ideological irritant' rather than it being a process of joining the dots to hold power to account and to learn for the wider good. Also, making reflection and learning from the past a mere option feeds the view that all we have to do is ignore trauma and it will go away without us having to feel unsettled or upsetting the status quo. But as history has shown us, this is not the way things work personally or culturally.

Rather than travelling in this direction, we need to be exploring further how we can expand our horizons rather than sitting in our silos. Psychology, psychotherapy, theology, sociology, and political science all claim, at times, to understand a phenomenon and offer ways forward, yet the reality is often that these can only be partial insights, skeleton strategies of change – especially when taking an ahistorical perspective to their disciplines.

Our systems do not like us to admit these limitations though – you might not get the grant, the book sales, or promotion if you dilute the 'brand'. For all of our talk and bluster, the human science disciplines so frequently under-deliver in terms of interdisciplinary work.

There is, of course, some diversity of literature drawn upon and produced in the human sciences. We have a spectrum with biographical and ethnographical approaches on one end and the objective analysis of 'truly' independent variables on the other. While both of these two approaches are somewhat helpful, a need for skilful integration of the objective and the subjective remains. The challenge is to move beyond this split and explore the analysis of life as it is experienced – by individuals and by communities. And limiting our work to one of the positions on the spectrum can mean it suffers. There are scholars who try to integrate these perspectives but only occasionally is it as stupendously well done, as in this book. The rigour and skill evident in these pages is reward itself for engaging with complex, powerful and dangerous factors that affect many people's lives.

It is rare that an academic, scholarly book gives the reader cold shivers and goosebumps and moves you to tears – but this book does. The account of how children were subject to institutional abuse – condoned, facilitated and overlooked by both Church and state – cannot fail to move the reader. The impact this has on siblings, parents and wider families is important to recognize too. This book doesn't just assert what we know happened (and is still happening), but helps us understand the power relationships and processes that facilitate this longstanding dynamic.

The subject material and the personal style does make this a taxing book to read (and probably to have written), but maybe that is as it should be, considering the seriousness of what needs to be confronted. To consider these experiences one is exposed to traumatic imagery and may need to read passages over and over – so as to understand the complexity, the multiple levels of involvement and implication for psychological and social health, for political and religious policy and for ways of overcoming this long-term process that has damaged so many lives. But it is important that we do.

Mea Culpa is a brave and impressive contribution to the field. It is going to help us understand gay men's experiences of life in Ireland – and those they are close to; it offers insight into the social and religious attitudes that are finally being taken seriously; and it promises to trigger widespread discussion and development. After all this is not only a story of interest to scholars and professionals, but as it is a story that seldom gets the attention it warrants, it should prove to be an important contribution to those who have been silenced for so long, providing, as it does, a powerful validation and confirmation of experience for all that have been affected.

Prof. Martin Milton
London
October 2018

Preface

If there was one principle that literally took possession of my mind in time, it was the ruminating noise of *mea culpa*. In my socio-historic environs, I was moulded and shaped by this oppressive idea. In my early life, I was directed to self-dissociate by this dominant mode of intelligibility in historic Ireland. To this day, as an adult, I often feel I have yet to transcend its power.

A way of imagining the persecutory power of an oppressive and traumatic social situation is when one thinks of people living in desperate situations, where the weighty presuppositions of social-historical environs narrow our horizons for making meaning of our own psychological experiences. For many of the souls in this book, it often felt like there was a finger pointing at us. In the public domain, when the disturbing behaviours of my deceased father were publicly exposed, the front-page of our local paper described our home as 'The House of Fear'.

As a young boy, I found myself immersed in the centre of an intense drama. In my historical household, I had this sense that I had to do magical things to transform a tsunami of hurt that had enveloped so many lives. In this repetitive trauma, I seldom trusted my own reactions to events. In my upbringing, I kept secret my shame, thinking I was to blame for the suffering I simply could not fix. In the circumstances of my young life, I was seldom at ease. I am now in my early fifties. Through my own persistence, relational love, and study, I feel I have a better grasp for how my historical consciousness was socially formed. It is not enough to say my family environs captures this dynamic. Rather, how I interpreted dysfunctional family dynamics was further informed by the way I soaked up the value orientation of the wider Irish society.

This atmosphere of pathological self-blame was not always incident related, in overt language/actions. While there were very traumatic and painful episodes, it was the imagined and real gaze of others, that gained distinct power over us, signalling social approval and/or disapproval. Such signals clearly have adaptive value for self-care and an alertness to the potential for danger. However, in my modes of self-understanding, those messages got very confused, creating a distorted mode of self-relation, where I started to doubt my value as a worthy and lovable person. At the time, I did not have a language for grasping this, other than pray that it would magically disappear. As a young boy, I did not want to be seen as a failure and wanted to be significant. I had little insight how fear and trauma had wound me up. I soaked up ideas that the noise in my head was of my own making. I felt I was the one with the problem.

For example, as a boy, the historic culture I grew up in, validated easily graspable stigma for being gay. In Ireland, tainted ideas of self-neglect and danger were prophesied as a predicted outcome for being gay. Within the preordination of this national script, I felt like a non-entity, a peripheral figure, worthy of contempt, not deserving of sustained love from others. The ideological ground I was born into was of a culture that stigmatized gay people, saying that gay people had no inalienable right to expect protection, and that gay sexual desires were highly offensive to God's law. Backed by legal laws, this pragmatic moral teaching was a dominant mode of social perception. In my young life, a shared reality was not visible. I struggled to find other gay people whom I could enjoy a shared affinity with. With the exceptions of disrespectful social inferences, an affirming gay narrative was a non-starter in routine conversations. In the rural town I grew up in, being a straight male was the acceptable and expected norm. As a young adult, moving to the City from country towns, lessened the fear of others knowing I was gay.

The historical traumas of my young life, combined with shaming social representations, back-footed me, making me feel guilt-prone for so many stressful situations outside of my control. My authentic core struggled to transcend the stressful imprint of trauma and sexual exploitations. While some recommended sympathy, I distrusted the intent of most persons. I also feared violence and intimidation. In this book study, I clearly illustrate how the foregrounded arbiters for the meaning of my sexual desires, constructed gay desire as objectively disordered development. Dire papal warnings suggested new trends in sexual liberties/freedoms were a moral sickness that threatened the moral fabric of society. Historically, the political and legal establishment reinforced religious stigma. This was how the state monopoly created modes of surveillance in Irish history, informing and shaping Irish people's attitudes and beliefs about gay people. This was the social terrain I grew up in. To limit possibilities of harm, making oneself invisible, and not drawing unnecessary attention, felt wise.

In this book, the trajectory of the narrative stories, paints a multifactorial tapestry of what twentieth-century Ireland was like, what happened, and what it is like now. I briefly describe the historical antecedents of Ireland's modern history; how the foregrounded pre-ordinances of my social terrain envelopes and captures the character of a 'my fault' ideology within Ireland's development. In the early to mid-twentieth century, as Ireland moved away from the remnants of British rule, an oppressed Roman Catholic majority was well positioned to redefine a new sense of sovereignty. This appropriation was keenly felt in all the practical domains of Irish life.

My book follows the stories of many damaged lives. I consider myself fortunate to be alive to write about these issues. I am aiming to unravel noxious social inputs, where high sounding ideological ideals were continuously reinforced in micro transactions. These contexts limited the power to act in significant ways. I describe how dominant thought-forms reached deeply rooted experiential capacities for making meaning of key experiences in time. Social messaging is so easily transferred, taking possession of our modes of self-understanding (Rochat 2014; 2013; 2009). In other words, 'The world exists in our heads every bit as much as our heads are in the world' (Chandler and Reid 2016: 295). Repetitive traumas generate a pathway of stress and fear, damaging our reflective capacities to make meaning of the external messaging system.

While I am trained in the psychological disciplines, this book positions psychology in historic/socio-political contexts. In our modern history, the overarching subcontract to Roman Catholicism is fundamental to understanding the character of Ireland. I describe a series of historic events, where the Church/state modes of thought merged as ideological fields of normative regulation. This foregrounded regulation within key spheres of Irish life became a holding container for our national/individual identity. As a historical accumulation of social capital, the power of the Church is by no means negligible in present-day Ireland.

One of the critical tasks in this book is to shine a light on how Roman Catholicism, as an applied social/pragmatic philosophy, became a visible arbiter of social norms in Irish life. From a grounded survey of our recent history, my focus will be on the macro and micro activities that enabled Roman Catholicism to become a foregrounded reference point for our cultural identity. I critique a de-politicized mode of analysis, suggesting that a transcendental impulse for interpreting this applied philosophy is socially weightless (McNay 2014). As Olson (2016) sees it 'politics precedes sovereignty, and sovereignty can only be claimed within politics' (p. 178). I examine the historical moments of commonality of religion and state, where the state largely underwrites the cross-pollination, even though religion insists that its social identity was not a 'political incarnation' (Vazquez-Arroyo 2016). However, this book argues that denying the political and social achievements of Roman Catholicism in Ireland is not a plausible position and cannot be defended. Religion's involvement in ethics is simply no accident (Kitcher 2011). In the book, I ground loss of power and vulnerability in religious ideation, an experience that imposed a restrictive and punitive scrupulosity. In my young life, I thought religious ideas would enact transcendence from pain. Religious explanations were spell-like in generating quietude, coupled with an expectation to conform to the national prescription. This creates false selves.

Religion rarely admits how its normative and dialogic ground was a significant political achievement in history. These 'good authority' arrangements in Irish history have had significant implications for the bearers of responsibility, particularly for those who found themselves in precarious situations throughout their lives. Religious belief system often added insult to injury, an oppressive messaging system, inflaming and damaging so many people's lives. Noxious atmospheres create stress, stigma, misrecognition and sometimes devastation. Thus, the book illustrates how many Irish people have been radically constrained in their capacities to make meaning of their own lives. In these situations, the bearer, as a needy or wounded subject, are impressed into thinking that they have brought misfortune onto themselves. These normative understandings of responsibility shackled so many. If one was a recipient of supports in these contexts, many were expected to be grateful, and not complain. If they protested bad treatment, they were constructed as engaging in suffer-mongering, promoting victimhood, engaging in a politics of pity. The arbiters of conduct were able to create suspicion about victims, sometimes leading to ostracism. Self-abnegation was pre-ordained with no inalienable right to challenge.

According to Medina (2017) epistemic injustice(s) can also manifest as 'the loss of one's voice, and one's status,' (p. 41) where a level of repression/oppression can 'run so deep, as to annihilate one's self.' Medina (2017) says these dynamics, 'occur when subjects are not simply mistreated as intelligible communicators, but prevented from developing and exercising a voice, that is, prevented from participating in meaning-making and meaning-sharing practices' (p. 41). In this book, when confronted with this past, esteemed players in Ireland's history are shown to minimize, efface, ignore, disbelieve, deny and even cover up this poisonous legacy. According to Honneth (1995) misrecognition can constitute a social injustice 'because the normative self-image of each and every individual being ... is dependent on the possibility of being continually backed up by others, the experience of being disrespected, carries with it the danger of an injury that can bring the identity of the person as a whole to the point of collapse' (p. 132, cited by Congdon 2017: 248). Not grasping how the mechanisms of social domination and oppression are enacted in psychology is a significant issue, contributing to loss of power, loss of agency and loss of opportunity. Renault (2017) says: 'contrary to widely held assumptions, the discourse of suffering does not lock individuals into the position of victims; rather, silence and the inability to express suffering are what condemns people to powerlessness' (p. 5).

In my younger life, it is no exaggeration to say I was heavily traumatized in these historically oppressive situations. I was told I was preordained for religious vocation. I was invited to sign up to religious life for transcending bad situations in my early life. In the culture I grew up in, I was explicitly instructed to always look inside myself, to discover the root cause of my unease. Looking inward yields little insight. I was seduced into thinking that it was a totally fruitless activity to point a finger at external authority figures, and to search for the holy inside myself to expunge interior sin. In my case, even as sexual crimes were being committed against me, I felt a subtle and overt pressure to offer it up, to turn the other cheek, as a way of transcending my unruly state of nature. Finding my right size beyond a feral state was about rigid self-discipline. I was thought to believe that noisy selfish desires exampled my own defects of character and shortcomings. Once I kept handing over my poorly trained will over to God, I would soon recognize that my self-will had edged out self-transcendence. Once I submitted to this preordination, the promise was I would attain mastery over any sinful and defective desires.

Over time, this value orientation moulded my thoughts and feelings. If I engaged in ritualized practices on a day to day basis, the promise was that I would overcome my own vices. If I was doubtful on receiving God's grace, the prophecy was that my unaccompanied will could mean my life would turn out bad. The better choice was to believe that I was handpicked from obscurity to follow God's commands by joining religious life. As mediator of God's will, I was told by my self-appointed religious confessor that my great sacrifice, in service of others, would bring great delight and joy to many. As a way of transforming bad circumstances, the De La Salle Vocations Director informed me I would be following the line of the great doctors of the Church. This recruiter in my national school informed me that the narrative of my harrowing home situation was consistent with the stories of the great saints. As a young boy, I was on fire with excitement. I felt I had a purpose and mission. I was eleven years old. I travelled to the birthplace of our local bishop's favourite saint, St Thérèse of the Little Flower, in Lisieux in France. During this period, it was consistently reinforced to me that my decision to join religious life would transcend any shattered assumptions from my unhappy home existence. Talbot (2005) says historically 'religions typically admonish their adherents to follow the directives of the relevant moral authority unquestionably, and not to exercise their own moral judgement' (p. 4). Admonishment was not a dominating feature of my religious identity but the spell of seduction was. I was being chosen by a recognized figure of God's masterplan for my future destiny.

Being moulded into religious ideation from a young age, I felt preordained to gravitate toward these sacrificial ideals, expecting resilience and warmth. I thought this was how I could build self-esteem. Once I rigorously owned up to the limitations of my unaccompanied will, admitting bad habits and temptations, my religious confessor/recruiter assured me that a divine grace would propel me towards a new dimension of existence. I would find my higher self-worth by deferring to religious ideals – surrender to win. Ego is often termed 'Edging God Out.' In Ireland, these redemptive logics from fallen states of nature, enjoy normative leverage, anchored in our history. I had to accept I was imperfect on the road to perfection. These ideals felt like law-like in my development, a constancy principle woven into the interior horizons of my being, demanding a repudiation of the self to gain mindful insights about the world.

In the book, I describe how the self, moulded by these preordained values became the fuel for intended suicide. In Irish history, the devastating impact on many people's lives is undeniable from the legitimated cross-pollination of religion with politics, law, education, media, mental health/social care. Poorer people have been significantly damaged by this distorting legacy in the historic imaginary. Psychological disciplines also increase distrust. It is not negligible to say that there is a social perception that existing psychological theory adds to stigma. Rather than disentangle structural stigma/oppression on modes of consciousness, psychological understandings remain weightless in their ways of conceptualizing and formulating human experience. The book is aiming to effect change by making intelligible how immersion in persecutory and oppressive contexts distorts meaningful modes of self-understanding. In working through the past, I aim to illuminate how citizens can struggle in the pursuance of a stronger sense of self-confidence, self-esteem and self-worth. I am critical of weightless and lofty explanations which simply do not transform social discontent into lasting social change. As a disclaimer to the content of this book, I would lean toward the hypotheses that historical and political contexts do matter in the development of human potential. My book takes the position that structural contexts (e.g. the social contract) and intersubjective modes of dependency and interdependency (reliable relationships) are critical for human wellbeing and flourishing.

For the lives portrayed in this book, I am aiming to go the distance in providing better insight into regional histories on evolving/deceased lives. As a work of social criticism, truncated ways of knowing are criticized which fail to compellingly unpack and disentangle instances of social injustice. This should be of concern, when citizens end up diminished, when some of our citizens can be oblivious to the ways social tariffs produce cognitive atrophy and alienation. Noxious social determinants which inflame modes of consciousness not only give rise to crude measures of health inequity, but also create modes of apathy and being stuck. This book is primarily focused on poorly grasped socio-historic traumas and adversities, sediments of which can still percolate in the porous membrane of present-day memories. Renault (2017) says, 'Social Suffering is, to be sure, not the only social problem in which concrete citizenship can be anchored, but to give up criticism of social suffering would mean depriving ourselves of an indispensable vehicle for making forms of politicization more concrete' (p. 202). As Bernstein (2015) argues in *Torture and Dignity: An Essay on Moral Injury*, 'Morals, emerge from the experience of moral injury, from the sufferings of the victims of moral harm' (p. 1).

I hope the stories of the ordinary lives will be informative for what can stretch our limits. Abstract conceptions of justice tend to take a bird's eye view of multi-layered contexts, a lofty position that is decoupled from a more concrete analysis of society (Honneth 2014). We lack credibility when we fail to grasp social harms. Powerful ideologies woven by certain ways of knowing create distrust. Adorno says such resistance may be 'the mere assertion of a mind that is incapable of looking horror in the face, and thereby perpetuates it' (cited by Allen 2016: 162). In the main, I unpack the historic costs of a blind allegiance to sacrificial ideals, how those ideals insulate us from a more multi-pronged conception of people's lives (Vogelmann 2018). Social hierarchies in modern states are supposed to buffer autonomy, not frustrate or destroy it. Our deeply rooted affirmation in the idea of social progress and enhanced freedoms is often guilty of censoring, remaining blind to diminished lives and communities. My book is interdisciplinary, drawing on repertoires from psychiatry, psychology, sociology, philosophy, critical theory, neuroscience, developmental science and historical scholarship. Such broad reading, beyond demarcated cells of encrusted privilege, aims for greater criticality and better problem-solving strategies. This book deals with significant violations that rob people of expansive autonomy.

Resisting the Power of Mea Culpa captures the root of a socially induced problem in Ireland's history, one of the many examples of the unscrupulous treatment of people, by those who held and hold power. For individuals who shoulder trauma, the appropriation of *mea culpa* often has devastating consequences on their deep psychological make-up. Taking on board the belief that events, or what was happening, was 'my' fault, enfeebled and ensnared early development. *Mea culpa* was/is a silencing technique, where people find themselves back-footed, moulded into a pre-ordained belief-system that not only recommended conformity and quietude, but demanded it. As a young person, I felt hemmed in, feeling I was inauthentic and unworthy of love. Ireland, unpacked as a historic society, committed to secrecy and legal discrimination, made traumatic experiences more painful. A historic society that legitimated criminality with gay desire, and psychiatry, citing family traumas as the causal root of arrested development, translated into a poisonous social legacy. From recent history, my book unpacks the manifolds of stress, stigma and noxious shame. *Mea culpa* was/ is a non-transcendent idea, capturing the routinized value orientation of dominating moral norms. The transforming power of struggles for equality un-conceals historic oppression toward empowerment.

Acknowledgements

I want to thank the Peter Lang team, in particular the former commissioning editor Christabel Scaife for her interaction with this work from the outset. The approach taken by Christabel was friendly, responsive, efficient and inspired my confidence as a writer. Thanks are due to my anonymous peer review, whose positive approach really helped me.

Thank you to Dr Philip Dunshea, Jonathan Smith, Simon Phillimore and Michael Garvey for their able assistance in the final stages of the production process. I feel very fortunate and truly grateful.

Thanks to a colleague for her wonderful comments for the back-cover blurb. In particular, her idea of how self-beliefs are moulded by the repertoires of regional histories, how confronting this historical preordination, in solidarity with others, helps to transform latent self-determining potentials in a progressive direction.

Thank you to Tiferet Valentine for introducing me to the work of Bernadette Murphy. As women, both of you resiliently enact prosocial mindsets beyond fixed and limiting ideas.

Thank you to Dublin ActUP and KnowNow for their spirited advocacy in challenging HIV stigma in Ireland and for advancing the scientific message of PEP and PrEP (normally one pill a day). Undetectable = Untransmittable #UequalsU

Abbreviations

AIDS	Acquired Immune Deficiency Syndrome
CBIS	Christian Brothers Investment Services (set up by De La Salle Brothers)
CCSA	Clerical Childhood Sexual Abuse
CDF	Congregation for the Doctrine of the Faith (Catholic) based in Rome
CSA	Childhood Sexual Abuse
ECHR	European Court of Human Rights
ESRI	Economic and Social Research Institute
FF	Fianna Fáil (political party)
FG	Fine Gael (political party)
HIA	Historical Institutional Abuse Inquiry in Northern Ireland (one module relates to the De La Salle Brothers)
HIV	Human Immunodeficiency Virus
ICCL	Irish Council for Civil Liberties
IFSC	Irish Financial Services Centre
IWLM	Irish Women's Liberation Movement
NBSCCCI	National Board for Safeguarding Children for the Catholic Church in Ireland
PEP	Post-Exposure Prophylaxis (taking antiretroviral medicines (ART) after potentially having been exposed to HIV to avoid becoming infected)
PrEP	Pre-Exposure Prophylaxis (daily PrEP reduces the risk of getting HIV from sex by more than 90 per cent. Among people who inject drugs, it reduces the risk by more than 70 per cent. Your risk of getting HIV from sex can be even lower if you combine PrEP with condoms and other prevention methods. US Centers for Disease Control and Prevention, on 27 September 2017, stated

that people who take medication daily 'and achieve and maintain an undetectable viral load have effectively no risk of sexually transmitting the virus to an HIV-negative partner')

PSI	Psychological Society of Ireland
PTSD	Post-Traumatic Stress Disorder
UCD	University College Dublin

Introduction

> In the era of information and communication, issues of misinformation and miscommunication are more pressing than ever. Who has voice and who doesn't? Are voices acting with equal agency and power? In whose terms are they communicating? Who is being understood and who isn't (and at what cost)? Who is being believed? And who is even being acknowledged and engaged with? Epistemic Injustice refers to those forms of unfair treatment that relate to issues of knowledge, understanding and participation in communicative practices. These issues include a wide range of topics concerning wrongful treatment and unjust structures in meaning-making and knowledge producing practices, such as the following: exclusion and silencing; invisibility and inaudibility (or distorted presence or representation); having one's meanings or contributions systematically distorted, misheard, or misrepresented; having diminished status or standing in communicative practices; unfair differentials in authority and/or epistemic agency; being unfairly distrusted; receiving no or minimal uptake; being co-opted or instrumentalised; being marginalized as a result of dysfunctional dynamics.
>
> — KIDD, MEDINA and POHLHAUS Jr (2017: 1)

At the outset, I am aware how use of the first person 'I' in academic writing is caricatured, stigmatized and discredited. I want to suggest this form of distaste, displeasure and disavowal for the use of 'I' is somewhat consistent with the mind-altering theological impressions I imbibed during my younger years of living in rural Ireland. The patterns of Ireland's secrets are deeply rooted, keeping us ignorant about loss of power. In this state, what was imprinted was the idea that sin/pathology arose inside of us. For me, this form of self-abnegation, as an overhang from my early socialization was causally related to later suicidal intent and action. The book describes cascades of trauma and adversity across the lifespan that manifested as damaged cognition and health inequity.

In the book, the sacrificial structure of self-abnegation, as deep patterns of systemic censorship have a poisonous legacy in Ireland, equivalent to soul death, and even premature death in real time. Surely, academic genres have a duty to break the spell of these rigid codifications in our legacy? The descriptive stories are of my younger years and later life living in Ireland. I include some of my family history. As I go through the story, a potentially useful way to frame the content are at the levels of society, social interaction and personality (Cote and Levine 2016). The invalidation of human potential did not take place in a social vacuum. Referring to historical society, I am primarily referring to immersion in state-religious regulatory concepts and ideas, as adopted and legitimated in political, legal, social care, education and further enacted as traditional values in Irish society.

When stigmatizing and disrespectful laws were the background to personal adversities in a young boy's life, the transacting imprints of oppressive social modes of thought wove a very dark impression on the practical ways I related to myself, consciously/unconsciously. The book examples how this multi-layered tapestry was carried, creating a coercive demand to be somebody I was not. It was like a preordination of higher ideals where I understood failure as subjective and personal to me. In this context, bad treatment for who I was becoming felt deserved and par for the course. If 'creativity is the unique and defining trait of our species, and its ultimate goal: self-understanding' (Wilson 2017: 3), I was back-footed from the off, not able to read situations, feeling captive to dominant and oppressive modes of intelligibility. Stigmatic social structures can enact a heavy cost.

In very explicit and shaming ways, being gay was constructed as an unmentionable vice, which one must overcome. In the historical scenes that I grew up in, I also learned to think there was something terribly insufficient about me being gay, signifying that gay men were not really men. It was so easy to be intimidated by this normative discourse in historic times. Situating a relational human being within social conventions aims to bring alive 'systems of values, ideas and practices' (Jaspal Carriere Moghaddam 2015: 268). I grew up in a fearful context where concealing insult and damage was normal. Over time, I did not have to make a special effort to be highly self-critical in a non-productive way (Shahar 2015). From an early age, this inflamed tariff was woven into my intentional modes of self-understanding. The shame I felt for a desire to be who I was, was intensely painful.

In history, there were no effective mechanisms to argue against the state privileging of religious discriminatory concepts in Irish culture. Rather than think these foregrounded ideas were unreasonable, I thought my restlessness was the outcome of a sinful soul. The book is particularly critical of religion in Irish history, largely because of its tentacle like grip over Irish customs and traditions. I am not anti-religious. I recognize the key contributions that religion has made to Irish life. Resurrecting my pained family history in the present is a tough choice to make. It feels like I am going against the tide, when progressive social change is said to define the current age.

My hypothesis in the book is that much of our early socialization remains as a congealed/submerged imprint on our enacted psychologies, often dissociative, distorting how we relate to ourselves and interpret experiences in the present. In the book, I shine a light on the often devastating impact of unjust social experiences in historic times. I hope my scholarship will be of benefit to others who have felt silenced, their self-confidence crushed from being situated in noxious social terrains. I keep being persistent in my attempt to better grasp how the social intentionality of historic ideation encrusts and hyper-arouses the ego in the present, the causal roots of a great deal of social suffering and misery. Making these patterns transparent is my goal. The German critical theorist Axel Honneth (2009) suggests historical explanation can be utilized for better understandings of present-day injustices and sufferings:

> In contrast to the approaches that have achieved dominance today, Critical Theory must couple the critique of social injustice with an explanation of the processes that obscure that injustice. For only when one can convince the addresses by means of such an explanatory analysis that they can be deceived about the real character of their social conditions can the wrongfulness of those conditions be publicly demonstrated with some prospect of being accepted. Because a relationship of cause and effect is assumed to obtain between social injustice and the absence of any negative reaction to it, normative criticism in Critical Theory has to be complemented by an element of historical explanation. A historical process of the deformation of reason must causally explain the failure of a rational universal, a failure that constitutes the social pathology of the present. The explanation must at the same time make intelligible the de-thematisation of social injustice in public discussion. (p. 30)

In the stories that follow, I take a sociocultural lens, trying to illuminate historical conditions that gave rise to social suffering with significant costs for the persons involved. My story aims to capture how the transference of dominant ideologies had damaging implications for developing self-confidence. In the book, persons are significantly burdened by societal experiences and social arrangements. Persons are often unaware of the impact of the social structure, and have little insight for how unfair their social learning is. In other words, the persons that come to life in the book have unreasonable expectations about their own power and agency, which keeps them subordinated. In my experience, I learned to spiritualize what was happening through religious rituals. Secrecy was good, politics was bad. Enacting this ideology was disempowering and not emancipatory. Those who experience toxic stress in their young lives may not be fully aware of the impact of encrusted ideation, and how they end up carrying this tariff as an invulnerable personae. Many of our citizens end up depleted, enfeebled and angry, not grasping how this position has come about. Mills (2017) says 'oppression negatively affects social cognition' (p. 101). Lack of psychological and societal awareness of noxious stress/trauma are unacknowledged for long periods of time. Symbolic recognition of social suffering is too late for many persons. Too much time is lost. We cannot enact legitimate struggle against social injustice and oppression without effortful awareness and effective mobilization and responsiveness from others in society. The right kind of persistence is critical.

PART I

A Multivalent Spotlight on Ireland's History

CHAPTER 1

The Context of Early Childhood

I was born in Longford in 1966. In birth order, I was the second last child within a large family. My deceased mother Anne (d. 2014) was a traditional housewife. My deceased father Peter was a very troubled, cowardly and violent man. His acts of kindness were few and far between. He threw his weight about erratically with tragic consequences for my family. Our family stood out. We were talked about, because of my father's shameful behaviour. While he was here, his presence on this earth left some mark on us.

My mother's parents hated my father. Despite how kind my grandparents were to us, my devout grandmother, particularly as she aged, became so embittered. My father never held down a steady job. While my father lost both his parents at a very young age, this can hardly be an excuse for his psychotic behaviour throughout his short life and his tragic end. The negative atmospheres he created at home is something I only have tacit awareness of. I was very young. I sought his approval. In many ways, I had to struggle to exist around him, as if I meant very little to him. His erratic pattern made me feel disposable. I felt I did not register in any significant way in his presence. The chaos he created made me feel anxious and guarded. I did not feel free around him. I felt fear. For others in my family, they were trying to escape his blows. Other siblings overheard my mother weeping late at night. My memory of my father is largely dependent on how others thought of him. I felt I was not central to him. Adult attachment figures can certainly dampen and depress the expectations of young children by not recognizing their needs. He was no role model. And my mother could not escape him.

My father was a popular figure in local sporting organizations and in the public 'drinking' houses in Longford. That said, despite how small in size he was, he would get into fights in the town. After a night out, I remember my mother being so upset about the state of his clothes. I remember how my mum knitted lovely cardigans for my father. She cared for him like a child. Yet, he punished her with harshness. At a young age, one of my siblings, saw my father forcing himself on my mother before I was born. He was expressing his right. When my father arrived home, he could look fearsome. He would have promised my mother that he would be home early and would cause no trouble. Sometimes, he disappeared for weeks. That was a relief. At other times, he was hospitalized for alcoholism and bad mental health. Some psychiatrists referred to him as a 'bowsey'. Whatever he was, he was trouble from the word go.

As a young boy, being compared to my father by my religiously devout and ailing grandmother was particularly cruel. A heightened antennae for micro-slights and hurts is something I have always been hyper-sensitive to. Whatever it is about those early undercurrents, they can manifest as a constancy principle in memory registrars. Referring to this developmental and social pattern in evolutionary terms, Rochat (2013) says 'the gaze of others gained unique power as a social signal' (p. 210). For myself, bad early prophecies created a hyper-vigilance, with lasting impact for how I thought about myself and appraised life situations. I could not cognitively work out that what was going on around me was not of my making. I had no language to express this upset.

In my early life, I simply did not possess the right set of tools to cope. My early home life was so broken. I did not create this pattern. Irish history was there in my family before my arrival. The ideational logic of this historic time period encouraged dissociation rather than opposition. Mills (2017) in his chapter on ideology says: 'one's processing (via socialization) of empirical inputs through a conceptual and affective grid that so transforms them to reinforce rather than challenge dominant framings and narratives' (p. 103). Psychological literature on shame and guilt evaluates these emotions as personal and in the context of interpersonal relationships. This lens seriously truncates how oppressive social beliefs and customs play a significant role in concealment. In these normative modes, to be healthy is your responsibility with no critical evaluation of social traditions.

To enact opposition to dominant ideologies, people need to have some sense how oppression corrodes self-control. Resilient and agile people probably cannot imagine how the pre-ordinances of one's social environs can damage the cultivation of optimal self-confidence. This lack of understanding for multivalent stressors feels so dominant in my culture. To others, my family may have appeared resilient, while the truth beyond these appearances was very different. My family was more than vulnerable, appearance is very different from reality. As some of us have aged, it is evident how the early toxic stress pattern damaged psychological equilibrium. I think of this as social transfers.

Normal stressors can be productive for adaptation and resistance. However, toxic stressors are strongly associated with cascading negative health equity in lifespan development. When policy stakeholders reflect on the implications of bad social conditions, they try to buffer the social contract to protect people from harm. WHO (2013) in its Mental Health Action Plan (2013–2020) 'An emphasis is placed on the developmental aspects, for instance, having a positive sense of identity, the ability to manage thoughts, emotions, as well as build social relationships, and the aptitude to learn and to acquire an education, ultimately enabling their full active participation in society' (p. 6). Perhaps there are many persons who view such sentiments as idealistic and think such utopian notions create victimhood. In other words, a social demand for protective buffers creates expectations. Perhaps, a critic of rights protections, might suggest a theory of social justice/equality based on subjectivist claims of moral injury collapses normative justice concerns to a politics of the wound, a mere suffer-mongering, giving rise to a bloated compensation culture.

When considering children's rights, human rights declarations may also be subject to the charge that they weaken the motivation to be resilient, to be robust and hardy, where children should be able to withstand bad treatment. Thus, those who moan and complain are of weak character and should be treated with suspicion. In response to such criticisms and popularized ideas, the majority of adult persons aim to buffer and protect children from being harmed, blighted and badly treated. Fundamentally, the protective intuition that the maltreatment and abuse of children is repugnant is the correct call. While social recognition of childhood harms has increased, Putman (1997) says, 'A deeper understanding of children's responses to trauma has been slow to emerge' (p. 21).

When you study Irish history, it becomes evident that we were regulated by the social hierarchy to rationalize bad treatment as normal. My book tries to grasp this heritage where people were led to believe they can only look inward not outward. Defects arise from character, not the social order. That value orientation in Irish history proved harmful, where many people were routinized to take on the blame and guilt for crimes committed against them. The hierarchy of knowledge in Ireland felt alienating when it was able to deform, frustrate and amputate core capacities for making meaning of lived experience. The moribund legacy of *mea culpa* as a foregrounded preordination cannot be merely conflated to shame affects. It's a much a deeper invasion. Spanning many decades, I will illustrate how repetitive traumas enfeebles and subjugates the intentional structure of consciousness, where people pull the rug from under themselves, and cannot trust each other to make it better. Violence, abuse, exploitation, oppression and discrimination are not innate to personality but are social creations that enact punitive costs and tariffs on human potential. Veena Das (2007) anthropological and ethnographical reflections are useful to describe the themes in this book: 'it narrates the lives of particular persons and communities who are deeply embedded in these events, and it describes the way that the event attaches itself with its tentacles into everyday life and folds into the recesses of the ordinary' (p. 1). Striking a similar note, Taoiseach Leo Varadkar on the occasion of the 2018 papal visit to Ireland by Pope Francis described how 'brutal crimes were perpetrated by people within the Catholic church and then obscured to protect the institution at the expense of innocent victims' (McKay 2018). The Taoiseach also acknowledged that the state created the subcontract for religious domination. The rest of my book positions my family history in the prevailing context of this recent history.

CHAPTER 2

A Summarized History that Shaped Irish Values from the Mid-Nineteenth Century to the Present

In my early years, my mother lived close to her parents. In my teens, I remember her working as a child-minder to support us. Historically in Ireland, as elsewhere, the gendered roles of women and men had a static and prescriptive like form, as if the roles of 'men' and 'women' were pre-ordained in distinct ways. In the lower socioeconomic classes, upward social mobility for women was certainly much harder to achieve (Daly 2016; Kennedy 2001). On a cultural level, Ó Tuathaigh (2018) captures the normative grounding for a significant period of twentieth-century Ireland:

> The constitution and statute law reflected Catholic moral and social teaching in sensitive areas, such as marriage and the family, contraception and family planning, and censorship (print and cinema). Indeed, social cohesion, such as it was, was the outcome of high levels of conformity to the social values and teaching of the Catholic Church. This was not surprising. Constituting over 90 per cent of the population of the Irish national state, with overwhelming control of schools and commanding a network of church-run hospitals and charitable institutions, the Catholic Church infrastructure gave it enormous influence on all aspects of life. Politicians – for the most part – were deferential or politically attentive to the wishes and warnings of Bishops. A formidable network of organized Catholic laity exercised a wide supervisory and morally vigilant role in the main arteries of social life – from charitable organisations to library committees – ensuring that all such bodies, public or voluntary, would do 'the right thing' by the Church.

In the town I grew up in, class position and status had a naturalized feel of inheritance. For example, when going to church, I was so conscious of different classes of people and how people were treated differently (Earner-Byrne 2017). This kind of social inequality was limiting and silenced my mother's voice in significant ways. It was a social/historical dynamic that was continuously reinforced for much of my mother's life, shaping how she felt about her position in life. More objectively, Lucas, Ho, Kerns (2018) state:

> It is difficult to imagine groups of any substantial size in which there are not differences in control over resources (power), variations in respect and esteem (status), and stereotyping that leads to social distancing and discrimination (stigma). In part because these processes are so fundamental, they have important implications for health by shaping access to treatment, nature of care, health-related behaviours, and other important outcomes. In addition, the concepts mutually influence each other and vary together in important ways that we propose can lead to cumulative consequences for health. (p. 69)

My mother's early experiences of social stigma were experienced within the context of 1950s Ireland. In the decades beforehand, my mother had certainly interiorized historic religious norms. When she became mentally unwell for long periods of her life, I remember thinking her mental state was genetically predetermined, that her suffering was specific to her and not anything else. My own magical thinking about mental illness was not that dissimilar to how many others conceptualize wellbeing.

As a young boy, I never really made the connection that my mother's threshold had been breached and how her modes of consciousness had been distorted by the social suffering inflicted on her shoulders. I do not think my mother grasped how social objectification of her womanhood made her so unwell. I do not think the psychiatrists who treated her explained to her how her social pathway devastated her mental health. Instead, my mother's erratic moods were heavily sedated by medications and psychiatric sympathy. The dominant modes of thought in traditional psychiatric formulations downplays historical thought forms and how they manifest in client presentation. My mother was polite and deferential to authority. She would not have had a voice to contest their truncated versions of her life history. Given all that she had put through, my mother would have struggled in working out, who to trust, given her life circumstances. Ó Tuathaigh (2018) gives a flavour of my mother's preordained status: 'Sexual behaviour and women's reproductive capacity were the most sensitive areas in which Catholic Church teaching sought to exercise control of public policy and morals'. As Cote and Levine (2016) succinctly frame the effect of religious traditions on human development, 'For the common folk, religions typically provided ready-made answers about their existence on a personal level; at the same time, societies were rigidly structured to unequivocally tell people "who they were" at a social level' (p. xi).

For the birth of my mother's first baby, prior to my mother's eventual marriage to my father, my mother was forced to go to a Mother and Baby Home in Castlepollard, Co. Westmeath. At this time of extreme social/religious conservatism, a child born outside of marriage was a major source of secrecy and shame. My mother was simply led to believe that she had brought this shame on herself. This shaming gaze weakened her and set her up for much worse to come.

The building at Castlepollard has been variously described as an austere and bleak three-storey building. My mother was just one of the 23,000 women in Ireland who gave birth in these homes mostly run by the Catholic Church (*The New York Times* 2017). The Castlepollard Mother and Baby home was run by the Sacred Heart Sisters. As a historical antecedent, Larkin (1997) says by '1914 Irish and Catholic had not only become interchangeable terms, but Catholic had come to be the inclusive term' (p. 91). Dillon (2002) describes: 'the long tradition of Catholicism in Ireland and its historical coexistence with the long struggle against British Colonialism as formative of Irish political and cultural identity' (p. 47). In the nineteenth century, the administrative and organizational skills of Cardinal Paul Cullen is often cited as a key precursor to the enactment of the inseparable Church/state relationship in twentieth-century Ireland (Keogh and McDonnell 2011).

Prior to this, the American and French Declarations in the latter period of the eighteenth century 'articulated key ideas about the rights of individuals' (Kelly 2015: 6). The broader Enlightenment period (1650–1820) is further cited as a pivotal period where old religious ideas, taboos and customs began losing their superordinate grip on European customs and values. Increased urbanization and industrialization, allowed citizens to exercise more control over their lives. Thus, the modern state expanded its remit to regulate social attitudes and behaviours (Peakman 2011).

Ireland's historical path ran a completely different trajectory to the paths of many other European countries. The notion of rights in Ireland was expressed more in terms of national self-determination than individual/

self-determination rights (Jackson 2014). According to Sangiovanni (2017) the Roman Catholic Church in the nineteenth century

> was hardly a friend of either socialism or liberalism, often inveighing against the self-ishness and individualism of the rights of man proclaimed in the French Declaration and in the revolutions of 1848. The nineteenth-century church, furthermore, had at most an ambivalent relationship with democracy (e.g. the widening of the franchise), religious freedom (e.g. the separation of church and state), and the natural liberal rights that had come to the fore in the wake of the American and French revolutions. (p. 29)

With Catholic emancipation in 1829, the ideas of Catholic emancipatory ideology continued to shape self-understandings in the overarching context of the pressing challenges which Ireland was to face from the 1840s (e.g. famine, poverty, unemployment, disease, emigration). As a pragmatic and functionalist religion, Irish Catholicism was keen to create an applied social identity in the social imaginary, deeply embedding its practices in key domains of Irish culture. Its methods of social activism struck a chord with key political figures.

A key ingredient of Catholic ethics is the notion of sacrifice. This pattern, while emphasizing prosocial responsibility, also encourages infantile thinking and deference to authority. As a regulatory tool, the psychological self is expected to abnegate to greater social causes. Citizens must cultivate the presence of God through their daily lives. Observance and attendance at Church rituals were key to social indoctrination. Unlike Enlightenment values, the confident expectation of greater personal freedom and liberty is significantly lowered in the social imaginary. Objective states of affairs are God centred. In the middle of the nineteenth century, Paul Cullen returned from Rome, fulsomely equipped to impute his sectarian and anti-enlightenment ideas onto the social imaginary of an oppressed Catholic majority. Cullen was a subsequent key supporter of papal infallibility at the First Vatican Council in Rome in the 1860s and also supported the dogma of the Immaculate Conception of Mary in 1854, both defining features of Pope Pius IX reign. Cullen, as a former president of the College of Propaganda in Rome was keen to invoke this thinking on his return to Ireland. Larkin (2011) writes that

Shortly after his arrival in Ireland, he began his great work of reform by convening the first national synod in the history of the Irish Church. The synod, which was convoked at Thurles in August 1850 with Cullen presiding as the Pope's apostolic delegate, proceeded to legislate a comprehensive canonical frame that would provide for a thoroughgoing and radical transformation of the Irish church for a generation. The legislation at Thurles proved to be particularly effective in four main areas. It provided, first, for the containment of the very considerable power and influence the British state had recently acquired in the education of Irish Catholics; second, for the reorganization of the structure and government of the Irish Church, third, for the regularization of the celebration and administration of the sacraments; and fourth, for the reformation of the conduct and manners of the Irish clergy. (p. 21)

Archbishop Paul Cullen (later cardinal) disliked the pastoral/folk pattern of Catholic religious preaching within the villages of Ireland. Cullen's approach in Ireland set about creating a more disciplined clergy and formal architecture to promote a structured institutional faith, one that would be capable of inscribing its ethos into self-identity and national sovereignty. His approach recognized the key significance of education for the enactment of catholic identity.

From the mid-nineteenth century, Archbishop Cullen expressed his displeasure for how the British authorities constructed educational policies in Ireland: 'In an early pastoral to his Armagh clergy, after the Synod of Thurles, he stated unambiguously that the role of the clergy '[extended] to the supervision and control of every system of education proposed or instituted for the children of the Catholic Church' (Doyle 2011: 190). Larkin (2011) says Cullen's 'ascetic temper cut him off from the cultivated, easy, tolerant ecclesiastics of a past generation. To him Rome was everything' (p. 15). In that dynamic, Cullen emboldened sectarian beliefs which would mean that Ireland was to entrench a path of deep and divisive religious identity struggles that have lasted all the way through to twentieth-century Ireland.

In the nineteenth century, many religious orders in Ireland were well positioned to resist the revised British rules from 1855. Those rules had proposed to dilute denominational ethos in school curricula (Doyle 2011). A further key variable during this time period was the hostile sentiment felt by the Catholic majority tenancy toward the minority Protestant landlord class. Landlord tenancy agreements were largely oppressive for the majority Catholic tenancy in Ireland, many of whom felt and were dispossessed by the Protestant ascendency class. The British also got the blame for the famine and the patterns of mass migration out of Ireland (Jackson 2014; Biancalana 2009; Towey 1980).

Catholicism under Cardinal Cullen and subsequent key historical figures in Irish Catholicism recognized the importance of alignment with the key concerns of an oppressed majority. Apart from the power bases of control of education and social care, a deference to Church authority also became aligned with the nationalist cause against UK influence over Irish affairs. Significant swathes within the Catholic priesthood, religious orders and the hierarchy were favourably disposed to the Republic cause of Celtic revival. Some others were more aligned with the pragmatism of home rule and advocated against violence and Church alignment with political causes.

Moving forward a century, Hogan (2012) describes the precursors and events that led to the formation of the Irish Constitution in the early decades of the twentieth century:

> The Constitution of the Irish Free State entered into force on December 6, 1922 after six turbulent years that saw rebellion against British rule, the success of the Sinn Fein party at the 1918 general election, the War of Independence, the partition of the island of Ireland and, ultimately the Anglo-Irish Treaty of December 1921. The 1921 Treaty had provided for the establishment of the Irish Free State, with Dominion status within the emerging British Commonwealth. While the new state was to be internally sovereign within its borders, its external sovereignty was, at least theoretically, compromised by the uncertainties associated with Dominion status. Yet, within a space of fifteen years, that Constitution was itself replaced following years of political and constitutional turmoil and debate, a process which accelerated following the accession of De Valera to power in March 1932. A new state thus emerged whose external sovereignty was now put beyond question. (p. 1)

Ireland's first female president, Mary Robinson (2012) in her memoir *Everybody Matters* captures the immersion of religion in 1950s as normative:

> We grew up with this sense of the importance of the Church, the importance of prayer and faith. We did not question it. This was Ireland in the 1950s. Our relatively new constitution – enshrined in 1937 – placed God and the Roman Catholic faith as its centre. This was a stratified society where people knew their place and did not question it. Priests held a status that was high and implicit and trusted. People did not look behind the white collar. In this Ireland, single mothers were pariahs who

had their children taken from them to be brought up by good Catholic parents while they paid for their sins, working as slaves to the religious orders in institutions such as the Magdalene laundries. Of course, we have since found out how some priests abused this power, preying on the vulnerable behind closed doors, and how some were protected from the force of the law by the highest echelons in the Church. This is an episode of deep shame in the nation's history. (p. 10)

The Sacred Heart Sisters ran St Peter's Mother and Baby Home in Castlepollard, where my mother had to go to give birth to her first baby in the early 1950s. This order of nuns arrived from England to Ireland in 1922–3. By 'late-1933 or early-1934, the Sisters bought the third and last of their homes, the old Manor House in Castlepollard, County Westmeath, with 110 acres of land' (Redmond 2015). Through the period from 1948 to 1973, 278 babies were sent to America from Castlepollard: 'They are known as the Banished Babies' (Redmond 2015). From the 1940s, the Castlepollard home started to secure a poor reputation. In its early days, the original Mother Superior was from the local area and was keen to make a good impression (Redmond 2015). However, this nun was struck down with illness and died young. Her replacement seems to have been less empathetic in her job. Paul Redmond (2015) who was born in the Castlepollard describes this home where his own mother gave birth:

> Babies were kept in large rooms or wards on the ground floor while mothers stayed on the second floor in dormitories, housing anywhere from six to 12 women, depending on how many were held at any one time. The third floor had two large rooms at the back, where all the births took place, with mums and new born babies remaining on the third floor for a couple of weeks after the birth. The third floor also had a few 'private' rooms, where well-off families who could afford to pay, handed over the huge sum of £100 for privacy, and a speedy exit. There was a small standalone room built in the middle of the back lawn that served as a delivery room of sorts. Since no screaming was allowed during labour as part of the punishment, any girl who couldn't help screaming was put out into the outside delivery room. It is nicknamed the 'Screaming room.' (Redmond 2015)

My own mother never told me of bad experiences when she was in Castlepollard. However, in her later life, she said she feared ending up in a nursing home run by religious nuns. She never wanted to be dependent on nuns again. She fell out with many nuns when she sensed the cultural tide was turning against religious authority. My mother did not like how religious sisters exerted their authority. In time, she came to realize their ideas were baseless. This came too late for her, as the damage was well and truly done by the time of her awakening.

When my mother left the Mother and Baby home in Castlepollard, she managed to persuade my grandmother to allow her hold on to her firstborn for a short period. Her parents thought my father was not a suitable man for their daughter. Their intuitions were right on this front. My mother was the only surviving child of my grandparents. My grandmother helped care for my mother's firstborn. My grandmother then changed her mind and insisted that my eldest sister Yvonne be fostered/adopted. At about ten to twelve months old, Yvonne was placed for adoption with the Sisters of Charity at Temple Hill Blackrock.

From the 1940s to the 1970s, many Irish children were acquired by US adoptive (foster) parents (Adoption Rights Alliance 2015). The Roman Catholic Church held the position that there was no inalienable right to contraception (Ferriter 2009). The new Irish state consistently deferred to religious authority as the sole arbiter of sexual desire and conduct. These arrangements were punitive and stigmatic, causing untold suffering and hardship in women's lives and for their babies developmental capacities, many of whom experienced significant traumas.

My sister Yvonne was one of the reported 572 adopted children sent to the USA from Temple Hill (Adoption Rights Alliance 2015). In Dublin, Dr John Charles McQuaid, Archbishop of Dublin oversaw these adoption arrangements. He was of the opinion to ensure the purity of moral values, it was best to place the illegitimate babies somewhere else – out of sight, out of mind. While in Temple Hill, my mother told me she gained access to see her first baby. My mother said she was permitted to view Yvonne through a partition. She described how the babies were kept in cots in a large open ward.

My eldest sister was fifteen months old when she finally left Ireland for America in 1954. Her US foster parents had a specific pre-order request for a boy and a girl. A priest from Pittsburg, Kansas, visited Templehill in 1954. Yvonne arrived by boat through Ellis Island on 15 May 1954. She and her foster brother were among nineteen babies. They were accompanied by twelve nuns. Back home in Ireland, my mother and her own father were grief-stricken. They were left feeling they had done something wrong.

In the US, my sister told me she felt different to other children in her local area, perhaps 'less whole and worthy than others' (Luca, Hos, Kerns 2018: 69). And in the lowered sense of self-worth horizon, she was expected to compensate with gratitude for her new home. In her early years, she was told her biological parents were dead in Ireland. In the case of my sister, her attachment style was dysregulated by stress and anxiety as a young baby and child. Yet, she was expected to contain all this 'by tampering down egocentrism and narcissism in favour of taking the perspective of another' (Saarni 1999 cited by Harter 2017: 85). From the off, my eldest sister as a child was expected to be altruistic. Without in-depth critical analysis of social objectification, the weight of blame and shame is more often carried by the wrong people, silencing them, with potentially devastating consequences for their lives (Bernstein 2015, Thompson 2013; 2013a).

Traditional American culture is one where autonomous citizens are expected to build and consciously configure their self-confidence to take responsibility for the consequences. Furthermore, American religions have tended to be functionally pragmatist, and in many cases fundamentalist in their orientations and beliefs. With regard to Irish history, Murray and Feeney (2017) write

> Knowledge, they say, is power. One manifestation of the power of the Catholic Church within the independent Irish state in the middle decades of the twentieth century was the virtual monopoly its clergy and the educational institutions under their control possessed over the discipline of sociology. The first university posts in this discipline were filled in 1937, the year in which the voters of the twenty-six-county state ratified a new constitution that blended Anglo-American liberal democratic norms with distinctive new provisions reflecting Catholic teaching. Verbal genuflection before the social prescriptions of papal encyclicals was to be found in this document although, as Joe Larragy (2014 : 201) notes, 'Catholic social power rather than Catholic social teaching was the prevalent factor in the Irish case and for a long time the formula suited an authoritarian church in a parsimonious state dominated by the rural petit bourgeoisie.' But times, churches and states change. In 1973, when both parts of Ireland entered what was then the European Economic Community (EEC), a secular, professional association of Irish sociologists was also founded.

Shortly after Yvonne left Ireland in 1954, my mother was pregnant with her second baby by the same father of her first baby. My father was one of seven children, six boys and one girl. He was the youngest in the family. My mother empathized with my father's situation: his mother died when he was seven years old and his father died when he was eleven years old.

In drink, my father was a violent and aggressive man. On the night they got married, my mother recalled how my father threw her down a flight of stairs. Ireland's society was deeply patriarchal. The concept of feminism was unknown to my mother. For example, I do not remember her talking of the 1970s Commission on the Status of Women (1970) which started the incremental process of social change for women in Ireland (Ó Tuathaigh 2018).

In the mid-1950s, as bad happenings escalated in their early days of marriage, accompanied by her father, my mother requested a church annulment. The Church had the power to annul a marriage in special circumstances. My mother's request for an annulment was refused. In the mid-1950s, a Jesuit priest based at Berkeley Road Church, in Dublin 7, informed my mother and my grandfather that she had made her decision and that she must remain married to my father. This refusal disgusted my grandfather. Ireland was now a Catholic country and it no longer permitted divorce. As Articles 41.3.1/2 of the 1937 Irish Constitution stated at the time, 'The State pledges itself to guard with special care the institution of Marriage, on which the family is founded, and to protect it against attack. No law shall be enacted providing for the grant of a dissolution to marriage' (Hug 1999: 18). With our newfound Irish independence, the writers of the new Irish Constitution in 1937 ensured divorce and the right to remarry would never be an option in civil laws. Prior to the new constitution, Daly (2016) says, 'Divorce had been largely absent from the Irish political debate since the 1920s, when the Irish Government introduced a law to prohibit divorce' (p. 182). We were a new Catholic Republic and we were moving away from liberal ideas on marriage, consistent with UK laws. My mother told me my grandfather turned against the Catholic Church after her request for an annulment was refused. After the birth of her second baby, my mother went on to have five more children with my father.

On the rare occasion, my father took my mother out, she remembered him getting into a brawl with another man. She recalled to me how my father's shirt was bloodied on their way home. Another man had asked my mother to dance. At the dance, my father had been paying no attention to her. He was acting the big man with his mates. For a time during the 1960s and early 1970s, my mother managed to separate from my father. According to one of my older siblings, they lived with our grandparents for a time. Late at night, my father regularly came to the door of my grandparent's house, demanding his wife be returned to live with him. She eventually returned to him and had more children.

In 1995, in her sixties, my mother was reunited with her firstborn baby. They had both been trying to locate each other for a long time. At this time, my sister Yvonne was forty-two years old. When she visited, I accompanied her to Temple Hill Blackrock where she had been handpicked for a special order by a US visiting cleric for his parishioners back home in Pittsburg, Kansas. In 1995, from the old pictures that adorned the walls of Temple Hill, my sister was able to recall how her tiny legs had been securely fastened to her cot in a large communal ward. She was filled with a huge amount of emotion when she recalled this experience. The other baby who went to the same US foster home had been born in the Rotunda Hospital in Dublin. After his birth, this baby was also transferred to Templehill in Blackrock. His birth mother had a Dublin address at an inner-city home for destitute women. The hostel was called the Regina Coeli hostel located in North Brunswick Street, Dublin 7. It was set up by Frank Duff, founder of the Irish Legion of Mary (Kennedy 2011). Duff had tried to avoid separating mothers from their babies. In a clerical culture, his lay missionary efforts were against the tide and found little support. Duff was also fearful of state inspections, as the building he occupied was not fit for purpose (Kennedy 2011). The Archbishop of Dublin, Dr John Charles McQuaid was not supportive of Duff's efforts (Kennedy 2011). He clearly viewed Duff's work as meddling in Church matters. In an extended quote, which captures the broader societal context of birth control during this historical period and beyond, Daly (2016) states:

Younger, educated middle-class couples were consciously trying to limit their fami-lies. Research into falling fertility suggests that changing attitudes are the first cru-cial factor. Couples take the decision to control fertility and then find the means of doing so; most of the fall in the fertility over the past two centuries was achieved using methods that would not be regarded as reliable today: coitus interruption, abstinence and perhaps abortion.

Fisher's research on fertility control in Britain prior to the 1960s shows that the key decisions were taken by men, and that most British couples relied on methods of fertility limitation that were available in Ireland: coitus interruptus and abstinence. If we apply Fisher's argument to Ireland, it suggests that the continuing high fertility in Irish marriages reflected a failure/unwillingness by men to control sexual activity and perhaps an unwillingness to consider the needs and wishes of their wives. The teaching of the Catholic Church, especially in confession, may have been critical. The 1935 Criminal Law Amendment Act and the 1929 Censorship of Publications Act made it a crime to print, publish or distribute works providing information about contraception or advocating contraception. Literature on the safe period, which was tolerated, and indeed approved by Pope Pius XII in 1951, was not banned in Ireland, but it was not readily available. By the 1950s, the Catholic Hierarchies in Britain, the United States and the Netherlands (to take only a small sample of countries) were instructing couples on how to limit family size in a manner that was compatible with Catholic teaching, but the Irish Catholic Hierarchy made no efforts to inform Irish couples. It was only in the late 1960s that branches of a Catholic Marriage Advisory Council, which provided pre-marriage courses and advice on the safe period, opened in Ireland, and these services were poorly advertised ... Although some couples obtained manuals outlining 'the safe period', access was probably limited to middle-class couples, who could get individual advice from a sympathetic doctor; the advice columns in Women's Choice in the late 1960s indicate that many couples were keen to learn about the safe period, but lacked even basic information on the subject. (Daly 2016: 145–6)

In my eldest sister's retelling of her circumstances, Yvonne says her foster mother waited until she was eighteen years old, before telling her that her parents were living when she left Ireland as a baby. My sister also informed me from the time she was seven years old up to twelve years old, her foster father regularly came to her room and sexually exploited her. Another female sibling was later fostered into the same family. She was adopted from another state in America. She was nine years old when she was adopted. My sister thinks her foster mother knew what her husband was up to with her and her foster sister. Yvonne says her foster mother was hyper-vigilant and that she had a tendency to project blame onto her. Once the third child arrived at nine years old, Yvonne's father lost interest in my sister at post-puberty age. This third child died in her forties. My sister's foster sister drank alcoholically throughout her adult life. More recently, my sister's only son died in very violent circumstances. Today, my sister's overall health is poor.

In the mid-1960s, Yvonne confided in a Catholic priest about the sexual abuse when she was twelve years old. The priest said he would pray to find the right answer to resolve this problem. Years later, Yvonne discovered how this same cleric she confided in, ended up in court for sexual abuse of minors. Subsequent inquiries in the US, Ireland, Canada and Australia confirm the concealment of sexual abuses and physical violations of minors (Australian Royal Commission: Final Report 2017; *Boston Globe* 2016; BRA 2015; Holohan 2011). Like so many scholars, Daly (2016) says 'lack of interest in such stories, and a failure to generate a public outrage, was undoubtedly a feature in the delay' (p. 180).

Without a sense of shared fate and discourse, this form of invisible suffering can be so corrosive to wellbeing. As well as her separation trauma from my mother, my sister had to take on the perceived social affordance that she was different because she was fostered and was of lessor value than her peers. When combined with dominant religious values of this time period, my sister was left with little choice but to take on the sins of others, as if the weight of their crimes was saying something about her rather than the father who violated her. Yvonne did not have the legal vocabulary to understand the exact nature of human rights violations. Kelly (2016a) says the 'term "human rights" refers specifically to rights that a human being possesses by virtue of the fact that he or she is a human being. Human rights do not need to be earned or granted; they are the birth-right of all human beings simply because they are human beings – no other qualification is required' (p. 34).

Regarding my eldest sister's adoption, John Cooney (1999) cites Dublin Archbishop John Charles McQuaid's published guidelines for adoption for this time period in Ireland. His six conditions were:

1. Obtain a written recommendation from their Diocesan Director of Catholic Charities.
2. Supply their baptismal and marriage certificates for inspection.
3. Supply a reference from their Parish Priest.
4. Submit a statement of their finances so as to ensure a good home and good prospects in life for the adopted child.
5. Submit medical certificates stating age, physical and mental health, and that they were not deliberately shirking natural parenthood.
6. Swear an affidavit that they were Catholics, guarantee to rear the adopted child as a Catholic, undertake to educate the adopted child, during the whole course of its schooling, in Catholic schools; and that if the child went to University, it would be to a Catholic University, and that they undertook to keep the adopted child permanently, and would not hand it over to any other party or parties. (Cooney 1999: 247)

Once the Dublin Archbishop had published his guidelines, 'Government departments accepted and enforced them. He went completely unchallenged in his activity' (Cooney 1999: 247). Within the broader context of 1950s US culture, Catholicism did not enjoy the same level of systemic influence as it did in Ireland's culture. However, Blanshard (1954) does note 'All but one of the nine-born Cardinals of American history have been the sons of Irish immigrant workers. The Irish dominance explains many of the characteristics of American Catholicism' (p. 30).

Everything about my sister's early life reads as shocking, toxic and so wrong. Now in her mid-sixties, her present-day suffering is significant. The root cause of this suffering is the imprint of a self-fulfilling prophecy, where the violated human being is caught in the tentacles of enacting a trajectory of self-harm. It is simply too much to expect individuals to unravel these harms when their oriented modes of feeling and thought are so engineered against them. Traditional value orientations that suggest looking inward is not helpful because the devastation was social. I think of what happened my sister as structural harm. My sister's social context ensured dissociation, altering how she could interpret the severity of her trauma. She was not protected in a secretive culture.

Yvonne's challenges cannot be considered normal challenges of childhood. She got off to such a tough start in life, through her separation from my mother and to be dehumanized by her foster father as a child was so wrong. In an EU court ruling, O'Keeffe v Ireland (2014), Irish judge Peter Charleton states that 'sexual violence is indisputably torture within the meaning of Article 3' of the EU Convention on Human Rights (p. 71). The Executive Summary of the Australian Royal Commission (2017) reads:

> The sexual abuse of a child is a terrible crime. It is the greatest of personal violations. It is perpetrated against the most vulnerable in our community. It is a fundamental breach of the trust that children are entitled to place in adults. It is one of the most traumatic and potentially damaging experiences and can have lifelong adverse consequences. (Australian Royal Commission 2017)

Spiegel (2003) says, 'Empirical research, clinical reports, the media and social movements soundly maintain that childhood sexual abuse is one of the most serious forms of interpersonal violence among both boys and girls' (p. 3). Regarding my sister's repetitive violation at the hands of her adoptive father, Messler-Davies and Frawley (1994) say:

> Frequently, the silence obtained from the child is so deeply internalized that the victim reaches adulthood with the secret of her violations intact. When the child does disclose the abuse while it is occurring, she is often ignored, disbelieved, vilified or further abused rather than validated and supported. (p. 86)

As people age, social science says the imprint of early toxic stress combined with additive factors (comorbidity) can take its toll on human beings (Juster et al. 2016). The World Health Organization (WHO 2013) acknowledges this burden of early adversity in children's health. Consistent with International Covenants on Civil and Political Rights, I certainly feel duty bound to speak up for my sister given the scale of what she was confronted with. Any of the major reviews in the science of childhood sexual abuse and exploitation agree in their fulsome recognition that the negative footprint for maltreated children is a substantive injury/moral harm. Most parents naturally intuit that it is so wrong to violate a child. Not so in my eldest sister's case.

Even when a priest was made aware of same, he did nothing as he himself was a perpetrator. This concealment also meant her foster sister, adopted at nine years old, was also exploited. When I met my sister, we had a great deal in common. We shared a similar discourse of recovery from addiction. In her early forties, Yvonne was very emotionally present to me. We got on very well as brother and sister. On one of her subsequent trips to Ireland, Yvonne brought her youngest daughter with her. On a couple of occasions, I travelled to see my eldest sister in the US. For the first time, her own family and friends saw a biological sibling who looked just like her, both of us sharing the same mother and father.

While our shared spiritual principles of addiction recovery for my sister and myself were benign in reducing unmanageability/powerlessness, the AA discourse is not very helpful for those who have experienced the complexities of early violation and trauma. The core AA philosophy tends to encourage people to think that their troubles are of their own making. This model takes the position that the only way to be rid of self-character defects is through God's help. For example, the AA *Big Book* (2002) states the following:

> So our troubles, we think, are basically of our own making .... We had to have God's help. This is the how and why of it. First of all, we had to quit playing God. It didn't work. Next, we decided that hereafter in this drama of life, God was going to be our Director. He is the Principal; we are His agents. He is the Father, and we are His children. Most good ideas are simple, and this concept was the keystone of the new and triumphant arch through which we passed to freedom. (p. 62)

In other words, these spiritual principles are often interpreted as an extension of religion, promoting the idea that characterological defects are critical to overcoming innate selfishness. The claim that 'the ethical politics of religion and culture constitute notorious instances of depoliticized politics,' (Vazquez-Arroyo 2016: 409) is an apt criticism of these approaches. Much social suffering remains under-analysed when people feel there is something innate about them that is wrong, not the society that has exploited and disempowered them in theological ideology. The orientation of that ideology were enshrined in beliefs, values and wider traditions. Metaphysical and transcendental ideas can extend too much wriggle room for abuse of power. Their misapplication can be very disempowering. Such traumatized persons should not be encouraged to take on the sins of the father, reinforced by a culture that rewards concealment and interiorizing self-blame.

In 2016, my sister's foster brother came to Ireland with his own family. As I had done with Yvonne, I brought him to Temple Hill in Blackrock. On arrival, we discovered the site had been totally redeveloped. Templehill Blackrock is one of the most expensive real estate areas in Ireland. When we visited, building works were in progress. In 2016, since my visit in 1995, the only aspect of the site that was recognizable was the historic facade of the main house. The rest of the green land was fully populated with small town houses and apartments. Many of these lands, formerly owned by religious orders in prime real estate areas were sold off for substantive sums of money.

In 2016, this was the first time that my sister's foster brother visited Ireland. As a baby, he had been fostered from Ireland to America in 1954 to the same family as my sister. On the morning of my US visitor's departure in 2016, the national radio reported that Irish Prime Minister Enda Kenny was visiting the Vatican in Rome with his wife (RTÉ News 2016). After a meeting with Pope Francis, and ending months of speculation of an impending visit, it was confirmed to Enda Kenny that Pope Francis intended to visit Ireland in 2018. The Pontiff visited Ireland at the end of August 2018 for the World Meeting of Families in Dublin. The former papal nuncio to Ireland, Archbishop Charles J. Brown, who was appointed as papal ambassador in November 2011, described the Church's rebirth 'as the spring after 20 years of winter', saying he sees 'green shoots. You see a renewed enthusiasm among young Catholics in Ireland now' (Gately 2014).

On our way to the airport in 2016, we drove past the Archbishop of Dublin's high walls in Drumcondra. I remarked to my US visitors that this was the house where Archbishop McQuaid had drafted up the guidelines for sending babies to America. Again in 2016, I was so aware of the longevity of the close alignment between Church/state. The previous week, Pope Francis himself had celebrated mass with a newly appointed Irish born Kevin Cardinal Farrell (MacDonald 2016). Cardinal Farrell was educated by the Irish Christian Brothers in Drimnagh, Dublin. Farrell joined the religious order Legionnaires of Christ in 1966. Prior to his elevation to cardinal, Bishop Farrell served the Diocese of Dallas where my US visitors now live.

Ireland's former president Dr Mary McAleese recently captured how the Roman Catholic Church continues to act as a 'primary global carrier of the toxic virus of misogyny', and 'a male bastion of patronizing platitudes to which Pope Francis has added his own quota' (RTÉ 2018). A precursor to these words relates to how Dr Kevin Farrell advised of his objections to Ireland's former president delivering a key note speech to a '2018 Voices of Faith' conference to be held at the Vatican in March 2018 (MacDonald 2018). Cardinal Farrell was one of the key figures overseeing the preparations for Pope Francis' visit to Ireland in Autumn 2018. He is from Dublin Ireland and has spent most of his tenure in Church leadership positions in the USA. The *Irish Independent* journalist says,

> Correspondence seen by the Irish Independent reveals a stand-off occurred between the conference organizers and Cardinal Farrell over his withholding of approval not just for Dr McAleese but two other speakers as well. The Irish Independent understands that Dr McAleese's views on gay rights is the reason the prelate objected. She has previously spoken about how son Justin, as a devout young Catholic, was bullied because he was gay. She said that Justin went through 'torture' when he discovered what his Church taught about homosexuality.
>
> Another conference speaker Ssenfuka Joanita Warry is a Catholic who campaigns for LGBT rights in Uganda and is herself gay. This is the first year the Vatican has withheld approval of any speakers for the annual 'Voices of Faith' gathering, which brings together high-profile international speakers to address issues of concern to women around the world. For the past four years, the conference has taken place within the Vatican. But the 2018 event ran into trouble with Cardinal Farrell, who heads up the Congregation for Laity, Family and Life and had taken up oversight of the conference. Chantal Götz, who is executive director of the Catholic philanthropic Fidel Götz Foundation and is the main organizer of the conference, took the decision to move the venue of 'Why Women Matter' from the Vatican to the Jesuit Aula in Rome rather than cave in to the Irish prelate's demands. (MacDonald 2018)

Tighe-Mooney (2018) says in her book *What About Me: Women and the Catholic Church*:

> I was rather taken aback by the Vatican's 2010 decision, under the papacy of Benedict XVI (2005–13), to upgrade the 'sin' of ordaining a woman. Considering the context

at the time –with worldwide revelations about the child abuse scandal, the vast scale of cover-up and secrecy, and the hostile stance taken towards victims – this was, to my mind, a rather strange move. In addition, given that women are forbidden from ministry in the Catholic Church, as well as being personally unaware of any specific public call for the ordination of women, I was puzzled by the timing and curious about what the move actually meant for women. First and foremost, it suggested that the Church meant business on this issue. There was to be no more discussion, and all pertinent people, such as seminarians, ordinands, clergy and theologians in Catholic institutions, are now obliged to take an oath affirming this position, among others, on Church teachings. To close down all avenues of discussion, as John Paul II (1978–2005) had similarly done, seemed a defensive action. For me, it prompted question of what it was that the men of the Church feared. Why make something that was already sinful and forbidden a more serious 'sin'? I was also curious to see what it said about the Church's attitude to women. Why at that time? What was the motivation, and more importantly, what were the implications.

Back to my own mother: I think of her preordained status as a woman within broader cultural conditions in Ireland. My mother was born in 1932. This was the same year that the International Eucharistic Congress, a major Roman Catholic event was held in Dublin (Ferriter 2009). In 1932, the serving Pontiff did not attend the congress in person. Yet, over 1 million people turned up for the celebration of a mass in the Phoenix Park in Dublin (Jackson 2014).

In the 1940s, Irish Taoiseach's Eamon de Valera's broadcast speech on St Patrick's Day 1943, examples his vision of an ideal Ireland, guided by the foregrounded presupposition of God's master plan for humanity:

> The ideal Ireland that we would have, the Ireland that we dreamed of, would be the home of a people who valued material wealth only as a basis for right living, of a people who, satisfied with frugal comfort, devoted their leisure to the things of the spirit – a land whose countryside would be bright with cosy homesteads, whose fields and villages would be joyous with the sounds of industry, with the romping of sturdy children, the contest of athletic youths and the laughter of happy maidens, whose firesides would be forums for the wisdom of serene old age. The home, in short, of a people living the life that God desires that men should live. (Cited by Beatty 2016 p. 1)

In the 1950s, there were a stream of pilgrimages to Rome celebrating: 'Pope Pius's XII solemn declaration of the dogma that the Virgin Mary was assumed body and soul into heaven' (Cooney 1999: 248). Cooney's study of the Archbishop of Dublin Dr McQuaid places considerable emphasis on the Archbishop's personal papers and on Irish government records. In the 1950s, Dr McQuaid's documents contain details of European trips, lavish dinners, special audiences and a gala performance in his honour (Cooney 1999: 248–51). At the time of the Holy Year celebrations of the 1950s, the president of the Congress of Irish Unions, John Conroy, stated, 'In the circumstances, no one will question the cost of the delegations sent by Congress to Rome, nor will there be a single demur about it' (cited by Cooney 1999: 251). Cooney goes on to say that, 'The Trade Union Congress, numbering 181,040 members, went into debt on account of its Holy Year expenditures' (p. 251).

The national deference for these religious traditions and festivities provided ample photographic opportunity and international travel for government. Cooney (1999) says 'all Government Ministers put Rome on their Holy Year itinerary, except for the Minister for Health Dr. Noel Browne' (p. 251). This minister was renowned for speaking truth to power, critiquing religion's dominant social influence in Irish society. Dr Browne (1986) had received his secondary school education in the UK. From this experience outside of Ireland, Noël Browne learned: 'English Catholicism had none of the hectoring arrogant triumphalist contempt of other religions which I later came to associate with Irish Catholicism' (p. 59). When working in Ireland, Dr Browne refers to workplace discrimination, because he had chosen to study medicine at Trinity College Dublin:

> I was suspect and unwelcome within the state medical services. To admit to a medical training in TCD, irrespective of the quality or extent of one's subsequent training, was an automatic disqualification from posts in any of the local authority sanatoria, the only sanatoria which provided medical care for public patients suffering from pulmonary tuberculosis. There were plenty of doctors ready to treat private patients, but this work did not interest me. (Browne 1986: 85)

From my own experience, I remember an aged lady from Wexford, recounting how a friend of hers had received a warning shot letter from Archbishop McQuaid. The Dublin Archbishop insisted that one of her children should not proceed with the study of medicine at Trinity College. This request was complied with. The medical student subsequently left Ireland to study medicine in America. It took until June 1970 for the Catholic Church to lift this ban (Ferriter 2012). Dr Browne (1986) refers to 'the cap tipping deference' (p. 80) toward a medical doctor's authority in the Irish hospital system. While acknowledging 'the British had no small opinion of themselves,' (p. 81) Browne says the UK hospital staff in the 1940s: 'all contributed equally to the struggle to help and to care for our patients. There were no titles; we all used Christian names. Technicians, technocrats, male nurses, doctors, porters, ambulance drivers and administrative staff, were all on equal terms, and co-equal members of a fine social and recreational club' (Browne 1986: 80).

Noël Browne (1986) was primarily known for his innovative efforts in the eradication of TB in Ireland. He also strongly advocated against the close Church-state relationship within legal discourses, education, health care and cultural norms. Browne grasped how his own life course had been externally shaped by institutions and the favourable opportunities that came his way and prevented him from being hemmed by a narrow-minded philosophy that stifled dissent and opportunity during a socio-historic context of deep oppression/repression in Ireland. He suffered personally for his independent mind. Status quo majoritarian rule defenders often seem inordinately invested in silencing opposition and alternative viewpoints. Browne did not last long in government as a minister. In the early 1950s, a controversy erupted over the Mother and Child Scheme in Ireland (Earner-Byrne 2013). This controversy is frequently cited as the rationale that brought down the Irish government in 1951 (Fanning 2014). Dr Browne went public on the direct interference of the Catholic hierarchy in Irish government health policy. Browne appears to have been a lone voice in Cabinet critiquing religious interference in government policies. The Archbishop of Dublin, Dr John Charles McQuaid, was able to exercise pressure on government to put an end for what turned out to be a short ministerial career (Cooney 1999). Former government minister Pat Rabbitte (2018), in an analysis of this period, talked of Irish government ministers being summoned to the archbishop's house in Drumcondra before proceeding with social legislation: 'When McQuaid crushed an attempt by a reforming young health minister, Noel Browne in the 1950s to introduce a free welfare system for mothers and their children, he boasted that the defeat of the Mother and Child Scheme "was the most important event in Irish history since Daniel O'Connell had achieved Catholic emancipation in 1829" (Rabbitte 2018).

In his autobiographical writing, Browne (1986) refers to the deeply sectarian nature of Archbishop McQuaid's thinking. Also, Ferriter (2017) citing Archbishop McQuaid's boast from 1955, proclaiming:

> I have now, at length, been able to take measures in the University [UCD] to have Catholic philosophy permeate all the faculties, and I hope that our educated lay folk in the near future will no longer show themselves to be infected by the Protestant English liberalism that had caused, and is still causing so much confusion in our country.' He hated the idea that 'history, commerce and technology are striving to override the world. (Ferriter 2017)

Even when it came to treating fatal health conditions, the former government minister, Dr Noël Browne (1986), highlights the sectarian-mindedness of Dr McQuaid:

> Our attempt to form a TB association was sabotaged by religious complications. Those of us who had started the project hoped to include doctors from all hospitals concerned with pulmonary tuberculosis .... To my surprise the steering committee, of which I was not a member, received an instruction from the Catholic Archbishop of Dublin, Dr. John Charles McQuaid, that he would not permit Protestant doctors to sit on our committee. The committee accepted this ruling, the usual practice at the time, at all levels in the country. (p. 86)

MacLellan (2018) says 'At the beginning of the twentieth century, tuberculosis was the third leading cause of death in Irish children. It was predominately an urban disease and the death rates in Ireland's capital city compared unfavourably with death rates in other cities of similar population size' (p. 253). As previously outlined, the history of suspiciousness for Protestant religion predates Dr McQuaid. In the previous century, Catholic children were even refused the sacraments by some Irish bishops because they received their education in Protestant schools, even when there were no Catholic schools in close proximity to where they lived (Privilege 2009).

Capturing the persistence of this deference for the Church in Irish life right into the mid-twentieth century in Ireland, Daly (2012) states:

In 1951, during a Dáil debate on the ill-fated mother and child public health care scheme, which the Hierarchy opposed as contrary to Catholic social teaching, the then Taoiseach John A. Costello informed the House: 'I, as a Catholic, obey my Catholic authorities' – to whom he offered 'complete allegiance.'

A Labour Party leader of the era, Brendan Corish, similarly declared: 'I am an Irishman second, I am Catholic first, and I accept without qualification in all respects, the teaching of the church to which I belong.' (p. 7)

Cooney (1999) says 'behind the extravagant external displays of religious fervour, Catholic Ireland in the mid-twentieth century was a grim, inward-looking and deeply repressive society' (p. 277). Research reports and books depicting harsh social realities were banned and suppressed. Keating (2015) traces the literary-journalistic censorship of the Irish Free State to the Censorship of Publications Act 1929 (Committee on Evil Literature). He argues it was introduced:

By an insecure state at the insistence of the Irish Catholic Church ... an institution that the Free State depended on for its very survival. The church, for its part, viewed the Free State and its people as a uniquely positioned vehicle to fulfil God's mission, a mission that the church believed was under attack from foreign influences. Additionally, Irish Catholicism would be shown to be deeply conservative and authoritarian with an overstated pessimism regarding the people of Ireland's ability to withstand foreign vice without the application of rigid clerical discipline – a feature born of Irish Catholicism's particular theological underpinning, which led to the Irish people being viewed as 'children' in need of 'parental' protection and guidance by both church and Nationalist ideologues. (p. 289–90)

When I think of my mother's status in the context of this history, it was normal for her to feel she had little power over societal arrangements. McGarry (2014) describes how the historical antecedents would have played out in the interiority of my mother's early life in Ireland:

Although the 1922 Constitution granted women equal voting rights, they became increasingly inconspicuous in political life, except as the widows or mothers of the patriot dead. In addition, their status as citizens was eroded by their effective exclusion from civil service examinations (1925) and juries (1927), as well as the introduction of a 'marriage bar' for female teachers and civil servants. The commitment of Free State politicians to gender inequality, which transcended party affiliations, culminated in

1937 with the dispiriting, if largely symbolic, commitment of De Valera's constitution to safeguard the place of women 'within the home.' (p. 662)

McNay (2012) says 'one of the effects of internalized domination is that oppressed groups often find it difficult to give voice to their experiences of suffering and injustice' (p. 235). My mother could not question those who had power over her. And I think over time when a pattern becomes so normalized, its dispiriting effects eat away at a person's ability to give voice to such cruelty. It was difficult for my mother not to feel undermined in the way Irish society was organized against her: 'Silence that is frequently a feature of oppression ... it is the effect of the incorporation of structural violence into the body which is then lived in euphemized form of a habitus of acceptance or resignation' (citing Bourdieu and Honneth, McNay 2012: 235). To think of my mother as biologically pre-determined to experience poor mental health in these psychotic contexts makes very little sense to me. My mother was up against dominant social values that fed a logic for very unfair treatment as normal. Practically, it is hard to imagine how a person's disposition could not have been impacted by these social scenes of disempowerment. When we were in distress as a family, some of us often turned to God to relieve our stress and fear. This was so seductive, weightless and delusional. We offered up our sufferings to a transcendental power. Even dire poverty was spiritualized in Irish discourse, creating an infantile mindset, devoid of a political understanding for how social disempowerment embeds itself, as mind-in-the-world.

In the 1950s, Daly (2016) refers to the slow and uneven pace of economic development in Ireland:

Throughout most of Western Europe, the 1950s was a decade of economic transformation with unprecedented growth, near-full employment, modest price increases and steadily rising living standards. In Ireland, it was marked by economic stagnation and the highest level of emigration since the 1880s. (p. 19)

In this context, Redmond (2015) offers a vivid description of the Mother and Baby Home which my mother had to go to in Castlepollard in 1952/3. He states that residents in the 1960s were given 'house names' upon arrival and provided with a rough cloth, shapeless uniform, drawstring underwear and hard clogs. Bras were not allowed. The girls were not allowed to talk to each other or form friendships. They were underfed and undernourished and forced to do hard work as 'penance'. They remained for two years on average, working on the farm or in the laundry or cleaning and scrubbing floors. They picked fruit and made jam, anything to 'repay the debt' they owed for their care. Many stayed for three to four years. (Redmond 2015)

Marking women out in this way, created the idea that these women were a distinct species and that they were different from others. In Castlepollard, Redmond (2015) says,

> Days began early with daily mass with fire and brimstone sermons from the local priests, particularly Father P.J. Reagan. Girls sat at the back of the chapel and nuns entered from the corridor from the Manor house. Girls would faint at mass and were punished for their 'disrespect'. Father Reagan was heavily involved with the adoptions, particularly foreign adoptions to America; he also ran the Saint Claire's Adoption Society which also handled adoptions from Saint Clares in nearby Stamullen – a huge 'Holding Centre' for unaccompanied babies and children. Fr. Reagan also had some involvement with another M&B home named Ard Mhuire in Dunboyne, County Meath. (Redmond 2015)

O'Toole (2017) refers to societal compliance and deference to 'what we might call the moral-industrial complex – the vast archipelago of industrial schools, Magdalene laundries, Mother and Baby homes and Mental hospitals – was that it used shame and fear to get families to collude with it.' A further vivid example of 'the vast archipelago' in Ireland's history is Tom Wall's (2013) very moving account of being brought up in the Irish Christian Brothers-run St Joseph's industrial school at Glin in Co. Limerick. In the early 1950s, Tom was separated from his mother. From the age of three years old to his late teens, Tom lived at Glin industrial school. Tom says of his time there, he was 'regularly beaten, bullied and left cold and hungry and worst of all was sexually abused'. Regarding the political and cultural backdrop of the horrors he and others experienced, Tom Wall (2013) says the Irish Christian Brothers 'were held in high esteem. No newspapers would print anything to discredit them'. In the context of the wider influence of the Church, he says of the Christian Brothers 'they were a law unto themselves and no authority seemed willing or able to challenge them'.

In the late 1960s, the school changed its functional purpose. For a short period, young brothers came to Glin on retreat and summer holidays. When talking to one of the new Christian Brothers at Glin, Tom was asked about the conditions at the former industrial school: 'I told him the truth. I told him about all the terrible beatings we got, the sex abuse, I told him the lot'. Later that evening, Tom was summoned to the superior's office:

> When I arrived he closed the door because there was young Christian Brothers about. He was furious with me. 'In future, I do not want the Industrial School mentioned here. When you are speaking with the young Christian Brothers, you are not to mention the Industrial School. This is a new college that we are running here now. If I hear any more about the Industrial School, you'll be out the gate, I hope you understand. We do not want the Christian Brothers talking about what happened here. I hope you understand that.' I said 'Yes Sir.' (Wall 2013)

At this stage in the book, Wall had stayed on at Glin to do some labouring at the former industrial school. In reading the story, despite the intensity of the violations he experienced, Tom clearly felt the outside world was alien and unsafe. As a developmental story, his fear and lack of trust makes a great deal of sense. People who went to these schools were treated differently by society. Tom suffered separation, stigma, terrible violence and abuse at such a young age. Tom Wall also states how he was keen to track the whereabouts of his birth mother. He managed to meet his mother before she passed away (Wall 2013).

A further example in Irish history was the recent spotlight on a Mother and Baby home in Tuam, Co. Galway. A local researcher, Catherine Corless, had conducted some field investigation on St Mary's, a home run by the Bon Secour Religious Sisters from 1925 to 1961. In 2016, Minister for Children, Katherine Zappone supported a policy for excavation of this site (Siggins 2016). This approval arose from the concerns that Corless had raised on discovering that 796 babies were buried in mass graves in Tuam over a thirty-six-year period. Corless had obtained this information from public and civic records, combined with local knowledge suggesting that babies were buried in unmarked graves at a site in Tuam. However, Corless could not find the burial plots at the site. From the records she managed to obtain,

Corless said the deceased babies were: 'a few days old/month/year/s, with the oldest up to eight years old' (Corless 2017).

In a Dáil statement on 10 March 2017, Minister Zappone confirmed the existence of human remains on foot of the initial archaeological report. In the following quote, the Minister for Children once again states a familiar pattern in Irish history:

> Experience tells us it can take time to shine a light on dark periods of our history. The truth is the truth is hidden. Sometimes hidden in plain sight. It takes the brave testimony of survivors, long studies by historians and the dogged determination of investigative journalists to bring a spotlight to events which were previously only whispered about – in this case for generations. (Zappone 2017, Department of Children and Youth Affairs Press)

In a TV interview, Corless (2017) was keen to take the weight of shame and blame away from the parents and their children who were forced into these homes. With a state enforced ban on contraception, consistent with a dogmatic religious ideology, Corless said the dominance of religious teachings devalued these women who had sex before marriage. She said these women were explicitly constructed as having committed 'grievous sins.' During this historic period and beyond, the Catholic Hierarchy remained resolute in its opposition to contraception (Hug 1999). Corless (2017) in her *The Late Late Show* interview, recounted various episodes of how women who gave birth to children outside of marriage were subjected to ridicule by local clerics, sometimes rejected by their families, and subject to further demeaning inferences by society. The lower down the social rank, these women who had given birth outside of marriage, were at a major disadvantage. That is not to say women in the high social classes were not stigmatized giving birth outside of marriage. Dominant stigma can impact all women and concealed stigma is in no way benign for its ill effects on human embodiment. From 1973 onwards, the Irish bishops began to row back on its earlier dogmatic opposition to contraception 'by saying that what is forbidden by the Church does not have to be forbidden by the State' (Hug 1999: 109–10).

Of the same generation as my mother, the widely acclaimed novelist John McGahern (2005) recounts his experiences of rural Ireland at the time:

> The country I grew up in was a theocracy in all but name, but I had naively thought that in the early days of the State, lip service at least would have been paid to the proclamation of the Republic in 1916, which guaranteed equal rights to all citizens irrespective of class or creed; but here [the Catholic Church] was, without a miss of a beat, still in charge, even as the old dispensation gave way to the new. (p. 1)

O'Toole (2015) says in the 1950s 'a grand total of 4,500 students sat the Leaving Cert exam and the number in all our universities combined was 7,900. The entire output of Irish broadcasting was seven hours of radio a day. There were just 43,000 phone lines in the State, only a third of them domestic.' Garvin (2004) notes how

> Emigration, mainly to Great Britain, was, almost proverbially, a way of life and it seemed to many that the entire independence project was a failure. The apparently dismal performance of the Irish Independent State belied the high-flown and ambitious rhetoric of the founding fathers and also questioned the formula of independence as the magic cure for Irish underdevelopment. The belief articulated by many eighteenth-century radicals including Theobald Wolfe Tone and Jonathan Swift that the English connection was the source of all of Ireland's many woes seemed to be rebutted by the actual experience of political independence.

McGahern's later book *The Dark* (1965), which was censored at the time of publication, deals with significant human rights violations. In highlighting this historic work within their collection of important events in Irish history, Fanning and Garvin (2014) say that McGahern's book

> Depicted child sexual abuse, the savage beating of young children .... themes that struggled for attention for a few more decades before official Ireland professed to be shocked and set up its tribunals of inquiry. The Dark was, of course banned and its author was fired from his teaching job by the Catholic Church. (p. 125)

A further insight into this repression is offered by the lesbian poet and novelist Mary Dorcey (1995) describing clerical domination as having a normative grip on social customs:

> In the 1950s, all was silence ... an almost perfectly homogenous society brooking no divergence from the norm. Repression. Censorship. Long dark winters. Poor food. Nuns and priests everywhere. Drab clothes. Censorship of books and films. Fear and suspicion surrounding anything to do with the body or the personal life. The near

total repression of ideas and information. A Catholic State for a Catholic People.
It is hardly possible to imagine the extent of this censorship, because the cultural
climate has changed so radically by comparison. (p. 25)

Garvin (2004) adds that

Cultural activity was under political attack. This cultural war was being waged by
linguistic revivalists, Catholic fundamentalists and state censors; writing, paint-
ing, theatre, dance and the plastic arts were commonly regarded with indifference,
suspicion and even active hostility by the secular and ecclesiastical authorities. This
indifference and hostility were also popular in some circles; such activity was commonly regarded as snobbish, pretentious and 'West British.'

What is explicit in these atmospheric recollections is how power is exercised
in societies. Allen (2016) citing Kant's essay 'What is Enlightenment' captures the pattern of how 'powerful people who use their power to prevent
their subordinates from making free and undistorted use of their faculty
of intelligence' (p. 87). Thompson (2013) refers to these patterns as 'the
values of elites become the values of the community as a whole' (p. 38).

My own mother did not have the tools to confront her situation and
she suffered great pain from this as a woman. My suggestion is she felt a
low horizon of self-worth was deserved and normal. She did not talk about
her feelings in a direct way. I was really lucky to have her. Growing up, I
became more aware of her rapid disappointment with my father. She did
speak more directly in later years. My father's promise to be a better person
never materialized. He got progressively worse. My mother could not escape
the clutches of my father's reach. He was manipulative and deceptive. There
was very little anyone could do to transform him.

From my vantage point, my mother's situation and also that of my
eldest sister's upbringing in the US tells me they must have felt they had
little human right to question these toxic social arrangements. The views
of domineering others often inferred that they ought to be grateful for
their plight. Catholic ethics created weightless ideas about the dignity
of the human person as if personal dignity is free-standing and that dignity is untouchable despite adversity and social harm. Or that dignity
grows through adversity. I do not think this is necessarily true as people
should not be experimented upon to prove their hardiness and strengths.

Resilience is not an evenly distributed phenomenon in the population. Ireland's theocratic impulse conspired to create a disconnected self. As a national philosophy, this encouraged falseness.

My mother's kindly and caring dispositions meant she had little choice to acquiesce to societal dominance. The impact on her health was terrible and grotesque. Consistent with her personality, my mother had positive assumptions about the world. She understood the requirement of stability and she would not have drawn extra attention by publicly interrogating social arrangements. She was a private person. Despite her proximate daily challenges, she was not embittered. She never projected anger onto her children because of her situation. Because of her warm disposition, people were drawn to her and liked her. I feel very fortunate in this regard. I was able to anchor toward her warmth. I could never repay what she gave to me during very testing times.

Another aspect to my childhood was how cultural superstitions were par for the course in Irish society. In school, I was regularly within ear shot of bad prophecies. Immediate dates were often set predicting the end of the world. Combined with the disturbances going on in our house with my father, I completely believed in banshees and ghosts. Cats would often gather and congregate in our back garden and would cry for hours at night. When pictures fell off the walls in our house, I thought our house was haunted. It was a sign of bad luck. Some of my mother's friends often came to our house to read tea-leaves from cups, making dire predictions about the future. The overall context of being proximate to these prophecies was a narrowing emotional experience for a child.

In my early teenage years, I regularly went to the cinema with my sister to watch really scary horror movies liked *Dressed to Kill* and *A Stranger Calls*. I also worked in the local hotel during the school holidays. The stories that some of the adults used to tell me were really dark and spooky. That said, I enjoyed this experience immensely. I also got pocket money and gave money to my mother.

As a younger child, my father's pattern for disturbing the peace naturalized fear and doubt in my world. I did feel protected and loved by my mother. I knew she was under pressure and was very strained. My own personality was to think I must do big things to make things better, but I could never could focus on small things. I was always making mistakes. I was always distracted by the drama of my circumstances. I felt I could do nothing right, but I still felt I had to make everything right. In an uncertain home, it was the only way to feel in control. Yet, the persistence of either shame or guilt seems to drive a person's desire to remove all the badness. As a young person, a lack of experience, means children are prone to over-rating their personal power to fundamentally change things.

Findings from developmental psychology, say young children feel as if they are right at the centre of happenings in their surrounding world. This resonates with my own experience. As a child, trying to magically change things, drove my thinking. In particular, I wanted to make things better for my mother. However, the insights of developmental psychology alone, offer a truncated view of a nation's ideology. I am mindful that analysing social happenings in the home severs insight of broader social developments. That said, personal happenings in the home extend deeper insight into a historic period of social norms. This type of historic reconstruction will be different for each age group and different within an age group. Social ideologies are often constructed as natural and social beings often take on the mantel of those ideologies naively. The purpose of focusing on personal experiences works against the tendency of reading history in triumphalist narratives and generalist ideas of social advancement and progress.

The multivalent texture of reconstructed lived experience aims to enrich insight into multi-perspectives and experiences. This means social critique in advancing better social policies can be more grounded in real and diverse lives and that theories are less general, abstract and distant.

Regarding Ireland, the macro political context and ideology of the 1960–1970s is well captured by various historical and social scholars in Ireland. The impact of the Northern troubles, and acts of terrorism in the South kept up the theme of religious conflicts as foregrounded. Despite economic crisis, pragmatic advances in social protection were achieved. Regarding religious values, Fine Gael, were a party with 'an identity crisis' (Meehan 2013, 124), with significant differences in attitude within the party on social and moral change. Liam Cosgrave (1920–2017) led Fine Gael and went into coalition government with the Labour party from 1973–1977.

While Cosgrave was certainly not noted as a progressive leader on moral values, he did value democracy and the threats posed by terrorism.

For the episodes that follow, it is important to keep in mind that the objective social structure of rural Ireland in the 1970s was conservative and inward looking. Foregrounded ways of knowing felt preordained, prescriptive and distinctively Irish. There was a great deal of silence and suffering and repression. We did not have much of a discourse to explain it. This can explain why struggles lie latent beneath the surface but still manage to exert a great deal of pressure on the mind. Many families felt a strong sense of guilt and shame. This erodes relational trust and self-esteem. Sacrificial concepts actively encourage many damaged persons to take on the weight of a guilt feeling, where we end up feeling overly responsible for our own disempowerment. Sacrificial concepts also encourage self-righteousness and fundamentalism. Frieder Vogelmann's (2018) critical analysis, utilizing a Foucauldian methodology says 'where a sensitivity is lost, violence threatens to become prevalent and to translate into action'.

Academic theory and applied therapies have a truncated and noncritical discourse for grasping the multifactorial layers of repetitive trauma and its resultant impact on personality formation and development. Expert disciplines need to critique how historical traditions damage the development of personality. Current understandings tend to focus on innate temperament and interpersonal experiences in the development of trauma. This lens does not do justice to the way societies were historically organized. In the absence of such analysis, stigma is emboldened in shaming ideas. The question is how are individuals constrained by pathological social formations which distorts, undercuts and damages the development of social personality, their motivations and their autobiographical selves (McAdams 2015)? Right now, the focus is on significant clinical symptoms, decontextualized from social traditions. Those symptoms are discoursed in disorder terms and are often not helpful for capturing the fulsome impact of repetitive traumas on human beings. Disordered individualist concepts devoid of historical analysis is partial and stigmatizing and does not encourage openness. The social representation of innate character defects dominated my early socialization. Being constituted by stress in an unconscious way modified my responses and reactions to external events and had significant process consequences for thought and mood. Lack of internalized security and stress disabled important transitional strategies in adolescent cognitive development. Surface meanings of history are also surface meanings of self-control and loss.

For a long period, my home situation had been spiralling out of control and was chaotic. This danger had been brought to the attention of many, but nothing substantive was ever done to remove my father from our family home. Instead, a fake idealism of moral perfectionism prevailed, a society characterized by concealment of its key secrets. As a boy, I was ill-prepared for carrying the enormity of thinking that this patchwork and template was all of our own making and had nothing to do with the way our society was constructed in historical time. This lack of knowledge made the burden feel very personal rather than social. When something feels that personal, there is much less inclination to make the experience socially intelligible and relatable to others. It is easy to fly in the face of one's experience as a way of coping. This dissociative feeling inscribes aloneness, intensifying the chatter of an elevated critic. My culture encouraged introspection to discover the cause of any unease. At the time, I never worked out how the symbolic meaning structure of this culture weaved its magic in making meaning of our self-experiences. I was not conscious of how underlying cultural convictions had shaped and influenced our beliefs as a family. I do not ever remember being able to stand back, reflect and analyse what was happening. I also thought we were the main architects of our own family problems which had engineered our silence and our shame.

In thinking this way, I was looking at life the wrong way round. I did not understand how the orienting template of social convictions precede our individuation and our families. Easily graspable social heuristics become core self-beliefs, our psychological armoury for dealing with life's vicissitudes. The social intentionality of customs and traditions were the core constituents for our self-beliefs. Fortunately, my mum was a natural nurturer and without her, our situation would have been a great deal worse. She had an extraordinary capacity for warmth and heartfelt duty to her children. Despite all the obstacles put in her way by society, her innate empathy and exceptional skills as a mother can never be questioned. Some part of her remained untouched by the violence she had to endure. In terms of my relationship to my mother, something significant changed after what happened next in our family history. I do not think anything can prepare a family for such traumas. Witnessing and being part of a trauma narrows a horizon for making meaning of the experiences that followed. The next section contextualizes the personal story of what happened more explicitly. It is the erupting story of a family worn out from trouble. Particularly for my mother and brother, what came next was shattering.

CHAPTER 3

The House of Fear

My father had always created uncertainty and fear around our house. I picked this up from my mother and sisters. My father's behaviour had forever been a source of great anxiety for them. My mother did her best to protect us from his late-night disturbances. He regularly came home drunk and rowdy. We had to seek refuge in our grandparent's home nearby. We would leave until my father calmed down and fell asleep. It was like as if my mother felt she had little choice to put up with him. He was expressing an inalienable right, a preordained right where he felt he could behave in whatever way he wished and get away with it. Up to this point, how he expressed this right went unchallenged. To evaluate a dysfunctional scene severed from the national ideology is meaningless.

My mother could not get a Church annulment or civil divorce from him. Furthermore, I think my mother's integral sense of self had been fractured by his violence. I do not think she fully grasped how much her life had been undermined by him. The oppressive effects of social meanings in Ireland merely reinforced the naturalness of social cruelty. She adapted to it. My mother was also fearful of public dissection. She always wanted to self-present as able to cope and manage her situation. This was very stressful for her. She had wanted a smaller family. She knew how difficult her economic situation was for her first three children. Yet, my father behaved as if it was his natural right to have sex and more children. My mother had no right to contraception. The provision of contraception was illegal in the 1960s. I would not have been born if my mother had a right to contraception. She was caught in a desperate and dangerous situation. She could ill afford more children with a husband who was only interested in drinking and not working or applying himself to anything meaningful. My mother sobbed silently. The normative idea in Irish culture that a woman was here to suffer, acquiesce and endure pain – this interpretation holds true for my mother. Shame silences people. When the arbiters of sexual conduct were moral/political/socio-relational, these 'good authority' arrangements shape and alters self-esteem.

After the refusal of a Church annulment in the 1950s, almost a quarter of century later, the civil ban on divorce was still operative in the 1970s and remained so until 1995, with only a narrow majority in favour of lifting the ban. No matter how bad my father was, my mother felt preordained to stick by him, even as his behaviour got progressively worse. What is inescapable is how the enacted social attitudes, traditions and beliefs lowered her self-confidence, how my mother interiorized oppressive norms. I embrace Sangiovanni's (2017) rationale for the inclusion of anti-discrimination in international legal human rights:

> Practices of discrimination are wrong when and because they express, instantiate, or enable interiorizing social cruelty. They therefore share the crucial relational feature that makes them instances of violating another's status as a moral equal. It is for this reason that they deserve to be considered in the same class as more severe violations of human rights, such as genocide and torture. (p. 211)

To explicitly say, as the Church did, that 'she made her bed' no matter what happened was also endorsed by state logic of this time period. My mother's choices were irrelevant. As she aged, my mother would say, 'Jesus only lived until he was 33.' Indeed, this sacrificial philosophy in the story of Jesus, for how Jesus handled his suffering is significant for how she should weigh up her suffering. This story was held up as an exemplar model of endurance and restraint. Viewed in this way, the message is abundantly clear: 'stop moaning.' After decades of living with such cruelty, my mother was showing signs of poor physical and mental health. Her subjective point of view about these tortuous conditions were not vocal. Bernstein (2015) refers to this as 'the morality of principles that undermines women's experiential knowledge of the moral harm of rape, while tacitly leaving the deformation of patriarchal assumptions about embodiment and reason untouched' (p. 313). To escape from the violence of my father, my mother needed a society that was really committed to denaturalizing discrimination and cruelty against women. I do not even believe my mother knew she had a right to physical security to protect her and her family from domestic violence. Neither, did she know that my father's imposition of sexual intercourse against her will constituted rape. My mother's sense of empathetic agency was forever preoccupied in protecting us. She carried the tariff of Ireland's false consciousness, as normalized in her education which contained foregrounded emphasis on theological principles, a defining ethos in which to interpret lived experiences. There was nothing hidden about this, it somehow seemed acceptable, even though the shared fate texture of harms were socially silenced in normative social discourse. The paradox is social suffering is both seen and concealed at the same time. My father demanded that his children should start work quickly so that he would have more money for his drinking habit. He created a false narrative around this, saying his children had to get out to work early for our mother's sake. My father saw no value in extended education. He tried to enforce his wishes on his children. There was nothing reasonable or sincere about his dictates. He was out of control, an erratic law onto himself. His behaviour was no outlier. He found enough cues and support in his culture to strengthen his inordinate right to be out of relationship with others, affording him no substantive insight beyond stereotypical formulations of manhood. Yet, thankfully, most men of his time were so unlike him.

One evening, out of nowhere, a very unsettling incident occurred in my family home. The previous month, my brother Eamonn had just finished secondary school in St Mel's in Longford. At the time, I was just nine years old. My father was forty-seven years old. On this particular evening, 14 July 1975, my father arrived home with drink taken. He was erratic and fearsome. In the main, I do not have many recollections of my father paying much attention to me. I remember him bringing me into a pub on one occasion. I remember him showing me off to his friends in the pub and telling these men I was his son. This is the only time I can remember a specific episode of him paying direct attention to me in an affirmative way. He was registering my presence. He could not be consistent with this. Most of the time, he was in an inflamed state of deception and he got away with it. My siblings have stronger recollections of how violent my father was around the house. Some of them were hypervigilant and fearful of his physical assaults and potential for more. When he was not in the house and gone away, I remember feeling much freer and happier. Perhaps, I felt like a child.

On the evening in question, in the sitting room of our house, my father became agitated by the twin noises of the television and a hair dryer. My father was so easily rattled. So, I jumped up to unplug the devices. I thought taking them out of the wall would please him. The exterior part of the adapter was cracked. Immediately, I yelped from the electric shock. This reaction angered my father. He thumped me across the head. He was shaking me and shouting at me. I was crying. I cried easily back then. I do not cry as easily now, if ever. I remember my mother intercepting to stop him from hitting me. She took the impact of my father. My older brother Eamonn then tried to stop him and my father turned on him. As Bernstein (2015) states very concisely, 'people not principles are what get harmed, broken, violated in morally wrongful behaviour' (p. 75).

In July 1975, my older brother Eamonn was sixteen years old. I only have a patchy recollection of the struggle which ensued between my father and brother. Everything happened so fast. Another sister was also in the room that night. It was an overwhelming experience for us all. In 1976, the following year, a local newspaper recounts that my father gave me:

> A box with his clenched fist in the face. With that Gerard fell to the floor and started to cry. His father said, 'What are you crying for? Are you looking for notice? Do you want more?' At that stage, Eamonn intervened and said 'This will have to stop. Can't you leave him alone? Gerard is not long out of hospital.' Gerard had been in hospital in Crumlin for investigation for nose bleeds. (*Longford Leader* 1976: 1)

I can remember my mother, running out of the house, hysterical, pleading for the support of near neighbours to rescue the situation. All to no avail. The nearest person she could see on the street was the father of a boy I had previously hit with a stone across the head while playing. I got into awful trouble for this shocking incident. Around the time, I felt this neighbour's reason for not coming to our rescue was my fault. When the police arrived, my father was unconscious and could not be resuscitated. A report in the local paper stated:

Guard M. McCann said that around 8.12 pm on the 14th July he received a request to go to Teffia Park where there was a disturbance. He travelled in the patrol car with Guard Kane and on arrival at the house he was admitted by the defendant whose shirt was covered in blood. He was in a very shocked condition. He asked him whose blood it was and he said it was his fathers. He asked him where his father was and he showed him into the living room. His father was lying on his back on the floor and was unconscious. Witness shouted to Guard Kane to summon a doctor and a priest. He tried artificial respiration without success as also did Guard Kane. He saw his mother also and she was in a very hysterical state. The deceased had a cut over his left eyebrow and there was blood coming from his mouth and nose. There was also blood on the couch. The defendant kept asking him how his father was. (*Longford Leader* 1976: 1)

My older brother was taken away by police: 'Dr G. Donnelly gave evidence of being called to attend the defendant at the Garda Station at 11 pm. He said he was very agitated and appeared to be in a state of shock' (*Longford Leader* 1976: 1). In the direct aftermath of this socially induced trauma, I remember my mother was so unwell. She lost all sense of reason. She was hospitalized for over three weeks. As my mother aged, she was subsequently hospitalized for manic depression (bipolar) on several occasions. Given her long history of persecution, it is hardly surprising her sense of self was breached and shattered. Over many decades, the chronic stressors and the social stigma she had experienced had enacted a very heavy price on her. My mother internalized this social enactment as something about her. It was never anything about her, but the cascading and repetitive social feedbacks she experienced, naturalized shame. It was never society's shame and how a moral society's profound appetite for secrecy weakened and damaged her. That is not to say that people were not kind to her and that she was not kind to them. But deep down, my mother's secret horrors were so unfair on her. She could never tell on society because she would not have been listened to in a meaningful and in-depth way. Often with the best will in the world, experts tried to capture and medicate her psychological state. Medication did help her cope but she felt deeply ashamed of having to be admitted to hospital, so often, over a long time period.

After the incident itself, we were supported by grandparents and near relatives. Some psychological support was offered to our family. I remember the psychologist as formal but pleasant. I think she may have ran a series of psychological tests on my sister and me to check core cognitive competencies. I think she determined we were fine in her objective tests of measurement. Terr (1990) says: 'Over the past centuries ... even physicians shied away from examining kid's real experiences' (p. 5). In 1975/6, I do not remember the child psychologist trying to explore the story of what had happened to us. Out of loyalty to my brother and mother, it was expected that certain matters were not spoken about after what had happened. As young children we got used of carrying experience in a particular way which concealed a great deal, where anxieties lie latent, appearances are key, eating away at our ability to interpret and make sense. In observing a code, we were not really talking to each other. A quote from Sangiovanni (2017) seems apt where we 'feel as if we are merely playing a part in a play that we don't understand' (p. 79). It is called getting on with it.

The court trial followed in 1976. The Guards gave evidence in court when questioned. One of the Guards said: 'He was not surprised to hear of a disturbance at Teffia Park. There had been a number of disturbances over the years which usually arose as a result of the deceased indulging in alcohol. Guard M. Kane gave corroborative evidence' (*Longford Leader* 1976: 1). My brother's statement was read into court:

> As far back as I can remember, my father gave us a terrible time and was a complete tyrant in the house. Many times, we had to send for the guards with his brutality and many times he put us out on the street in the early hours of the morning. His drinking had a terrible effect on us. He used to beat us all .... Had this been an isolated incident I would not have done anything at all .... At no time did I hit my father with anything other than my hands. When I hit him it was only on the spur of the moment because he had hit Gerard, but I hated him for all the trouble he had given us down the years. (*Longford Leader* 1976: 1)

My brother often recalled how another sibling expressed great relieve that our father was deceased. No one in my family ever had a good word to say about him. After the case in November 1976, the local paper carried the story on its front page as a main headline 'Longford Family Lived in Fear: Youth Cleared of Father's Manslaughter' (p. 1). A jury returned a verdict of not guilty on the charge of manslaughter. For over a year and a half, my brother had to wait for this verdict. This was a huge worry for my mother.

Judge Peter O'Malley said of the verdict: 'It was a very proper decision. He was sure that they all wished that this unfortunate family would have no more trouble in the future' (*Longford Leader* 1976: 1).

My brother Eamonn died at fifty-eight years old in 2017. Eamon did extremely well to exercise the levels of responsibility that he did in his short life. I feel so sorry that he lost his life so soon. He made a very strong contribution to life despite the violent context of his early life trajectory. My father really had it in for him. To block out his trauma, Eamonn drank very heavily all through his life. Some may interpret addiction as self-induced, a choice he made to suffer. I remember his attempt at recovery from alcoholism in a treatment centre. His wife and children, members of our family, work colleagues and friends participated in this intervention.

After treatment, my brother stayed sober for a while. As my brother aged, his sober periods were few and far between. This is how he coped. His behaviour became more alienating as his drinking was so repetitive. There was no inherent badness in my brother's nature. How he interiorized, interpreted and carried the corrosive effects of what had happened to him was so hard to watch. He was unreachable in many ways and I did not try hard enough to reach him.

At his funeral service, I do not recall any mention being made of anything my brother had been exposed to in his early life. In general, the Church struggled to find the words to adequately capture its share of responsibility for creating a cultural backdrop where some Irish women, like my mother and her young family, were preordained to endure bad fates. The moral logics of the Church-state prohibition on divorce in Ireland was punitive. That said, the priest at my brother's funeral was respectful and nuanced. I was very moved by the many people who turned up to sympathize with my brother's two sons, their mother, siblings, relatives and close friends. Eamon had good friends who looked out for him. It is hard to believe his remains lie in a cemetery. Eamonn was found dead in his home. When I received a late-night call, I expected the worst.

My brother Eamonn had a particular gift for helping people out all through his life. He was a perfect advocate to have by your side. However, I felt he could never translate this advocacy to himself. In the same way that Eamonn saved our deceased mother and his family from psychotic violence, I really felt my brother had enacted false ideas about himself. Taking up a sacrificial stance was so corrosive to his wellbeing. Like my mother, I felt he carried a sacrificial complex learned from historic socialization. In his early development, taking on the mantel of an elevated sense of responsibility absolutely wrecked his emotional life. My brother was lonely in this space. Eamonn was not a violent man like my father. He was absolutely nothing like my father. He was empathetic, warm-hearted, with many diverse interests.

My brother could have enjoyed a more balanced perspective on life if our mental health services were better equipped in understanding the weight he carried and how the death of my father, the psychotic violence he experienced and witnessed as a boy rearranged and damaged his life. I believe my brother always wanted to be seen as optimally in control of outcomes. Most of us value being in control as we build our identity. As he aged, it became harder for him to bounce back. He was depleted.

The early photos of my brother show him to have a bright and sunny disposition. More recently, I saw my father's younger photos and he too had a sunny disposition. When my father's last remaining sibling died recently, I discovered how my father as an older teenager/young adult had shown some kindness to her children. Despite the not guilty verdict in relation to my father's death, my brother was burdened about what had happened. He carried the blame and found this very difficult to talk about. Most theoretical ideas on trauma and addiction appear to come up short in understanding how social discourses and social arrangements act as key .transfer points for making meaning of social suffering.

During the 1970s in Ireland, the prevailing norms of society did not encourage open reflection of family traumas. There were so many secrets and great resistance when people try to articulate these secrets. As *Sunday Independent* journalist Gene Kerrigan (2018) recently stated in his column, 'We simply don't know how many others have backed down, and retreated in obscurity, in the face of that brutality' (p. 32). He was referring to the recent Cervical Health Scandal and how a bullying institutional culture seems to resist victims of injustice. Kerrigan extends his critique to social patterns in our history, where wronged individuals have been consistently fought by the state in the pursuit of justice.

In 1974, 'there were only 235 social workers employed nationally' (Ferriter 2012: 375). Historically, religious patronage dominance of these institutions was so naturalized and so foregrounded in the public sphere. The Institute of Public Health in Ireland in partnership with the Centre for Effective Services says, 'the lifelong effects of the early years' experience include impacts across many aspects of health and wellbeing; including inter alia obesity, heart disease, mental health, educational achievement and economic status' (IPH 2016). These overt symptoms are often the manifestation of social oppression, where persons find it difficult to articulate self-limiting beliefs. The burden of stressed constitutions will compensate with maladaptive behaviours.

In my brother's and even my mother's case, to theorize this as an innate pathology to them is wrong. While traumatized persons have a level of psychological resilience to bounce back in our younger years, we have less resilience to cope with stress as we age. Feeling burdensome is very wearing. Comparing oneself to others in a beaten and depleted state is not a good idea for self-esteem. This lowers self-confidence even more.

As a young adolescent in the 1970s, I myself as a gay young boy had appropriated cultural ideas of badness about myself. I was religious and I regularly prayed to be good. I had no idea what lay ahead through this projection. As it happened, religion was certainly no place of refuge for transcending damaged self-confidence. Rather, further exploitative experiences that soon followed my father's death, inscribed further fear and even more distrust for the wider world. Carrying guilt had become second nature to me. If I got angry, I would feel guilty. This lack of ease and constant anxiety felt natural. I wanted to feel safe. Surrendering to God's will was such a foregrounded value in my social imaginary. Turning to God to relieve suffering was so easy to grasp. It was freely available to ritualize and routinize people like me who were struggling to understand life on life's terms. I felt that if I adhered to what my religion preached, I would overcome badness and anxiety. A critical characteristic of a self-confident person lies in their ability to create a reflective distancing from limiting social traditions and beliefs. I was too distracted and found it so difficult to forward plan as a young boy and as a young adult. I had no idea that by choosing to enact transcendental ideas, I would actually end up with a short straw. I could not clearly work out how social/religious ideologies manifested in my beliefs and attitudes. I could not make sense of so many things in my early development, largely because of the heightened and fearful speed inside my head. I winged it and kept up an appearance, but I knew I was not learning much. I was moulded to be enlivened by religious ideation. Magical, idealized self-righteous thought had a strong grip on me. It was a persona and façade. How Ireland's culture enacted its social conscience and discourse through religious ideas felt part of my identity as a person. Ireland's history encouraged repression of social facts. Positioning my own family experience within social repression is to say that the development of self-regulation/self-determination is a complex skill, particularly in early childhood and in transitions through adolescence and young adulthood (Oettigen and Gollwitzer 2015). Whitlock and Selekman (2014) describe process trauma in young lives as

> negative events, particularly as they accumulate, are processed by the amygdala (responsible for emotion identification and response) not yet in full dialogue with the cerebral cortex (responsible for higher order cognitive processing). As a result, children are likely to look for a concrete cause for negative events and to identify themselves as key causal agents. In addition, they often lack the experience needed to appreciate that the pain, which they and those they love may be experiencing as a result of difficult or traumatic life events or transitions, will pass with time. (p. 135)

Furthermore, the developmental approach of Crowell, Derbidge, and Beauchaine (2014) offers further insight:

> over time, children apply increasingly complex behavioural and psychological responses within the environment, ideally increasing the chances of navigating developmental challenges successfully. However, in extremely high-risk environments, such as those characterized by violence, behavioural repertoires that are adaptive in one setting (staying quiet around an abusive caregiver) can become maladaptive in others (e.g., school), conferring lifelong risk. (p. 188)

As I have been contending thus far, it is simply not fair or accurate to analyse subjective suffering as a developmental experience devoid of sociological/

historical explanation. The negative psychological experiences of my family were inseparable from the social and historical context. As both an academic writer and as a human being at the centre these experiences, I think I am in a good position to resist the 'sterile' tendency of truncated academic thought which 'amputates core characteristics of reality' (Devereux 1967, cited by Renault 2017, p. 12). Ideological cliques in academia are often very removed from the world which they research. What can feel even more oppressive, is when groups of academics, peers, politicians show a resolve to keep social suffering invisible, or if visible, status quo meanings are foregrounded, over others.

> Groups engage in epistemic activity all the time – whether it be the active collective inquiry of localized epistemic communities such as scientific research groups or crime-detection units, or the heavily institutionally structured evidential deliberations of tribunals and juries, or the more spontaneous and imperfect information-processing of the voting population. (Brady and Fricker 2016: 1)

Experts of mental health are often viewed as part of the problem where they try to medicalize social suffering, but do not identify the social/political factors that enable social transformation. The critique is that medical diagnosis may act as surveillance techniques to regulate societies, rather than empower critical thinking of social objectification, for the 'retrieval of a politic ethic of responsibility' (Vázquez Arroyo 2016). It should be clear that status quo politics enacted deference to theologically infused ideas. In the main, this value orientation in academic knowledge produced particular ways of abstract and idealistic thinking, often failing to grasp the rationale for loss of power in historical time. Oppressed people accept oppressive conditions without recognizing how objective structures of oppression has gripped their modes of self-understanding and bodily dispositions. This corrosive thread is more overt and obvious as people age. McNay (2012) says:

> In short, the internalisation of domination may profoundly affect the ability of individuals to act as effective agents of their own interests; it may prevent them from construing their problems as political in the first place and, even when they do have a critical understanding of their situation, their willingness to participate in corrective political action is far from assured (Mansbridge and Morris 2001; Bader 2007). From this perspective, one of the central problems for political theory is not

to explain why individuals rebel but why, in situations of unjustifiable inequality, they do not, that is, the problem of quiescence (Gaventa 1980). In order to ensure then that no sphere remains immune from a 'scrutinising concern' about injustice, political philosophy needs to be permanently attentive to the experiences of individuals in the pre-political sphere where domination and political exclusion have their roots. (McNay 2012: 235)

This analysis can also accommodate how males are never constructed as victims of real symbolic violence and exploitation. Boys and men are never victims of social injustice. Gay boys are unmentionable. Also, psychiatric terminology as a replacement for theological or folk theories can be regarded as another form of asymmetrical domination, particularly when its theoretical structure fails to grasp the instances of how internalized oppression undermines the capacity of autonomous agency (McNay 2014: 207). Biological psychiatry persists in underestimating 'how the social world plays a fundamental role in human functioning and experience, with causal effects on mental health and illness' (Kirmayer and Gold 2012: 307).

In defence of the idea of social suffering, one that finds its legitimate place as a critique of society, suffering can be studied with a substantive level of critical and empirical rigor in social science. The rigor of the lived experiential writing in this book may have implications beyond the described instances of social suffering in a certain historic period. More critically, descriptions of social suffering needs to be stated less opaquely or merely viewed as subjective sufferings of unfortunate creatures. Critical writing aims to analyse modes of intelligibility as decompressed transactions that are a constant and potentially explosive undercurrent. Poorly construed, harmed citizens can die prematurely, never to grasp what ailed them in life. Renault (2017) says:

Reporting on experienced suffering, making it an object of narration and knowledge .... aids in bringing whole sections of society out of invisibility. It helps to give back to the individuals concerned, the capacity to make demands and act collectively to transform the conditions of their existence. (p. 5)

Brendan Kelly, Professor of Psychiatry at Trinity College, cites estimates of 3 billion euro per year in lost revenues in Ireland but says 'the true cost of "mental disorder," of course, stems chiefly from the untold suffering experienced by patients and their families, in addition to the measurable economic and societal costs' (2015: 9). This empirical recognition is important. Also, I concur with Bernstein (2015) when he says:

> Standard moral theories – with their guiding ideas of autonomy, pleasure and pain, flourishing, and virtue, which are intended to tell agents what they ought to do – come nowhere near addressing the types of harm suffered in the two paradigm cases of wrongful violence, cases that are pivotal to our individual and collective self-understanding. Rape and torture require thicker, more complex conception of what makes human lives injurable by human others, one which brings into view our standing for ourselves in relations to others as human. (p. 175)

In the midlands where I grew up in, current repertoires of social recognition for historic institutional abuse have evolved, away from the normative impulse of silence, secrecy and defence of traditions. *Longford Leader* journalist Jessica Thompson (2018) describes the experiences of fifty-two-year-old William Gorry 'who survived horrendous sexual, physical and emotional abuse in an industrial school as a child.' As an adult, William has set up an organization to lend such survivors a voice (<http://www.risn.ie>). From the age of nine, he 'along with two of his brothers and three of his sisters [were] carted off to Mount Carmel industrial school in Moate, Co. Westmeath which was run by the Sisters of Mercy' (Thompson, J. 2018). William was at the school until he was twenty years old:

> Sometimes it was okay but mostly it was Hell, I was emotionally, physically and sexually abused over the years ... We would get beaten by priests, lay staff and nuns who were supposed to care for us. We were screamed and yelled at, I was told that I was useless, stupid, blind and hopeless, nobody would love or want me. I was isolated to confined space and often punished severely. Many times I got slapped and boxed across the face, I remember being locked in a hot press in darkness for hours until I was bruised and blistered. I find it hard to form friendships, getting close to people and trusting them is hard, I feel like I'm always watching myself ... I haven't been able to move on or have a life of love and happiness, it's like a tension inside of you and you're just supposed to be happy with what you have. (Thompson, J. 2018)

This idea of having to make do with what is on offer is a consistent theme in this section. Guilt is at the core of this shaming experience where the altered self feels interred. This historic dynamic feels like a preordination of social regulation, waiting for people to take on the mantel of self-sacrifice as a pristine ideal, where negation of self is connected to the official philosophy of this time period. The pull toward transcendental ideals intensifies a purist feeling of 'my fault.' Super-ego resistance was the demand expectation of national idealism. Furthermore, the adult who suffers early trauma can become a hero and burnout as their life unfolds. Can societal arrangements engineer, distort, pummel, damage and devastate modes of self-understanding? The answer is certainly affirmative. Ireland committed itself to a first principle that was easy to pick up in socialization and popular culture. This first order guilt principle of uber-responsibility ultimately cuts people off from relating to others, in being able to articulate exactly what they have soaked up. How Christianity interpreted this was to suggest that suffering was an exemplar experience, a test of character. Such ideas are seductive and expose 'ideology's pervasive and negative influence on social cognition' (Mills 2017). When I refer to social cognition, I am thinking about how traumatic events alter the trajectory of core developmental competencies in lifespan development. This is well captured by Jackson-Nakazawa (2016):

> early chronic, unpredictable stressors, losses, and adversities we face as children shape our biology in ways that predetermine our adult health. This early biological blueprint depicts our proclivity to develop life-altering adult illnesses such as heart disease, cancer, autoimmune disease, fibromyalgia, and depression. It also lays the groundwork for how we relate to others, how successful our love relationships will be, and how we will nurture and raise our own children. (p. 12)

The next sections have more of a focus on my own experiences, placing emphasis on how the tentacles of social/religious traditions objectified how I made meaning of early psychological experience. Gravitating toward the idea of a religious vocation which recommended sacrifice emboldened shame even more so. This scale of social introjects inscribed into personality structure kept me out of touch with reality. A naturalized tendency of going against myself proved shattering and terrorizing. I was naïve to its inverse quality. I felt I had to fight my own desires to give me rest. I remember the idea of turning against myself being the correct thing to do. While I have never experienced conversion therapy directly, this ideology was percolating below the surface of my personality. I was a young boy, and was easily exploited by a mind-altering religious ideology, as a way of coping with trauma. Spiegel (2003) says 'boys who experience childhood sexual abuse are more likely than non-abused boys to reside in a single-parent household or a reconstructed household with parents who are separated or divorced' (p. 24). I am now more aware how some clerics purposively created proximity to young people like me as substitute father figures.

CHAPTER 4

Recruiting Junior Vocations in the Diocese of Ardagh and Clonmacnoise

Attentive to God's voice, a voice calling him to place all his trust in Him.
— La Salle Organization 2016

This quote is from John Baptist de La Salle. John Baptist founded the De La Salle Order in 1680 in France. The quote captures the familiar dynamics of a religious calling. It is a theological way of thinking I am more than familiar with from growing up as a boy in Ireland. The Irish De La Salle Brothers opened their Junior Novitiate in Castletown, Portlaoise in 1880. The order's teachings resonated with the dominant Catholic ideology and traditions of the time in Ireland. The overall demand was high for religious orders in Ireland to teach and to provide social care service throughout the country (Ó Tuathaigh 2018; Towey 1980). It is worth emphasizing again how sectarian this theological structure was in nineteenth- and twentieth-century Ireland. Political and theological self-determination was Catholic emancipation from British rule. Even under UK rule, Kelly (2014) documents how the Catholic Bishop of Galway had oversight of the Mental Asylum Committee in Ballinasloe in 1904. The bishop was able to get his way in suggesting that Catholic psychiatrists run the hospitals. Despite the subsequent controversy in the House of Commons that a Protestant candidate was rejected for the post, the Asylum Committee in Ballinasloe, when asked for a rationale of their decision, responded 'that the Lord Lieutenant had 'no right to ask them for any reason' (p. 52) on who they appointed. In the UK Parliament debate, it was further highlighted that the 'first thing' that the new Catholic appointee in 'proving his suitability was to take out the emblem of England from the standard of the asylum.

He [Dr Kirwan] admitted that he did it, and when the attendants of the asylum were receiving their uniforms he was so faithful to his creed that the buttons had to have the harp and shamrock only upon them' (p. 52). This episode merely illustrates the close interconnections between Celtic revival, the autonomy of the Catholic Church and the drive for political self-determination in Irish history. My own Catholic patronage national school in Longford was still facilitating the De La Salle mission of evangelization up to the early 1980s, in the hope this arrangement would instil the concept of early religious calling as good and noble.

The fundamental purpose of religion is to regulate minds in the direction of its ethos tenets and to save souls. Roman Catholicism was not an abstract philosophy. Religion had an objective like reach, whereby its naturalization as a foregrounded identity felt like a holding container for self-identity. Transcendental philosophies can be attractive to teenagers because they reach into stereotypical categorization that is childlike, immediate, simple and transcendent. Young teenagers often want to be the centre of attention and developmentally the seductiveness of transcendental ideas mimics their sense of autonomous functioning. Children need to be protected because they may oversubscribe to the idea that the world revolves around them. Stressed and traumatized children are probably less likely to decentre from stereotypical conceptions for their sense of selfhood. For me, religious ideas were comforting. Predators can really take advantage of this dynamic. When a religious figure promises redemption from pain and adversity and then betrays the trust preordained on him, immersion in these modes of intelligibility felt schizophrenic, twisting an adolescent's self-understanding in unimaginably painful ways. With sexual norms as they were, the evolving structure of my self-conscious desire were another secret, adding further insult to injury.

After witnessing the trauma of my father's death, I was desperate to transcend the pain I felt inside. So soon afterward, to be sexually exploited by an esteemed religious authority deepened a feeling that I must be so tainted in some way. My threshold for making meaning of own experience was violated. It was an extreme disservice to a young boy's dreams and I did not have the ability to communicate this awful pain to anyone. Powerful exploitative people embedded in an oppressive social matrix clearly make the determination that being out of relationship with yourself means you are less likely to possess a level of control and power to form relationships with others. Abusers empower themselves by being aware of their sickly secrets and transfer their sickness onto a child. This tricks the unwitting child into thinking they are responsible for the perpetrator's sickness. When the perpetrator is also the objective arbiter of making meaning of sexuality, this further twists the early teen's self-beliefs in a profound way. Unknown to me, I was set up to painfully resist myself. Other people could easily preordain meaning for me and then exploit me as a boy and teenager. I was carrying all this in a way that was unknown to me, but known to others who could see and seize on my vulnerability. For my part, effortful self-control to outsmart grander prophecies, predictions and prescriptions was so weighted against me. There was nothing roomy about this experience. The experience created terrible tension.

Being patrons of schools was just one of religion's enculturation techniques for the foregrounded enactment of its own identity capital in Ireland. Religion was construed as integral to the self. As if, we were innately born to discover the religious impulse, the deeper revelation and promise of a true, reliable and pristine self. Religion monopolized the application of ethical discourse in Ireland. It was a monopoly of populism in social discourse. A critical commentary from Kitcher (2011) captures the historical dynamic of religious enculturation:

> Each super-naturalist view rests on epistemically similar grounds – typically there was some revelation, long ago, that has been carefully transmitted across the generations to the devout of today – yielding a condition for complete symmetry. Under these conditions, no believer has any basis for thinking only he and his group are privileged to know the truth about the transcendental realm, while others live in primitive delusions. Further, serious inquiries into the ways in which canonical scriptures are constructed, into the evolution of religions, into the recruitment of converts, into the phenomena of religious experience, demonstrate how radically unreliable are the processes that have yielded the current corpora of belief. Nor can one isolate some core doctrine, shared by all religions, something capable of being viewed as a shared insight. If there are beings of a hitherto unrecognized sort, approximating some idea of the 'transcendent' we have every reason to think we have absolutely no clues, or categories, for describing them. Religious entanglement in ethical practice is no accident. (p. 4)

As an adult, I now view the fundamental claims of religion as a false consciousness, a false security, one that distorts the ethical project in significant
ways. The a priori claim of religious innateness extends too much wriggle
room for social control, to determine goodness and rightness. For me,
religious appropriation meant I was not a good problem solver. I could
not see beyond the normative arrangements. Secrecy ensures there is no
crisis, no shared fate. One is left with the contradictions. In my case, like
my mother and brother and others, it kept us in a state of veiled ignorance
on too many important things. For example, the ideas learned about guilt
and sin were so persecutory and mind-altering in an enclosed culture. I
learned nothing about the development of self-confidence in this system
of thought. If anything, doubting myself was encouraged. Self-abnegation
promotes concealment of harm. I thought this was model citizenship.
Alcoff (2017) ties this species of thinking to the 'transcendental delusion:
a belief that thought can be separated from its specific, embodied, and
geo-political source' (p. 397).

Growing up in Ireland, I never truly discerned that the genesis of religious enculturation was the historic product of real persons and groups. I
thought religious concepts were above all that. I thought religious people
were the sole and ultimate arbiters of truthful knowledge. Everything else
that anyone else said was relative to what the men and the people of God
said. In my young life, people who openly disagreed with religious ideas
were treated with a normative degree of scepticism, side-lined, not engaged
with. With the prediction that even these doubters would ultimately see
the error of their unaided ways and surrender to the divine authority of
human affairs, the invisible hand of God working in mysterious ways: 'Such
approaches brook no dialogue ... not putting themselves in the position to
be taught' (Alcoff 2017: 397).

In the idea of brooking no dialogue, I had no sense how my subject formation was been shaped in tricolour assemblage, modes resembling the holy
trinity of right, left and centre, a gravitational pull in which personhood
developed. Any significant disruptions to these 'normative and essential-
ist assumptions' (Haslanger 2017) were not known to me. The media-
tion of adults, serving at mass, confession, communion and confirmation,
my school, and our hospitals were key anchor points for naturalization. I

wanted to feel secure in the transcendent, because of how dysfunctional and distressing social reality appeared to me. Morality gave me a buffer against a disturbed reality. However, my religiosity literally normalized 'delusions, hallucinatory thoughts, poor social, cognitive, language, organization of thoughts, judgement and reality testing skills' (Caplan 2016: 951). These neurodevelopmental deficits are part of the onset diagnosis of childhood and adolescent schizophrenia. This is referred to as abnormal and maladaptive. This is stigmatizing when it is formulated this way. Viewed primarily as genetic antecedents, my suggestion is my own childhood symptoms were rational manifestations of trauma in a stigmatizing culture. There should not be no shame or secrecy about any of this. For me, these symptoms were the surface characteristics of a deeper psychic disturbance. In a stigmatic historic culture, if the child succumbs to the self-belief that he has brought this on, the child will keep up appearances, which unwittingly can set him off on a path of feeling estranged. My unease was normal but I did not feel normal because I did not grasp the historical mechanisms of social domination and how this historical scene of disempowerment had injected a noxious undercurrent which signalled my vulnerability to powerful others in the social hierarchy to exploit me.

At eleven years old, an opportunity to get away from my home in Longford presented itself. In 1977, in my final year at St Michael's Boys National School in Longford, a religious man arrived to recruit pupils for early religious vocations. This brother was the Vocations Director for the De La Salle Order. His name was Bro. Bernard Doyle (1911–1985). He had a heavy build. He was in his late sixties. I have a distinct memory of him being accompanied to my school by a respected cleric from our diocese. When I spotted both of them in the schoolyard, I wondered who the new cleric was. I had never seen the De La Salle Brother before. Religious people got my attention back then. In Bro. John Towey's study of the *Irish De La Salle Brothers in Christian Education* (1980) he describes a high level of social co-operation for the work of the De La Salle Order. This was achieved through the Irish bishops and the political establishment, who variously turned up for school openings.

The historical accumulation of this social capital in Ireland up to the present has been a major social and political achievement. While Ireland can no longer be characterized by devotional rituals, where the current dearth in religious vocations has certainly altered the old parish structure, religious patronage is still a key visual in key domains of Irish life. No other discipline or religion enjoys such an advantage in the collective intentionality and social imaginary of Ireland. The latter decades of the nineteenth century up to the middle of the twentieth century were major growth periods for the De La Salle Order in Ireland. Their growth as an order largely mirrors the pattern of many other religious orders in Ireland. During the same historic period of the nineteenth and twentieth century, French society was less fertile ground for the De La Salle Order (Towey 1980). After Catholic emancipation in 1829, the Irish Catholic bishops were able to secure significant autonomy for the historically oppressed Catholic majority. Baggett's (2009) analysis further defines the key aspects of the historical scene: 'After Emancipation in 1829, the positions of political debate were being reconfigured and the sectarian differences between Protestant and Catholic, Orange and Green, were transformed into oppositions, Ireland versus England, nationalist versus unionist' (p. 1). As Bejan (2017) recently noted in describing the historical antecedents of religious conflicts:

> long-standing anxieties about uncivil disagreement rose to new prominence in Western Europe after the Reformation, when – with the help of that recent advancement in communications technology, the printing press – Protestants and Catholics began to broadcast their polemics far and wide and hurl insults at each other at an alarming rate.

This survey gives some sociological context for how Catholicism aligned its identity to the key concerns of an oppressed majority Catholic population. As an applied ethics, Catholicism continued to develop its identity in the early twentieth century. As a young boy, this merger felt pre-ordained. I did not reflect on it, as the transfers of this ideology literally took possession of my self-reference at deeply evolved experiential capacities for making meaning of my life experiences. Inglis (2005) says there was a dominance of 'Catholic-church personnel in such key areas as philosophy, psychology, and sociology' (p. 10). It is not enough to say that structural institutions of education, law, politics, religious rituals and social policies are the only key sites to enacting a sense of national identity. It is also important to highlight how the domesticated scenes and rituals serve as reinforcements for the direct transmission of religious values. The power of religious values was more than evident and resonant in my family. The combination of micro and macro traditions, made me intuitively feel that religion was an intrinsic feature of my personality, my family and my wider society. I was not sufficiently resourced to refuse this national script. Fintan O'Toole (1998) writing towards the end of the last century refers to the historic Church-state relationship as 'undeniable' (p. 67). He specifies the levels of religious enculturation in Irish society from birth to death, which extends a greater degree of cultural specificity to how people enact their sense of self in culture. O'Toole (1998) says of the Irish, we were

> likely to be born in a Catholic hospital, educated at Catholic schools, married in a Catholic church, have children named by a priest, be counselled by Catholic marriage advisors if the marriage runs into trouble, be dried out in Catholic clinics for the treatment of alcoholism if he or she develops a drink problem, be operated on in Catholic hospitals, and be buried by Catholic rites. (p. 67)

These were the antecedent social conditions of my own emergence into the world in 1966. In my early life, I was an anonymous subject in this mass project of socialization, where one takes on the mantle of a religious thinking which shapes and informs self-beliefs regarding blame and responsibility. This is key to grasping the preordained structure of secrecy. Our bishops, priests, brothers and nuns were the mediating signals and cues of God's eternal presence.

Prior to my meeting the De La Salle Vocations Director in 1977, Bro. Bernard had served as school principal in a number of De La Salle Primary and Secondary Schools in Dublin. In the late 1970s, I had no sense of the hidden kaleidoscope of abuses simmering beneath the surface of Ireland's fake appearances of authenticity. Critically, as a young boy, I had not developed a conscious capacity to abstractly think through faith claims. What I did not know was that a-priori faith claims were cultural constructions and storied narratives in my history. I had certainly not internalized any critical suspicion for what clerical figures said.

When Bernard came to Longford, he lived in De La Salle HQ, Churchtown, Dublin. Bro. Bernard had served as principal at the De La

Salle School in Churchtown from the late 1960s to the early 1970s. During
his time there, he wrote an article for the school magazine Wine and Gold.
In his writing, Bro. Bernard Doyle (1970) thanked those responsible for spiritual formation. In his editorial, the principal states how four of the gradu-
ating secondary students 'are now in Arch-Diocesan and other Seminaries'
(p. 8). The De La Salle Brothers also had their own primary schools. When
he retired as principal, Bro. Bernard continued on his work as Vocations
Director for his order. He travelled all over the country to Catholic schools
to recruit young boys for his order's school in Castletown, Portlaoise.

Over the duration of my final year in primary school (1977–8) and
after my initial introduction to him at the school, Bro. Bernard called to my
home to cultivate and discern my religious calling. The practical purpose of
these visits was to get me ready to enter the De La Salle Novitiate situated
in Castletown, Portlaoise. I always felt these meetings were about discern-
ing my suitability for religious life. I also thought Bro. Bernard really liked
me and that he was going to care for me, look after me and that he would
see that no further harm would ever come to me again. The De La Salle
school that Bro. Bernard was recruiting me for was to serve as my secondary schooling too. At the end of my secondary schooling, it was planned
that I would then enter religious life. Recruiting young postulants was a
historic feature of the De La Salle approach for vocational recruitment
throughout the world (BRA 2015; Towey 1980).

Bro. Bernard came to my home on a regular basis. I so looked forward
to these visits. He took me out for dinner in local hotels. I really bonded
with him. In our conversations, Bro. Bernard kept repeating to me how
fragile religious callings were. He kept warning me about bad things that
might stand in the way of God's calling. I had told Bro. Bernard what had
happened in my home in 1975 and about the court case that followed in
1976. In 1977, Bro. Bernard stressed to me in a loving and caring way that
it was not unusual for me to feel I had a religious calling. He said many of
the famous saints of the Church came from vulnerable backgrounds just
like mine. I was so impressed with myself. These ideas were so powerful in
finding purpose and meaning to my development.

Anytime we met, Bro. Bernard just kept reassuring me that God worked
in mysterious ways. This was very soothing. I felt I had something to look

forward to. Bro. Bernard said given all my family had been through, a religious vocation would make my mother very happy. In Dr Towey's study of the De La Salle Order (1980) he refers to his colleague Bro. Bernard Doyle as 'better known as a Vocational Director in the best tradition' (Towey 1980, p. 541). There was nothing particularly mysterious about Bro. Bernard's talk to me, as it largely resonated with the normative repertoires and assumptions as enacted and re-enacted in the town I grew up in. As an eleven year old, I was very excited with all this attention shown to me by Bro. Bernard. It gave me something to focus on and to hope for. I was so sure that joining religious life would make me and others very happy. Bernard's message reassured me that I could build my self-esteem around him, within the splendour of the one true Catholic faith, as the universal Church. These were exhilarating and transcendent ideas for a young child to anchor towards. I trusted Bro. Bernard. He spoke perfectly and I listened intently to the rhythms of his speech. He was talking magically about me and to me. The idea of God hand-picking me made me feel great and exemplary.

Prior to meeting him, religion had had a very special import in my life. I had been a boy server in the local church. I loved getting up early to serve at 8 a.m. mass. Among the many priests in St Mel's Cathedral in Longford, I served Fr Colm O'Reilly, who went on to become the bishop of the diocese in 1983. He had a gentle presence and was always appropriate around me. I did feel guilty around him, because I was not intending on a local diocesan vocation. When I told Bro. Bernard about this conflict, he reassured me that the De La Salle Order had a special place in the heart of our serving bishop, Dr Cahal B. Daly. Bro. Bernard told me that Bishop Daly was an eminent theologian and that he was held in very high esteem. My memory of Bishop Daly (later All-Ireland Primate and cardinal) was of him smiling a lot and he gave very long sermons. The long queues for his confessions meant he took a great deal of time with each person. He was an old style theologian. I liked the mystic that surrounded him. It was magical just seeing him. Bro. Bernard was like that too.

As I reflect on this period, Bro. Bernard knew who to draw close to and whom to exploit. Taking on the normative spell of goodness was my attempt to build shattered confidence and esteem. I must have felt I owed this to the world. This made me feel useful. I was going to save others from sin. At the time, Bro. Bernard had impressed on me that he had been sent by God to free me from my broken circumstances. Once Bernard told me I had the calling, no one could take this away from me. I was pre-ordained to a be a saint. I got comfort from feeling blessed in an otherwise stressed state of affairs. My centre of gravity was at the mercy of false prophets. I did not grasp how vulnerable I was in the ways I responded and interpreted the world. To be virtuous, I literally had to engage in a fight with myself, not with the dysfunctional crowd who created this tension in the first place. I had to watch myself, not the normative spell of the ideology that degraded my mother, my sister, my brother, the rest and now me. Theological definitions had a tentacle like grip of the stock of meanings for making sense of experience. From this I deduced I was wrong, never them. I needed religion for a redemption from innate sin.

In my household, the way we talked of sexual purity was infantile, secretive, immature and consistent with the moral teachings of the Roman Catholic Church. Bro. Bernard's discourse was so consistent with purification ideals. When he met my mother, Bernard would have also spotted her vulnerability and her loss of power to repressive religious ideals. As a former school principal, he may have met many mothers who were deferential to religious people. In the public domain, my mother smiled. She had no voice to openly challenge the norms of a society that was so oppressively rigged against her (Duffy 2011). She would not have grasped how social power was exercised, and the extent of which religious belief traditions had constrained her. I think my mother thought religion contained her. She kept going to mass and charismatic groups. There was nothing peripheral about religion in my early life. I think my mother naively thought that religious and spiritual beliefs would make her life and mine more tolerable. She was dependent on her mother who was devoutly religious, and my mother was directly dependent on religious ethos providers for my youngest sister's social care.

In these contexts, I do not think my mother could ever have imagined that her son was being simultaneously groomed by a paedophile cleric. We were in a disadvantaged position to confront this criminal exploitation. This is how powerful religious ideology was in historic Ireland. To mask and carry suffering was a virtue, to reveal it, was our vice, not theirs. We were expected to carry the weight of their shame and guilt, thinking it was our shame. You were encouraged to clean your own side of the street. My mother always observed this. Those regulative ideals in culture were not abstract or distant. They were designed to normalize guilt as a super-ego ideal. Going to confession was designed to relieve us of any fall from a state of grace. Those ideals were deeply felt by persons and were mind-altering. Despite how impossible those ideals were in self-realization, some in key positions of power used these powerful concepts as a smoke screen to harm others. In the period between the 1970s and the mid-1990s in Ireland, blind allegiance to this ethos had pragmatic reach. Disadvantaged persons were at a significant disadvantage in being able to work out how this power performed its magic on them. As Hammack (2018) points out, 'The social world is not ideologically neutral but rather is the product of historical forces characterized by power asymmetries'. The job of the social critic is to 'denaturalize social phenomena so as to reveal how something that took the shape of a natural event in fact was a social construction' (Laitinen and Sirekela 2018: 2). Our historic practices encouraged silence.

The concepts of mindfulness promoted by psychology encourages ego-less states of mind. This philosophy is somewhat consistent with theological concepts. The noisy and restless self is the sinful or noisy dysregulated self. Powerful institutions had the resource capacity to create suspicion about the restless, irritable and discontented. Sacrificing truth in the avoidance of institutional scandal, hiding and exporting our secrets, has a significant audit trail in our history. Powerful people in enclosed societies seem less accountable and those same powerful people seem to intuit that this is their privilege.

We lived in a country town. I was hooked on transcendental faith claims as solutions to daily problems. This meant I dealt with nothing, which was consistent with a normative appetite for avoidance and resistance. Erroneous self-beliefs were my modus operandi. I had been trained to think that being open to God's will over my will was authentic and that the worldly world was dangerous. To be without God's given potential was predicted by powerful others as a slippery slope. These everyday beliefs were the socially engineered seeds of my own fear and self-doubt.

To feel protected from the world, I took refuge in a system of thought that explicitly encouraged me to think less of myself. The bondage of self was my problem to overcome. In my family history, the martyrdom syndrome was not in any way conducive to human flourishing and freedom.

To infer the familiar is comforting feels like a cruel projection. This was the power of the domineering introject, where victims were scoffed at, dismissed, laughed at, sneered at, spoken about behind their backs, disbelieved and discredited. These were the violating scenes where victims/survivors who were trying to articulate the wrongs that were being committed, can die prematurely. When our thresholds for making meaning of our experience are so badly breached, we externalize the stress. Poor mental health is then formulated by powerful others as personality disorders. This is our shameful legacy. The biosocial imprint is undertheorized. Instead, the pressure is placed on the depleted individual to overcome and be more resilient. This formulation can literally shame the core of deeply traumatized individuals into compliant quietude or hidden suffering. The surface trickery of elitist concepts do not come close for grasping how the development of selves are disrupted in bad social arrangements. In the psychological disciplines, the domineering and monolithic projections of current theories are not sufficient to unpack the introjected roots of violent histories enacted on human psychology. The echo-chambers of existing concepts, ideas and practices do not encourage openness. We have to be willing to enlarge our grasp of human disempowerment.

The next section of the story offers the regional historical context for how the De La Salle Order managed to gain and secure access to the diocesan schools in Longford. The De La Salle Order did not have a direct presence in the diocese itself, serving as another reminder of the normative reach and power that this order enjoyed. What I have also discovered from my reading, I was a prime candidate for predation. Clerical predators not only focused on boys without fathers. Many of their victims were pre-pubertal boys and girls (*Boston Globe* 2016).

CHAPTER 5

The Special Historic Relationship of the De La Salle Order and the Diocese of Ardagh and Clonmacnoise

Our local bishop Dr Cahal B. Daly (1998), despite his support for ecumenism, still favoured a distinctive Catholic ethos in schools. This religious identity of schools with public subsidy is still a foregrounded feature of education in Ireland. There is now significant pressure in Irish society to change these religious patronage arrangements. A recent advocacy campaign strongly argued for a deletion of the following archaic rule:

> Of all the parts of a school curriculum, religious instruction is by far the most important, as its subject-matter, God's honour and service, includes the proper use of all man's faculties, and affords the most powerful inducements to their proper use. Religious instruction is, therefore, a fundamental part of the school course, and a religious spirit should inform and vivify the whole work of the school. (Humphreys 2014)

In the 1970s, Ireland was still a very religious country. Set within a wider European context, Ireland's economy was viewed as a relatively poor country, with slow economic gains and uneven regional development in the urban/rural planning of Ireland (Daly 2016; Ferriter 2012). Combined with the backdrop of religious sectarian conflict, hostile Anglo/Irish relations, continuing socio-economic inequality, religious personnel were still foregrounded as key players in the public sphere. The Church was a key influencer on the traditions of Irish life (Norris 2012; Inglis 1998; Rose 1994). In 1980, Brother Columbia Gallagher, the Provincial of the De La Salle Order in Ireland captures the extent of the contribution of his order to education:

> Just as the Irish Church owes its strong Christian Heritage to the austere lives and arduous labours of the early monks, so the Irish Province of the De La Salle Institute is indebted to these pioneering Brothers for that distinctive Lasallian influence

and spirit that are a not insignificant feature of the Irish educational scene today. (Gallagher cited by Towey 1980)

Austereness and arduous labour exemplifies historical notions of self-control in service to others. A repression of self-interest is designed to promote societal betterment.

The father of our local bishop, Dr Cahal Daly, had trained as a teacher in the De La Salle Training College in Waterford (Daly 1998: 43). Cardinal Daly's father may have come into contact with the De La Salle Order in Roscommon where his father was from. As bishop, Dr Daly presided at my religious confirmation in 1977/8 at St Mel's Cathedral in Longford. Prior to his installation as Bishop of Ardagh and Clonmacnoise in 1967, Cahal Daly had studied in France during what he termed 'the revival of French Catholicism' of the 1950s (Daly 1998). Dr Daly wrote an article for the Irish Press newspaper in 1979 which illustrated his keen interest in French Catholicism (Daly 1979). After some studies in France, Dr Daly went on to enjoy a high-profile involvement for the three-year duration of the Second Vatican Council from 1962 to 1965. Dr Daly (1998) stated in his memoir, 'We did not know it yet, but the great revival of the Church which was to be brought about by the Second Vatican Council was already being prepared in France during those years' (p. 105). In his memoirs, Bishop Daly refers to his first visit to a seminary in Lisieux in 1952 which took St Thérèse as its patroness (p. 106). St Thérèse of Lisieux was one the his favourite saints (Daly 1998). When Bishop Daly left Longford to be installed as a senior bishop in St Peter's Cathedral in Rome on 17 October 1982, he recalled being helped by the 'words of St Thérèse "Anything you ask, Lord; but do have pity on me"' (Daly 1998: 243).

As part of my vocational discernment and recruitment process, Bro. Bernard brought me on a trip with other boys to France to the birthplace of St Thérèse of Lisieux, 'The Little Flower of Jesus'. On this trip to Lisieux, at breakfast, I distinctly remember Bro. Doyle placing me on his knee. At eleven years old, I really thought I was special compared to the other boys. During Cahal Daly's term as Bishop of Ardagh and Clonmacnoise (1967–1982), it is certainly not difficult to grasp how the De La Salle Order managed to gain the level of access to the national schools in Longford. Not unlike Dr John Charles McQuaid the Archbishop of Dublin, Bishop Daly was a strong advocate for obedience to papal central authority in Rome (Daly 1998). In his subsequent senior roles, Dr Daly, as Primate of All Ireland, and as cardinal, Cahal Daly took a dim view of clerics who strayed from Church teachings. While many viewed Dr Daly as socially progressive, his authoritarian positions were more than evident on the Irish state broadcaster when he publicly rebuked dissenting clerics who strayed from Church teachings. Many of the Irish clerics who were silenced by the CDF in Rome under the leadership of Cardinal Josef Ratzinger (D'Arcy 2015; Flannery 2013; Fagan 1997) were the same clerics Bishop Daly rebuked for going against magisterial teaching authority in Rome.

In a letter to the Archbishop of Dublin in 1967, Cooney (1999) advises how Cahal Daly 'confided his qualms that "all the aberrations in the Church today have been committed over and over again in the Church's history"' (p. 406). When Dr Daly took up his position as Bishop of Ardagh and Clonmacnoise, he sought direct assistance from Dr McQuaid for his first pastoral letter at St Mel's Cathedral in Longford in 1967 (p. 406). However, perhaps unlike Bishop Daly, the Archbishop of Dublin did not share the view that the Second Vatican Council was progressive for the Church. After the Vatican Council, McQuaid preached to his parishioners: 'You may have been worried by much talk of changes to come. Allow me to reassure you. No change will worry the tranquillity of your Christian lives' (Cooney 1999). McQuaid had exercised significant authority over the lives of Dublin citizens for almost four decades. He was determined not to let go. In later sections of this book, I will enlarge on how these alliances among Church leaders were fundamentalist and right-wing in orientation.

In my young life in the 1970s, it was easy for me to be hoodwinked and groomed by a representative of a dominant empire. In a stressed out state, I genuinely thought I was going to be significant someday by following in the footsteps of the great saints. All of the religious sayings had made a practical impression on my ways of thinking. I was excited about embarking on a path which would transform my distracted circumstances. I filled my mother's head with the joyous glory of God. My mother appeared happy for me.

Trauma theorists Ogden, Minton and Pain (2006) formulate cognitive processing as 'encompassing the ability to observe and abstract from experience, weigh a range of possibilities for action, plan for the accomplishment of goals, and evaluate the outcome of actions' (p. 8). I was performing well in national school. However, the talks with the De La Salle Vocations Director seriously distracted me. He was the proximate mediator for religious ideas that up to then were more general and implicit. According to Llinas, 'As with muscle tone that serves as the basic platform for the execution of our movements, emotions represent the pre-motor platform as either drives or deterrents for most of our actions' (Ogden, Minton and Pain 2006: 11). My motivation to be religious merged seamlessly with the wider social approval (Daly 2016; Duffy 2011; Ferriter 2009). Bro. Bernard literally came through my national school as part of a normal day at school. He represented a key institution which was an integral feature of my socialization as a young person. I felt pre-ordained and hand-picked within this system. I was not cognizant how much of my socialization had primed me for this mindedness of religious vocation. Again, my mother was comforted to see me so excited about this. She had absolutely no idea what lay ahead. I felt secure in the knowledge that Jesus was the son of God and I would be saved. This was to be my protection once I did not sin and I obeyed God's will. Then, I would feel secure and whole. Back then, these were exciting ideas. It never struck to lash out at them when all this went so terribly wrong. Why? I felt I brought this on. I thought I was responsible for what had happened. I had put up my hand in class to follow in the footsteps of the Church. Soon after, Bro. Bernard arrived in my home. I felt like it was a visit from the transcendental arm of God. I was the chosen one. Very quickly, Bernard would have known that his techniques and visits were making a big impression on me. Bernard encouraged me to think that God was the answer and that he alone could save me. This was to be my secure base, where I would be free from further harm.

Historically, my experience is just one example of the macro-outsourcing to religion, disclosing its power at a micro/everyday level in Ireland. Within my socialization, he was high status and I was a lower status. In terms of societal deference at the time, these everyday episodes would not have stood out. Regular attendance at religious rituals were not out of the ordinary. In a 1970s country town, religion was part of culture, my education, and a part of my life outside of school in the 1970s. Bernard's presence in my school was part and parcel of how religion socially reproduced its identity. The idea of religious vocation was not alien. It was a special gift, a grace bestowed on a poor family by God. At this stage, the De La Salle Brothers had been performing its work in Ireland for close to a century.

Within the educational architecture, the order had achieved a naturalized status. Its representatives could walk into family homes, take the 'special ones' away on religious trips and could walk into hotels with young boys, without anyone raising an eyebrow. That is the power of how religion built its social esteem in Ireland and elsewhere. Roman Catholicism had cleverly worked out that the transcendental requires grounded social and political capital to achieve its aims. When the power of religion is denaturalized and even exposed, credible questions are raised about its right to a foregrounded status. Why does religion need overall patronage of schools? The suggestion is that religious ethos in schools, social care and other cultural rituals, is the right holding container for a nation to make meaning of its practical activities. This is some structural advantage for religion to enjoy over others as a method of social reproduction of its social identity.

These critical questions were not on my mind in the 1970s. I was so swept up by the intensity of being told I was on a mission and was a chosen one. I believed their appropriations of what religious vocation meant, not grasping any hidden agenda. It was easy to be hoodwinked by the power of their messaging system. There is nothing too mysterious on how the spirit moves, it requires grounded political muscle to depoliticize human beings. I was off on the wrong footing while thinking I was on the right path. Religious fundamentalists can be like that – delusional. They take a high moral ground and pretend they are above the political. There was nothing progressive about any of this because of how harmful and disrespectful it was to our emotional lives. Jackon Nakazawa in *Childhood Disrupted* (2016) describes how our 'biography becomes our biology' citing how

> New findings in neuroscience, psychology, and medicine have recently unveiled the exact ways in which childhood adversity biologically alters us for life. This ground breaking research tells us that the emotional trauma we face when we are young has farther-reaching consequences than we might have imagined. Adverse Childhood

Experiences change the architecture of our brains and the health of our immune systems, they trigger and sustain inflammation in both body and brain, and they influence our overall physical health and longevity long into adulthood. These physical changes, in turn, prewrite the story of how we will react to the world around us, and how well we will work, and parent, befriend, and love other people throughout the course of our adult lives. (p. 32)

These well received insights were unknown to me as a child and teenager. I had no sense how my reactions to events were altering how I perceived and interacted with the world. I was ignorant. I can still be in denial on these research results despite the experience I have that confirm them.

The next section describes the situated texture of Bro. Bernard's grooming techniques, consistent with the dark profile picture of how many clerics abused their power over children. I did not grasp Bro. Bernard's true motives, not for a second. His true intent was behind my back, outside of my awareness. At this time, Bernard clearly knew he could do this and get away with it. Bernard knew what I was taught. He knew my situation. He could visibly see my excitement. Bro. Doyle had the advantage. He had the power. He could brush me aside when he was finished with me.

CHAPTER 6

Child Sexual Abuse in 1977/1978 Catholic Ireland

> Typically, a priest arrived in a parish or other Church setting sometime between 1960–1990. Often energetic and charismatic, he focused his ministry on youth activities. Gradually, he developed friendships with young people, frequently boys between 11 and 15 years old ... All had been taught from birth to respect and trust priests as Christ's representatives on earth. Eventually, Father introduced sex into his relationship with a young person. (Frawley-O'Dea 2007a: xi)

The leadership within the Ardagh and Clonmacnoise diocesan architecture continue to deny the systemic nature of these historic practices in their national schools. They treat such occurrences in the 1970s as outlier type experiences in the day to day running of their patronage schools, which they had no control over. In the latter sections of the book, I go into greater depth on how I experienced this effacement in my later adult years. Back to the history, shortly after my trip away to Lisieux in 1977/8, Bro. Bernard, the National Vocations Director called to my home as per usual to take me out to dinner in the Longford Arms Hotel. For the first time, another young boy was present. I remember feeling instantly attracted to this other boy's looks. Prior to this, as a younger boy, I remember thinking about older boys in my area in a similar way. However, on this occasion, there was an intensity to this attraction I do not remember experiencing before. He was not from the local town. He was from Birr, Co. Offaly. This seemed to afford me a much freer sense to allow myself to feel attracted to him. I had no idea that Bro. Bernard was using this occasion so that he could possibly monitor my reactions to this boy. Or, how, he was using the occasion to impress on me that I was not the only boy he took out to dinner.

As I approached my twelfth birthday, I still did not know how much I was been manipulated and groomed by Bro. Doyle. Prior to this occasion, we had always dined alone. When my mother had previously asked Bernard if she could join us for dinner, he told her his business was solely with me. This is what my mother told me in later years. At the time, my mother would not have questioned the authority of a religious person. Each week, Bro. Bernard would simply arrive at the house and bring me to the Fountain-Blue or Longford Arms Hotel. At a much later stage in my adult life, I learned that Bro. Bernard called to other boy's homes in the area. A week or so after this dinner with the boy from Offaly, Bro. Doyle returned as usual to pick me up from my home in Teffia Park. He brought me to the Longford Arms Hotel. After dinner, he took me up to his bedroom. I do not remember if there were two beds in the room. I know we ended up sharing a bed together. This episode went on for a good while. Bro. Bernard asked me to touch his genitals. He asked me if he could touch my genitals too. I remember him telling me he was teaching me the facts of life. After all my mother had been through, Bernard said that this would be too difficult for her. He had alluded to these ideas before. Bernard couched this talk as if he was my channel of communication toward God, my promise of freedom within an empire of saints. I believed him. I wanted to trust him, so that my special calling would not be taken away from me. I had been somewhat uncomfortable with some of his previous talk about the facts of life where I felt I could not get away from him when we chatted in his car outside my house. But this particular episode in the hotel room was so unexpected, unwanted and really confused me. It came out of nowhere. The way he set the whole episode made me feel I was part of it in some way.

In the hotel bedroom, I remember being totally uptight. I remember Bro. Bernard's tone was reassuring. It was fairly dark in this hotel room. The curtains were drawn. I think there was some light creeping in from the outside. It was summer time. The room was hot and sweaty. Bernard continued with this genital touching. He kept guiding my hand to touch his penis. Bro. Bernard said I would be okay. He kept emphasizing that he was doing this for my own good. He knew I was uncomfortable. This did not deter him. He was persistent but reassuring in tone. He may have ejaculated. It felt sticky. My frame was tiny beside this heavy and sweaty man. How did he think he could do something like this to me? In later years, my mother told me how distressed I was at this time. My mother later recounted, how a hotel porter comforted me in a corridor, where the hotel bedrooms were located. She said I had fled from the bedroom in distress. I have no strong recollection of this. She also told me when Bro. Bernard came back the following week, she told him never to come back again. She said when Bro. Bernard was at our door in Teffia Park, I was cowering in the corner of one of our rooms. I do not have much recollection of this either. Retired Irish bishop Willie Walsh (2016) says parents of abused children 'often felt guilty that they had not noticed the danger to which their child had been exposed and thus in some way had failed to protect their child' (p. 88). This makes a great deal of sense. I do not think my mother could deal with it.

Bro. Bernard's behaviour constituted a sexually inappropriate invasion of my space. He disrobed in front of me and had been making comments of a sexual nature for a long time beforehand. This was clearly part of his grooming and his advancement toward sexual exploitation. Up to this point in my life, I had never been exposed to anything like this. To share Bro. Bernard's bed was completely against age-appropriate development. He knew he was transgressing norms. In late 1970s Ireland, who was I, or my mother to raise an objection about the sexual abuse by Bro. Bernard? Within the proximity of my world in 1977, I would never have questioned the authority of religion. Each week, Bro. Bernard's words were similar to that of the founder of the De La Salle Order. 'You must destroy the man of sin who has reigned therefore in you, preached De La Salle' (Cooney 1999: 38). Cooney (1999) says 'central to French religious thought was a Jansenist concentration on mortal sin, especially sexual weakness' (p. 38). In order to situate this violation one must consider 'the value structure of the appearing world' (Bernstein 2015: 132). This writer says, 'Morally injurious acts are representations of the world that reveal how perpetrators regard their victims, and how they evaluatively regard themselves relative to them and relevant others (which could be everyone). Not all wrongful acts involve moral injury, but paradigm cases of criminally and morally wrong acts do involve moral injury' (p. 132).

Cooney's study (1999) gives a sense of the Archbishop of Dublin, Dr McQuaid's rootedness in French and Ignatian spirituality, when he preached: 'The saints become saints only in doing violence to themselves' (p. 37). This well-expressed social view of self-abnegation/sacrifice inflicted so much pain. Bro. Bernard's twisted behaviour in my social context was so weighted against me. At this time, I thought that any struggles I had were a sign of disturbance which resided within me. Psychologically, Bernard persistently reinforced what I had learned more tacitly and implicitly about the taboo of sex. Child sexual abuse patterns are well documented in social science research (Brady 2008; Gartner 2005; 2001; Spiegel 2003; Messler-Davies and Frawley 1994; Feiring, Taska and Lewis 1999; Dubowitz et al. 1993). The investigative team at the *Boston Globe* (2016) that inspired the Academy Award winning film *Spotlight* (2016) describes how an 'incorrigible paedophile ... calmly explained to therapists how he would single out his prey, the needy children of poor, single mothers' (p. 11). This was my mother too.

When my grandfather found out what happened with Bro. Bernard, he was very angry. My mother told me my grandfather never liked Bro. Bernard. He was suspicious of him. As previously mentioned, my grandmother was very religious. She said her husband's anger was another illustration of his communist leanings. Dr Noël Browne (1986) describes this as a fear for 'creeping socialism' (p. 26). These terms were used to dismiss my Grandfather and others like him, who questioned Church authority. I remember my grandfather as a kind and gentle presence in my life. He died of cancer in 1981. I remember going to see him in hospital. He had been a towering figure and now he was withering away in a hospital. As a young boy, I was very upset after he was gone. I always felt very much received as a young boy in his presence. Like my mother, my grandfather was caring. I felt he understood my childlike intentions and world. I felt he could see into my world. On my behalf, I thought I could feel a tearful and visibly warm empathy in his eyes for me. I always felt safe in his company. While he was an important and a comforting presence in my young life, I did not see much of him. He worked long hours, most days of the week, driving the bus from Longford to Dublin. When I did see him, I loved his company and felt cared for and protected by him. He was very good to me when I was sick. I knew I mattered to him. I was also aware of his pragmatic sense for injustice perpetrated by the Church. He had a very different reading of history. He was open to Marxist ideas and clearly believed that religion was the opium of the people. On reflection, I think his distaste for religion was more personal than a general distaste for the ideology of religion. But he got nowhere, because my grandmother dismissed his ideas as nonsense and he loved her. Because of my grandfather's age, he had witnessed first-hand the regression and the suffering the new arrangements of the Irish state caused his only living daughter and family. Meehan (2013) describes the disbelief expressed in literary accounts regarding the new foundations of the Irish state. My grandfather was more than familiar with the hopes and subsequent broken promises of these decades:

> 'What was it all for? The whole thing was a cod.' Michael Moran – the principal character of John McGahern's *Amongst Women* – found himself questioning the merits of what the independence struggle (1919–1921) had produced: 'some of our own jonnies in the top jobs instead of a few Englishmen. More than half of my own family work in England. Government spending had been hampered by the financial burden of reconstruction following the War of Independence and subsequent Civil War, the Great Depression stalked the 1930s, worsened by the Economic War with Britain, while frugality became the theme of the war years in the early 1940s, and rationing and strict controls remained in place after the world's theatres of war fell silent. The 1950s are often described as Ireland's 'lost decade,' characterized by high levels of emigration, unemployment and general poverty. These social ills were anathema to what the 1916/1919–21 period had seemed to promise and, like McGahern's Moran, many were left wondering about the value of independence. (p. 183)

Garvin (2004) says 'Alexis de Tocqueville's tyranny of the majority was alive and well in the emergent republican society of independent Ireland'. Regarding my grandfather, I subsequently found out how saddened he was for taking part in the adoption placement of his daughter's first baby to the nuns in Dublin in the 1950s. One nun in Longford said he cried a great deal about her parting. He was also angry with my father's behaviour and knew how the new laws of the Irish state prevented his daughter from getting a divorce. He had no power, as the state and Church were singing from the one hymnal, with no sign of effective mobilization against this systemic oppression. In such circumstances, it is easy to dismiss people's problems as merely personal. During this time, this dominating interpretation came from God's representatives on earth, who were so deeply conjoined to everyday practices. It was some level of control to exert over a nation, where objective modes of intelligibility were so fused with subjective ways of knowing. Politicians, the civil architecture and society were so enveloped in this multilevel phenomena.

In the 1970s, my mother was dependent on the generosity of local diocesan clerics for the placement of my youngest sister in residential care. This home was run by the Sisters of Charity of Jesus and Mary in Delvin, Co. Westmeath. My youngest sibling was born with significant brain impairment. She was born when I was less than three years old. Caring for her needs at home was very hard on my mother. When he was alive, my father could not accept my youngest sister's impairment. He did nothing to help her. This was a stressful atmosphere for my mother. On the day my sister left home, Bishop O'Reilly, then a priest of the diocese, transported my youngest sister with my mother to her new residential care home run by the nuns. My mother returned with him on the same day. She was very grateful to him for directly organizing a full-time place for my sister. As my mother learned to drive, she regularly went back and forth to see my sister. I regularly went with her. My sister regularly came home on holidays too. For my mother and grandmother, the Church was an important social outlet. In the 1970s/1980s there was not much else to do in rural towns. We did not have much money.

In my early to late teens, we lived with my grandmother. As she was ageing, and her husband deceased, she became very demanding on my mother. In my late teens/early adulthood, we moved from our own council house into a house that my grandmother purchased. Through this, I became more aware of my grandmother's distress. She was hypercritical and demanding on my mother. As a teen, she regularly compared me to my father. She often showed her displeasure and wrath to other siblings too. Her maledictions toward me were so shaming because of my father's violent history. My grandmother had a tendency to say cruel things to my mother too. My mother said that my grandmother once got down on her knees wishing that my mother was the one taken, rather than her only other child. My grandmother had lost another child, at nine years old, to leukaemia. My mother told me that my grandmother had a significant number of birth losses when infant mortality rates were very high in Ireland (Kennedy 2001). My grandmother often shamed my mother for her bad outcomes in life. I think my grandmother was grief stricken for so many reasons. My grandmother could never settle in the houses she had purchased. Later on, my mother had to transport her from one private nursing home to another. My grandmother could never settle in any of the nursing homes either. With my grandfather passed, my grandmother's ageing placed increasing demands on my mother's time.

When she was able bodied, my grandmother owned and managed a very successful eatery/restaurant in Longford. She was very well respected and was ahead of her time in the innovation she displayed. In our younger years, she was very generous to us with food when we visited her. She always served up beautiful food and dessert delights. An older sibling has strong admiration for our grandmother and says that without her support, her early life and others would have been much harder. My own mother was also a great cook and baker. Many visitors who came to our house positively remarked on her culinary skills and her great company over the years. Her meticulous precision in following and storing recipes are memories I will always cherish.

On a lighter note, I remember as a young boy been taken aback when a religious nun requested to use the toilet in my grandparent's house. Up to this point, I had thought nuns had magical powers and did not go to the toilet like the rest of us. Holding out for my innocence about the nuns been special, my grandfather explained to me that the figs in the fig roll biscuits were the nun's deposits left in the toilet. My grandmother had little patience for such talk and dismissed what my grandfather said. I do not remember my grandmother being too happy in the latter end of her life. She prayed a good deal. The nuns visited her in her house that we all now lived in.

One of the things that really strikes me about religious ideology and dogma is how it seemed to have an answer for everything. Many religious persons had ways of shutting down the conversation, having the last word on everything, what was permissible in conversation, and what they deemed morally inexcusable to even contemplate. Feeling bad about yourself and being joyless seemed to be noble virtues as a method of overcoming inherent vices. Over and over, I remember that feeling being reinforced. For a young teenager, this appropriation was narrowing and anxiety provoking. I had few resources for understanding this. I was under a spell of thinking that this badness was interior to me and that the responsible thing to do was to always feel at fault for everything going on around me and inside of me. This felt repressive. I was always on edge. My learning was that if I persistently willed against my own will, then the promise was that I would find an identity that would gain approval. When I struggled, I simply needed to persist harder in finding out that the root of any problem always resided in me. It was my job to overcome myself on the road to redemption.

Heading toward the arbiter of this meaning structure in the pursuance of a junior religious vocation was only going to make matters worse. I could not be persuaded out of this wish. I could not escape from thinking that this pursuit was a preordained calling from God and that I must respond to it appropriately. I had no sense how punishing and hard this motivation was on me. Self-sacrifice insists that God's command is more important. At such a young age, the guilt and the anxiety in not pursuing a religious calling was too much for me to deal with. Self-immersion in religious concepts literally felt part of my self-constitution. I was obsessed with the idea that personal will was insignificant to God's will. A normative repression in my early transition to teenage life weighed heavy on me. More than anything else, it was the ideas that Bernard inserted and how I interpreted his follow on sexual behaviour that made me feel very uneasy with others. It left me engaging in a provocative battle against myself where I would act in ways that were oppositional to my best self-interests. I could not decentre from the thought insertions of Bro. Bernard which seamlessly merged with the normative religious philosophy I had grown up with. Being traumatized, I was easy pickings for seduction into religion and subsequent predation. The gravitational pull in my thinking toward religious systems of thought felt like a rational stoicism toward higher ideals. I thought this would dispel the ingrained uneasiness I was familiar with.

Like many others, the way society was arranged allowed experts to diagnosis symptoms as particular to your personality and your home situation. This truncated lens was shaming and examples poor critical thinking skills.

At the time, I did not have the wherewithal to withstand the implications of dishonest discourses. Throughout her life, I think of how my mother got an awful belt of this philosophy. As a teenage boy, my capacity to judge and weigh up situations was significantly compromised. I would not work why I was so at odds with myself. My short-changing and defeatist behaviours were exampling all the reasons why children and teens ought to be protected from 'over-strong repression' (Klein 1921: 1), adding, 'We can spare the child unnecessary repression by freeing – and first and foremost in ourselves – the whole wide sphere of sexuality from the dense veils of secrecy, falsehood and danger spun by a hypocritical civilisation' (p. 1).

The next section examples how internalized oppression can create a motivation in a young person's life for more of the same. Circumventing information about danger felt like an unconscious repetition I had no control over.

CHAPTER 7

Entering the De La Salle Junior Novitiate in Castletown, Portlaoise in 1978

I shall nevertheless confess to you my shame, since it is for your praise.
— St Augustine

Despite what had happened with Bro. Bernard, I still insisted on going away to the De La Salle School in Castletown, Portlaoise. I persuaded my mother to let me go in 1978. I told my mother that Bro. Doyle did not teach at the school. I told her Bro. Bernard simply went around to national schools to recruit boys for his order's school. This was all true. My mother always tried to meet me in my expectations. She was never inclined to insisting on her way, over my way. I think my mother did not want to repeat any harshness because of our family history. She may have rejoiced that she was going to have a son joining religious life. I think she felt I would be safe as a brother. She certainly accepted that my vocation as something that could be good for me. She did not go against it. And she knew how much I had invested in religious ideas. It is not possible to theorize about young psychological development without grasping the overlapping tapestry of my social upbringing. My own temperamental sensitivity to context may also explain individual differences in a child's reactions to adverse situations (Alkon, Wolff, and Thomas Boyce 2012).

On one occasion in the school playground at the De La Salle school in Castletown, I remember seeing Bro. Bernard. He looked at me in his normal way as if nothing had happened between us. Emotional immaturity is a key trait of sexual predators (*Boston Globe* 2016; Terry et al. 2011). In looking my way, I knew what he wanted from me. I kept my distance and was nervous of him. I remember my defensive posture which was a front for the deeper disappointment I really felt inside. The former school principal clearly thought I might be willing for more or the same.

I did not last long at De La Salle Secondary School in Castletown, Portlaoise. When I went home, after my first term, my mother opened up a letter from the school principal. The principal reported I had been sleep walking. In the event of an accident, Bro. Charles said that the design of the boarding school was not suitable. In the letter, Bro. Charles said it was not a good idea for me to come back to his school. He felt I must have been homesick. I remember being devastated and inconsolable in not being allowed back to the friend I had made there. I was gutted that my religious vocation was over. I felt this was all my fault – again! After this fast exit from Castletown, there was never any follow-up from the De La Salle Order regarding my wellbeing.

Similar to the recruitment pattern in Ireland during the 1970s, The De La Salle schools in Australia often 'lacked sufficient pupils from the local catchment area' (BRA 2015). Historically, the De La Salle Brothers had arrived in Australia from 1905. Towey (1980) states how the local bishop, Patrick Moran, offered the De La Salle Brothers the site at Castletown, Portlaoise in 1881. Three years later, Bishop Moran left for Australia. One of his first duties was to visit Paris requesting 'a detachment of brothers to be sent to Australia' (Towey 1980: 389). Until 1920, the makeup of the brothers in Australia were primarily staffed by De La Salle missionaries of Irish descent. Referring to an institution run by the De La Salle Brothers in Australia, BRA (2015) say 'Some of the boarders in 1942 were disadvantaged, from broken homes, or boys whose families were disrupted from World War II' (BRA 2015, see 'Alan's Story', Appendix). At eleven/twelve years old, the theme of disadvantage and recruiting boys from other areas was very similar technique used by Bro. Bernard in his role of Vocations Director for the Irish De La Salle Order in 1970s Ireland.

A letter I recently received from my old friend who attended De La Salle Castletown at the same time as me, extended me good insight into my emotional state in 1978. Bro. Bernard had recruited him from his local De La Salle National School. My friend said that boys came as far as Kerry and Tipperary to the De La Salle School in Castletown. He had spent a number of years at the school and often attended school reunions for past pupils. He asked me had I ever received invitations for these reunions. I told him I had not. My friend's handwritten letter essentially confirms the reason given by Bro. Charles for my departure. In one section of his letter, my former school peer states:

> Another subject I want to talk to you about and I hope it doesn't upset you, is that you had a serious sleepwalking problem. This used to happen quite often and would usually start about an hour after the lights were switched off in the dorms. Sometimes you would talk in your sleep before you got up. Other times you would get up without saying a word and walk silently in a trance like state around the dorm. More often than not, you would rip the curtains off the rails from some lad's cubicle or drag the covers and blankets off his bed. When this would happen we would all get up to see what was happening. Then three or four of the older boys would try and restrain you and after a few minutes you would waken up. You would be very upset then and you didn't know where you were. The Bro in charge of the dorm then would awaken with the noise. The boys would drag you forcefully out of the dorm and away to some other part of the building – where, I don't know.
>
> Then, other times you would sleepwalk to different parts of the building and on one or two occasions you ended up in the yard outside. I remember one night before you were dragged from the dorm, you grabbed onto the doorknob and locked the door from the inside and wouldn't let go until the knob broke off in your hand. It was upsetting to watch.
>
> The next day you would be tired in class and we would ask did you remember what happened the previous night. But you didn't seem to remember and you would be embarrassed.

The learned pattern of hyper-arousal after repeated exposure to child and adolescent trauma and sexual exploitation is well documented in clinical literature (O'Donoghue and Ferguson 2016; Sanderson 2006; Pynoos, Steinberg & Aronson 1997; Pynoos, Steinberg & Wraith 1995).

In the context of my friend's description, I want to focus on how Bro. Bernard (1970) characterized my erratic behaviour. Through his previous role as school principal in De La Salle Churchtown in Dublin from 1968 to 1972, Bro. Bernard (1970) addresses the theme of 'really difficult' boys. Bro. Bernard is reflecting on the academic achievements of all secondary school pupils within various categories of educational attainment. Bernard says:

> Congratulations to our Leaving and Inter Cert students of last year, who did so well in their examinations. A special word of praise to the twelve Leaving Cert Boys who

won valuable University Scholarships. Academic successes are desirable and we all like brilliant results. We must not, however, forget the boys who work 'brilliantly' but fail to shine in exams. They must not worry unduly. Their years in College give them something very precious. They will have learned perseverance, courage and self-reliance. They cannot but make a success of their lives. What of the really difficult boys? Every school has its quota of these. Small though this quota may be, these boys are our really greatest problem. No amount of advice and admonition can make them see that they are their own greatest enemies. (p. 8)

To my mind, Bro. Bernard's thinking gives a good indication of how the De La Salle Order aligns itself to the higher status order. And Bro. Bernard then speaks with a significant degree of contempt and frustration for underperforming 'difficult' pupils. Some of these pupils were most likely from troubled backgrounds like mine. Furthermore, critical to the success of this strategy is the way a sexual predator chooses a young victim. These are the very young persons a predator might view as 'their own greatest enemies.' If the brothers exploit such boys, these boys are less likely to be believed. They have no status, only their youthful wilful and erratic responses.

The mission of the De La Salle Order was purportedly about helping the worst off in society. Across the world, subsequent Commissions of Inquiries illustrate a high percentage of disadvantaged young persons were cruelly taken advantage of in these religious run and religious patronage settings. The power of these orders on public policy allowed the religious orders monopolize these settings and set the discourse terms for how disadvantaged persons were viewed by the broader society. This is how the orders developed their social capital in education and social care. Not many in society seemed to suspect that the arbiters of moral norms would be the very ones who could actually commit such grave harm and exploit young children in their care and in the wider society.

When the orders privately educate the wealthy, religious educators suggest they are cultivating minds for social justice within the higher echelons of society. However, this trickle-down redistributive philosophy for social justice, as a way of reducing disadvantage is a problematic theory in practice (Aarte Scholte 2016; Salverda, Nolan and Smeeding 2009). From reading *The Boy from Glin Industrial School* (2013), an aspect of Tom Wall's work that really stood out was how his living conditions at the industrial school run by the Irish Christian Brothers were so different to the boys accommodation. By accident, Tom outlines how he discovers the living quarters of the Brothers, when a new duty Brother came to the boy's refectory. The recently arrived brother requested Tom to fetch a key from one of the other brothers in their main dining hall. Up to this point in Tom's story, a request for more bread was something that was unheard of. This newly arrived brother was of a different sort. Tom describes the Brother's varied appearances and the luxury of the Brother's dining area in detail:

> They kept themselves cleanly shaven and always wore clean white collars. Others were scruffy and stubble on their faces. Their kitchen and dining hall was on the Monastery side of the school which consisted of sitting rooms, parlour, and community room. Each Christian Brother had his own bedroom which was located upstairs. They did not complain about the cold as the entire Monastery was heated. They went for breakfast as soon as Mass was finished in the morning. Their dining room table was beautifully laid out with linen and serviettes, folded into serviette rings. Their meals were always served with the best of cutlery and china. (Wall 2013)

All of this was in stark contrast to the boys living conditions which were cold, filthy and the boys were always hungry and often resorting to desperate measures to secure food:

> The Christian Brothers went for dinner at 2.00 p.m. So by 2.30 p.m. we would try to get the discarded food from the Christian Brothers' dining room. If we were late getting to the bins the rats were there, and we had to abandon that exercise for that day. We were also able to raid the buckets for scraps of bread until someone found out and added water to make a mush out of it.

A further aspect of Tom's story was how he experienced repetitive failures in his early business ventures when he left the Industrial school. The Brothers did not provide a decent level of education for these unprivileged and blighted kids. After the boys finished up in these schools, the brothers did not seem to care what happened next. Wall (2013) says many of his peers ended up with depleted existences, with some of them taking their lives and dying young. Many of these brothers were so unsuited to these roles and were dangerous to youth. The Brothers instead of instilling confidence in blighted children and youth, made some of their lives worse with

violence and exploitation, shaping intense levels of mistrust and resistance
in many of the young boy's lives. I know the Brothers had their successes
in Irish education. That said, the cruelty exerted on children in industrial
schools was definitely above the cultural norms of chastisement in historic
Ireland. I engage with these dynamics in greater detail in the second half
of this book.

In the UK, like Ireland, public trust in religious patronage systems
meant the religious brothers were aligned to helping disadvantaged youth
(Inglis 1998; Coldrey 1993; 1988). Subsequent public inquiries into these
historic arrangements reveal a terrible pattern of abuses over a thirty-year
period from 1945 to 1975 in the homes run by the De La Salle Brothers for
troubled boys. These homes, approved by the state, were reserved for young
children and teenagers who were said to have committed petty criminal
offenses (Caulfield 2014). Testimony from a former UK resident, now in
his late sixties, reads:

> I kept the abuse a secret for 55 years. Mr Riley said he was raped by the headmaster,
> sexually abused by another brother and by a visiting priest. I remember lying in my
> dormitory, hearing the screams of other boys echoing through the house at night. I
> remember being beaten. I remember blood running down my legs. And then Brother
> Joseph tried to interfere with me. One minute you'd be singing hymns in church and
> everything and you'd come out and that's what they'd do to you after church. One
> minute you're on your knees praying to the Lord and then you'd be doing things the
> good Lord said you shouldn't do. (Caulfield 2014)

The Scottish Bishops' General Assembly (2009) in its assessment of the
dynamics and impact of CSA says:

> The sexual abuse of children is fundamentally an abuse of trust and of power which
> exploits the age-related differentials between child and abuser, as well as enlisting,
> abusing, distorting and disorientating the child's needs for intimacy, affirmation,
> security, trust and guidance. ... Its core dynamic is that of entrapment and isolation,
> through which social and physiological transcendence may be blocked ... A particular
> source of confusion is the incorporation of the child's active agency in psychologi-
> cally 'accommodating' the abuse and keeping it secret.

The psychological accommodation is an epiphenomenon of the social
structure that kept these violations under-wraps. Many of the well-worded

apologies from clerics never once allude to the economic costs of grievous moral harm to children and teenagers. An adolescent's effortful control needs to be sharply focused on preparation for the educational tasks ahead. In my own young life, I was totally messed up. I could not compete with my peers. I was caught in an intense spiral. I felt rudderless and fast-moving. I could not understand my acting out at school. It just seemed to be happening over and over. Most of the lads in my school were focused. They seemed to know how to pace and to learn. They were not drawing attention to themselves in the way I was. I was again sexually victimized in my early teens by another older man. It was a random assault. I was curious about sex but not against my consent with people who felt they could do as they wished.

The next section examples the dominance of religion in Ireland with the visit of John Paul II to Ireland in 1979. This period for me, during my early teenage years, reinforced a feeling that I was a total misfit. Deep down I felt inferior and disapproved of for simply being me. A stronger psychological interpretation would be to say that I am making choices, making choices to construe myself as a victim of socio-historic circumstances. I did not have a language for talking about what I had been going through. I thought if people knew my story and what I felt about it, this telling would invite revulsion from others. That persistent fear of rejection felt persecutory. Inside myself, I still did not grasp that those persecutory self-beliefs arose from being immersed in Catholic faith formation in historic Ireland. Can people discourage, disbelieve, make light of, discredit, efface and stigmatize others when they decide to open up about their experiences of child victimization? Certainly, the religiosity of 1970s/mid-1990s Ireland pretty much guaranteed the discourse concealment of clerical crimes against children, making victims suspicious of their own thoughts/feelings. Unequal power arrangements can work this way, where a pre-ordained higher social status rank is able to use and misuse its power through its accumulated stock of identity capital, setting the terms for a national conversation on how to deal with historical injustices. In 1979, I was an uneasy young teenager, with many interiorized fears. Teenage brain development is a key cognitive transition point for advanced learning, identity and formal/forward thought development.

As I started my secondary schooling in Longford, the next section describes the normative scale of the deference(s) for religious power. It was the biggest religious event ever to be staged in Ireland during my lifetime. The static presumptions of normative logics were on full view. These traditions had not gone dead in the late 1970s, involving ensembles of preordained social practices and rituals to solve many of the problems we continued to have in Irish society.

The Pope's Visit to Ireland in 1979 and After

We ascribe intentionality to an entity capable of having a particular set
of commitments and entitlements, namely those that can be articulated
and discursively instituted by social linguistic norms. (Gallagher 2017)

In my early years of attending secondary school, Pope John Paul II came
to Ireland (O'Neill 2014). The power of the Catholic Church in Ireland
was so well exemplified in the massive turnout of our population to greet
the newly elected Pope to Ireland. He was regarded as so charismatic and
different. Before and after the Pope's visit, I remember attending nine day
retreats given by the Redemptorist Order in St Mel's Cathedral. This order
of preachers came to Longford every year. My mother named me after St
Gerard Majella, a famous Redemptorist cleric. Some of the Redemptorist
preachers were austere in the way they preached. In the church on Berkeley
Road in Dublin where my mother was refused a marriage annulment in the
1950s, there is a shrine to St Gerard Majella in the top right-hand corner of
the church on Berkeley Road. It is now run by the Discalced Carmelites. To
this day, I often go in and light a candle in her memory at his shrine. I am
fond of visiting this old-fashioned church. It is part of my family history.

As part of the Pope's trip in 1979, John Paul II visited the pontifi-
cal seminary in Maynooth. He specifically addressed the contribution of
'religious brothers' in Ireland saying, 'Your call to holiness is a precious
adornment of the Church. Believe in your vocation. Be faithful to it. "God
has called you and He will not fail you"' (Thess. 5:23, cited by Towey 1980:
594). The redemptive agent in these moral repertoires is the responsible
agent. If he falls for less than, theological ideas suggest that the social is
never a constraint, rather moral character is above the social. This innate

formulation in theology, philosophy and psychology conceptualize innate dignity as preconditions for a resilient sense of agency. The resilient inner hero is someone who rises above adversity and trauma. No matter what happens, these tests from the external with prove the boy's strength.

All this talk resonated with what I heard as a boy. It was deeply configured in my modes of self-understanding. The idea of quieting my own noisy/sinful ego. My personality could not find a reasoned space to detach from this consciousness. I had not achieved an inter-independence from it. Thinking I was special from the viewpoint of theological development and experience was not that helpful. Thinking that I was picked from obscurity to serve a divine purpose was repressive to emotional development. At a time when my cognitive architecture at adolescence was designed to increase my awareness, I was still too caught up in a 'non-transcendent self' relying too heavily on concrete and literal deductions. Developmental psychologist Susan Harter (2017) says 'adolescence is a particularly precarious period for self-development, given the proliferation of multiple role-related self-images that are far from under cognitive control, as they vacillate unpredictably' (p. 92). Again, developmental psychology often truncates regional histories in favour of objective and abstract ideas.

For the Pope's visit, our serving Bishop Cahal B. Daly, was 'involved in the drafting of the Pope's sermons and addresses' (*The Telegraph* 2010). Out of a total population of 3,365,000 in Ireland (Towey 1980: 555), *Irish Central News* says that nearly 'three million people turned out to welcome the Pontiff at five different venues: Dublin, Drogheda, Galway, Limerick and Knock' (Walsh 2015). No doubt, many of the same people turned up for all the events in the Pope's itinerary. That said, despite the duplication, this was a huge turnout of the population. Ireland came to a standstill for the new Pontiff from Poland. This was my situated life space in Longford in my early teens. When speaking to priests and religious in Maynooth on 1 October 1979, our local Bishop Cahal Daly (1998) noted how John Paul II addressed the theme of religious vocations:

> The degree of religious practice in Ireland is high. For this we must be constantly thanking God. But will this high level of religious practice continue? Will the next generation of young Irishmen and Irish women still be as faithful as their fathers were? After my two days in Ireland, after my meeting with Ireland's youth in Galway, I am

confident that they will. But this will require both unremitting work and untiring prayer on our part. You must work for the Lord with a sense of urgency. You must work with conviction that this generation, this decade of the 1980s which we are about to enter, could be crucial and decisive for the future of the faith in Ireland. Let there be no complacency. (p. 226)

During my schooling, nuns were always coming to visit my mother and grandmother, almost every day. They would stay for hours drinking tea, bringing plain biscuits and saying rosaries. After school, I remember their sayings about the evils of the modern world. As a teenager, these nuns were the literal embodiment of John Paul's message 'let there be no complacency'. I remember meeting one of these nuns in later life and she told me that I was the one in the family never mentioned by my mother. This memory stays with me as it represents how micro-slights are communicated, as if who you are is insignificant – you are without qualities. The gay person is unmentionable, wilfully going against God's will and is not really a citizen in the proper sense of the word. Homosexual behaviour was designated criminal in the nation's laws at the time. As cited by Hewitt, Flett and Mikail (2017), Rosenberg and McCullough (1981) underscore that 'knowing that one matters to others is fundamental to the formation of a resilient and healthy self-concept, and ultimately shapes the sense of self-worth' (p. 115). In my youth, the concepts of health and self-worth were assigned to hetero-sexuals. And if there were gays in my local area experiencing distress from being silenced and insulted, I had not met them. All I had at my disposal were vile inferences from the social stock of national meanings in Ireland of this time period. In the late 1970s and early 1980s, I had developed no alternative language to contest the normalcy of social oppression, propped up as it was, by key stakeholders in Ireland. How could I have unmasked this domination when so much of my values were fulsomely constituted by this theological discourse? There were too many obstacles enacted in my own subjective dispositions that were literally tripping me up. As a teen, I did not understand how I was formed and shaped by the norma-tive judgements of my society and could not emancipate from them. In this way, oppressive ideas and templates have to fall somewhere, designed to regulate how people feel and think. Without an understanding of this overarching dynamic, the dominant philosophy is not transparent in the enacted horizon of our moods and thoughts.

On his trip to Ireland, John Paul II spoke to nearly a third of the population at the Phoenix Park in Dublin in 1979 (BBC 2005). In another of the papal addresses, John Paul II warned how the current age was 'endangering 'freedom, the sacredness of life, the indissolubility of marriage [and] the true sense of human sexuality' (Fuller 2002: 238). To his youth audience of 280,000 in Galway, the new Pontiff said: 'The desire to be free from external restraints may manifest itself very strongly in the sexual domain [and] Do not close your eyes to the moral sickness that stalks your society today' (Vatican 1979).

Social perfectionism was prescribed as heterosexuality in marriage or abstinence. Gay sex was a moral sickness, according to the new Pope. Yet, John Paul II told his audience in Galway he believed in each and every one of us and that he loved us all. The powerful inferences that the Pope was making about sexuality perpetuated stigma, prejudice and discrimination, even though the feeling of 'social disconnection is thought to be especially noxious' (Hewitt, Flett and Mikail 2017: 133). At this time, the Pope's prejudicial ideas were socially woven into Irish norms. He was here in Ireland to give us a top-up on our history. Rather than view my own life experience as an oddity or outlier, one can situate my experience within a 'central motivational impulse of dominant groups in unequal social relations is not hatred, but the desire to control' (Jackman 2005, cited by Tileaga 2018: 99). Tileaga (2018) adds Gordon Allport's (1954) definition on discrimination as

> wrong because it stifles public recognition of someone's social worth. When Allport writes about aspirational worth he brings into view people's rights to self-determination, self-definition, and inclusion into a moral community. Similar to recognition theory, Allport's (disvalue) definition points to a fundamental human motivation of striving for equality of worth, respect, esteem, and moral inclusion. (p. 99)

Tileaga (2018) adds an extra insight beyond 'negative evaluation' (p. 100), suggesting 'benevolent attitudes mingle with conservative and discriminatory actions and where sympathy mingles with resentment and contempt' (citing Jackman, p. 100).

In my rural setting, Honneth (2001) talks of 'being made invisible, of being made to disappear, that evidently involves not a physical non-presence, but rather non-existence in a social sense' (Honneth 2001 p. 111). Nell McCafferty (1985/2010) says the Pope's visit was an attempt by a charismatic religious leader to reverse the progressive benefits that came with Ireland's EU membership in 1973. The Pope wanted to reinvigorate conservative ideals. From the 1970s, McCafferty refers to the successes of the Irish Women's Liberation Movement (IWLM), a movement that confronted the state privileging of patriarchy/misogyny where women's second-class citizenship was naturalized in Irish history. Feminist movements were able to bring about progressive changes designed at eroding the historic legacy of gender inequality and repression in Ireland (McCafferty 1985/2010).

However, after the Pope's visit to Ireland, there was a resurgence of popular piety and Marian devotion in rural areas, with sightings of moving statutes all across Ireland (Fuller 2002, p. 243–4). Traditional Catholic values, perhaps more concentrated in rural areas, meant that Ireland still voted conservatively, rejecting a right to abortion and divorce. In 1983, the Irish electorate had voted to amend the constitution enshrining the right to life of the unborn with the addition of Article 40.3.3 into the Irish constitution. In 1984, the tragic cases of the Kerry Babies and the tragic deaths of Ann Lovett and her baby at a grotto in Granard, Co. Longford, were indicative of socio-religious conventions and ideals been upheld in Irish culture (Ferriter 2009). The *Longford Leader* editorial captured the Granard tragedy in the headline, 'Ann Lovett's Decision', posing the question 'Who is to say Ann Lovett did not die happy? Who is to say she had not fulfilled her role in life as God decreed?' (McGee 1984). Ann Lovett was 'the third youngest of nine children born to Diarmuid and Patricia Lovett. Ann's father, who was from the village of Kilnaleck, Co Cavan, moved the family back there in 1972. In 1981, they moved to the nearby small town of Granard' (Boland 2018).

In his headline on this tragedy, the *Longford Leader* editor is keen to impress on the goodness of the status quo of this time period. Rather than challenge the status quo, the local media editor rolls over and affirms the traditions as innocent and not complicit in the tragedy. The editor rails against the emergent logics of secular traditions, citing 'psychoanalysts, psychiatrists, family planners' and 'all the other do-gooders of Irish society.' Despite having attended the local doctor for 'shingles' when she was seven months pregnant, Boland (2018) says that the Chief Executive of the Midland Health Board in 1984, 'Denis J Doherty told the media that Ann had not accessed any of their services: the public health nurse, social workers, or community welfare officers.' From this, it is reasonably clear that Ann had absorbed the values of a clericalist culture and felt the gravitational pull of dominant religious symbolism in rural Ireland at the time.

Eugene McGee, editor of the *Longford Leader*, poses further reflections in his 1984 editorial, how Ann's relationship to the Virgin Mary was more important to her than anything that modernity had to offer her. This aspect of the editorial shows little appetite for investigative journalism other than to infantilize the grotesque death of a teenager and her baby in purity concepts and the editor interprets self-sacrifice to her faith concepts, as coeval with all that is good in Ireland's history, while dismissing newer trends that may lift the veil of ignorance in the status quo.

Regarding Ann's family context, *Irish Times* journalist Rosita Boland (2018) says her mother 'Patricia Lovett, née McNamee, was a private woman who kept to herself and attended Mass regularly. "Lily," a close friend now aged eighty-six and still living in Co. Longford, recalls her as "a lovely, lovely decent woman. She was a great parish worker and very religious."' Boland (2018) says Ann's father 'Diarmuid Lovett bought the Copper Pot bar on the town's Main Street and the family lived above it. The pub didn't seem to open much, or get much trade. He was also a carpenter, but was unemployed and didn't appear to have adjusted successfully to the role of publican.'

Ann Lovett was discovered by locals at 4 p.m. on a rain-soaked winter school day on 31 January 1984. Canon Gilfillan was the local cleric who went to the grotto to administer the last rites where Anne lay with her deceased baby. Boland (2018) continues:

> At 5.55pm, Ann was admitted to Mullingar hospital, and it was noted her lips and fingertips were white on arrival; a medical state called cyanosis. Her school uniform was soaked, and she was cold to the touch. The obstetrician in attendance, Dr Marie Skelly, directed that blood and oxygen be given. 'Momentarily there were signs of

recovery, but almost immediately she stopped breathing,' said Dr Skelly. She said it was difficult to ascertain whether Ann had hypothermia and exposure, or haemorrhage. Ann did not respond when her chest was opened for direct cardiac massage. Ann Rose Lovett died shortly afterwards, aged 15 years, nine months and 25 days.

Dr Marie Skelly, the obstetrician who had attended Ann in Mullingar hospital, told the inquest that 'I have known of five certain cases where pregnancy was concealed right up to the time of birth, even from people in the same house and I have known of two that were concealed from people sharing a room with the pregnant woman.'

Despite the status quo editorial position of the *Longford Leader* at the time, Boland (2018) highlights how the *Longford Leader*, in one its first reports on 10 February 1984, contained an admittance that others had knowledge of her pregnancy. Citing a more recent interview with the former *Longford Leader* editor, Boland (2018) says,

> 'From our investigations, we are satisfied that many of Ann Lovett's school pals did know, and several adults in Granard knew,' ran a sentence in Eugene McGee's and Jim Gray's report. How did they discover this, I asked McGee when I visited him. 'I picked up the phone and talked to people in Granard who knew me,' he says. It appeared plenty of people in the town had either suspected or knew Ann Lovett was pregnant. (Boland 2018)

Boland says, 'On April 22nd, 1984, less than three months after Ann died, her sister Patricia, aged 14, died by suicide. Diarmuid Lovett, her father died three years later, aged 57. Patricia Lovett remained living on Main Street, Granard, until her death in June 2015, aged 81.'

At a subsequent Sunday mass shortly after the death of Ann and her baby, Canon Gilfillan said,

> 'The secret of what happened is with that little girl in the grave,' he said. 'What happened should have been left to the town to deal with in its own way. My firm belief is what happened should not have been covered by RTÉ or the newspapers: it should have been kept parochial, local. They gave us loud-mouthed publicity of the worst kind, but God is good and able to triumph over evil reporting.' (Boland 2018)

A week after the first local report in the *Longford Leader*, the next edition's front page contained a statement from Granard Town Commissioners, who had met 'and adjourned their meeting as a mark of respect to the family of late Ann Lovett and her baby' (*Longford Leader* 1984). The Commissioners expressed their deep upset at the 'insensitive and distasteful reporting by most of the national papers ... In our opinion, the appalling reporting was characteristic of the British gutter press in dealing with Irish affairs' (*Longford Leader* 1984). A further letter was received by the Town Clerk from Albert Reynolds, local FF TD, to convey his sympathy to the family. Reynolds was also highly critical of the media:

> In such personal and community affairs, I believe that a dignified silence is infinitely more beneficial than headline seeking and cheap political opportunism. My attitude is shared by all caring Christian people throughout the country, and together with them, I reject what can only be described as an objectionable intrusion into a very personal and private tragedy by some poisoned pen pushers in the national and international media.
>
> I am well aware of the depth of community spirit which exists in the Granard area – their concern for the underprivileged, disabled, disadvantaged, and all who need and seek their help, and it is to be hoped that the uninvited attention of the media will in no way diminish the fine traditions of the area. (*Longford Leader* 1984)

On the same front page of this edition of the *Longford Leader*, a small section reports how a fifty-four-year-old man died 'on Friday night last after sprinkling himself with petrol and setting fire to himself at the door of St. Mel's Cathedral. Pat O'Connor was single and lived alone. He was rushed from the scene to Mullingar Hospital, but was dead on arrival' (*Longford Leader* 1984). Also in the direct aftermath of the deaths in Granard, an official within the Catholic Archdiocese of Armagh wrote in a letter to the poet Christopher Daybell (February 1984), 'I think her sad death reflects more on her immaturity than on any lack of Christian charity amongst the family and people with whom she lived' (cited by Gartland 2014). Daybell, in a further covering letter to Dr Garret FitzGerald 'dated March 3rd 1984', told the Taoiseach that the girl's death 'coupled with' the letter from the archdiocese, had driven him 'almost mad ... The letter goes beyond hypocrisy – that man in Armagh is incapable of feeling beyond the walls of his office and the great institution into which he has built his being' (Gartland 2014). In another letter to Dick Spring, the Tánaiste (Deputy Prime Minister) and leader of the Irish Labour Party, Daybell 'said it could emerge, "considering the hideous attitudes of men toward women in rural Ireland," that Ms Lovett "was driven by forces other than those within herself. I await the result of the inquiry in a now cool anger, and hope that it will stiffen the resolve of your government on divorce and contraception"" (Gartland 2014). In essence, these tragedies are particularized to outlier types of experience, something innately immature to the young teenager. The clergy completely de-contextualizes the role of its traditions in the tragedy.

On 5 May 2018, *Irish Times* journalist Rosita Boland (2018a) wrote a follow-up article entitled, 'I was Ann Lovett's Boyfriend'. For the first time, Ricky McDonnell, her teenage boyfriend in the 1980s, came forward for interview. Now in his early fifties, McDonnell revealed their sexual relationship, gossip about her pregnancy and about a further violent attack Ann was subjected to. Ricky saw the bruises on Ann's body and inquired if she had been raped. She did not respond and she implored him to stay silent about it.

After her death, Ricky further described how family members came to him with an open letter addressed to him that Ann had written just before her death. She had also left a letter for her family. Ricky provided further information on a meeting with local cleric Fr Quinn. Ricky advised how Fr Quinn told him to burn the letter. Shortly after, Fr Quinn was said to have set up a meeting with the local Bishop of Ardagh and Clonmacnoise at his Palace in Longford. Ricky McDonnell claimed the bishop swore him to secrecy about the letter's contents. He was reminded that by kissing the ring of the bishop, his secret was sealed through a direct apostolic line of succession to St Peter in Rome, Christ's representative on Earth (Boland 2018a).

McDonnell also claimed he met with the Minister for Defence, Patrick Cooney, a FG TD for the Longford-Westmeath Dáil constituency (Boland 2018a). Cavan FF TD John Wilson also showed up as a mark of respect at Ann's and her baby's funeral in Granard (*Longford Leader* 1984). Both John Wilson and Albert Reynolds went on to serve again as government ministers, with the latter serving as a future Taoiseach from 1992–4. Through Fr Quinn's solicitors, Boland (2018a) says the cleric denied a meeting took place with the bishop in Longford and that he had demanded that the letter be burned. Now retired since 2013, Bishop O'Reilly told *The Irish Times* 'he had never met Ricky McDonnell' (Boland 2018a). Former minister Patrick Cooney, now eighty-six years old, 'Initially, when The Irish Times contacted Patrick Cooney and asked if he had ever met Ricky McDonnell, he said, "No". When asked if he had helped recruit him into the Army, Cooney replied: "I have no recollection of any incident like that at all," adding, "anyway, I couldn't offer to recruit him into the Army; he would have had to go through the recruitment process"' (Boland 2018a). But when told of Fr Quinn's account, that a meeting did take place, which Fr Quinn set up, the former minister Paddy Cooney responded, 'If Fr. Quinn remembers it happened, I have no difficulty with that' (O'Keeffe 2018). This type of behaviour by esteemed institutional players examples the length they are prepared to go to isolate and undermine individuals.

In Ireland's case, the dysfunctionality in the social order has been slow to change. In a recent penning on the Kerry Babies case, in an article entitled 'The Legal Crucifixion of Joanne Hayes,' Nell McCafferty (2018) captures the tone of the 'vilification and humiliation' at the tribunal: 'What kind of young lady do we have here?' This question examples how many Irish women were treated, as if their sexual behaviours were a menace to the good moral fabric of society. The lines of questioning in the Kerry Babies tribunal by an all-male tribunal; combined with humiliating practices of interrogation by law enforcement officers; a dependence on discredited pseudo-science at the tribunal itself; a narrow-minded rural political and legal class. Despite the local support of men and women in her community and across Ireland, Joanne Hayes and her family went up against a deeply rooted ideology (McCafferty 2018; 2010/1985). The case examples once again the cross-pollination of Church and state apparatus, where the power tentacles of the legal and moral architecture share the same ideological mindedness. Given the monolithic control that the Church enjoyed over primary and secondary education, this cultural dynamic of shared ethos is hardly surprising. McCafferty (2018) describes the background context of the Kerry Babies case itself:

> Joanne Hayes had three pregnancies by her married lover Jeremiah Locke, already a father of two, in the early 1980s. The successful campaign to amend the Constitution

and outlaw abortion in all circumstances took place between June 1981 and September 1983.

Joanne's first pregnancy resulted in a miscarriage in June 1982. Her second pregnancy resulted in May 19, 1983, in the hospital birth of one daughter, Yvonne, who was reared in the Hayes family home near Abbeydorney, four miles from Tralee. The third saw a baby born to her in April 13, 1984, as she stood alone in a field outside the family home late at night.

The boy died at birth. His lungs did not inflate. There was a mark on his throat, indicating how Joanne, who suffered a perineum tear, had pulled him from her womb. She hid the dead baby in a bag, in a pool, on the farm.

She had been treated in St Catherine's hospital in Tralee for a miscarriage, a few hours before the body of 'baby John' was found in a plastic bag on a beach near Cahersiveen, 70 miles from Abbeydorney, on April 14, 1984. The new born baby, estimated to be 48 hours old, had been stabbed to death. (McCafferty 2018)

Joanne Hayes had been initially charged with the murder of the Cahersiveen baby, a case which was subsequently thrown out by a judge. McCafferty (2018) says, 'It took 90 minutes and three phone calls to come up with the name of Joanna Hayes as the prime suspect in the Kerry Babies Scandal.'

The Gardaí were forced to drop the charges four years later. However, it took the Gardaí until 2018 to offer Ms Hayes an apology for their botched investigation in 1984, also citing that DNA testing was not available in the 1980s. The Gardaí confirmed a criminal case was ongoing for the murder of 'baby John.' The Irish government quickly apologized to her and family, promising speedy compensation for what Joanne Hayes had been put through by the Gardaí and the adversarial behaviour of the Tribunal (Lucey et al. 2018). The Taoiseach, Mr Varadkar (2018), speaking from the EU Parliament in Strasburg, said

> He had only recently learned the full facts of the Kerry Babies case, as he was very young at the time, and that it had been an 'eye opening' experience. 'It reflects the extent to which Ireland was such a different place in the 1980s than it is now,' he said. 'I absolutely want to add to the apology made by the Gardaí and make that an apology on behalf of the State as well.' (Lucey et al. 2018)

Back to my own family history, over the course of her life, my mother suffered with a bipolar illness and was regularly admitted to mental hospital over many years. At the time, I think bipolar had a different term – manic depression. When I visited her in St Loman's Psychiatric Hospital in Mullingar during the 1980s and early 1990s, I often came across the infantile and distressed state of some of the female patients in the hospital. Like my mother, many of the women were heavily sedated and very sick. The words of Axel Honneth (2008/1995) captures how social conventions and poverty can enact a heavy price on people's lives: 'The successful integration of physical and emotional qualities of behaviour is, as it were, subsequently broken up from the outside, thus lastingly destroying the most fundamental form of practical relation-to-self, namely, one's underlying trust in oneself' (p. 44).

Honneth's writings sensitively capture the noxious stressful pathway of my mother's history of suffering in Ireland. During the period from the 1970s to the 1990s, community mental services were only beginning to replace the traditional pattern of admission to psychiatric hospitals (Walsh 2017; Kelly (2016b). Kelly (2015) also charts how the nineteenth century witnessed significant expanse of institutional approaches to the treatment of the mentally ill. For example, 'In 1859, there were 1.16 asylum inmates per 1,000 population in England and by 1909 this had risen to 3.7. In Ireland, there were 3,234 individuals in asylums in 1851, and by 1914 this had risen to 16,941' (p. 10–11).

Recognition of my mother's mental health pattern is one that should acknowledge how her cumulative pains were largely induced by adverse interpersonal, economic and societal determinants. That said, this was not how I conceived my mother's health as a young boy. In the front of my mind, I felt so tied to my mother's situation, where one 'develops a sense of being highly responsible for others' (Hewitt, Flett and Mikail 2017: 115–16). The shame and guilt in not being able to fix things was always there. Psychological interventions had done little to help us understand our family trauma and resultant PTSD and paranoia. In this space, you are left thinking there is something innate about you as a person that is intrinsically sick, that trauma related behaviours are distinctive to your temperament and have little to do with the social menu you have been served up. This was mind-altering to the extent that it concealed the true nature of the suffering. But it was not irrational in the sense that we were regulated and swept up by a foregrounded value that we were here to suffer.

A key feature of Roman Catholicism is an expectation that you engage in a fight against yourself as a subjective defender of their faith belief system. This idea of self-control had taken root and possession of our minds in time. This conception of responsibility was an inward/essentialist formulation, one that encouraged self-abnegation and silence. These normative methods of self-control enacted our conscience in action. It felt law like inside of us to obey this superordinate command. Rather than help with self-control, this repression created hypervigilance, a demand expectation involving approval and disapproval. We lost touch with ourselves in this inverse dynamic. Very little peace was to be had. Too much stress and disconnection arising from Ireland's commitment to self-abnegation and fear of stigma. While I have never been officially diagnosed with schizophrenia, I identify with many of its clusters as associated to my early development. The fantastical thought-insertions of theological concepts took me out of reality. Consistent with most developmental research on adolescence, Lisdahl et al. (2018) say 'converging lines of evidence suggest that adolescence may represent a sensitive period during which exposure to substances increases the risk of substance use disorders (SUDs) and neurocognitive impairments compared with adult exposure' (Brown & Tapert 2004; Spear 2015; Spear & Swartzwelder 2014, cited by Lisdahl 2018: 51).

This psychotic distrust for the self in the normative order could be felt at the core of individual human beings. I do not think psychiatry has ever got to grips with the damage that social contexts enacted on human intentionality and embodiment. The adherence and privileging of certain ideas over others ensured that a mutual recognition was often concealed from the persons who suffered most. These tariffs lie latent and devoiced in socially oppressive/repressive contexts of experience. In these contexts, it is difficult to alert others when loss of self-confidence is normalized as good. Without question, I felt this pressure and compensated in maladaptive strategies. Lack of enlightenment on how we end up disempowered is a corrosive thread that works its way through a stressed mind in the world. As a younger person you are better able to withstand and conceal social suffering. McNay (2012) says

> the idea of social suffering is not intended as a subjectivist elevation of injury as an incontestable sign of injustice. Rather, it is a relational category that draws attention to the co-implication of body and power and, in particular, to the way in which certain types of oppression are rendered political invisible by being internalised as corporeal dispositions ... one of the effects of embodied domination is silence. (p. 230)

This is a controversial formulation because it suggests affects infect the motivational capacity for agency and this can happen behind our backs. Certainly, during my adolescent development, I remember well an elevated and distracted speed that was normal (Monti, Colby, O'Leary-Tevyaw 2018). What I had picked up and internalized in my childhood and teenage years was a feeling that I had to perform to be liked by others. I acted from my emotions and did not seem to have the cognitive bandwidth to think beyond my situated environs. This was a self-defeating pattern. It also felt distinctly non-relational. I was too constituted by a romanticized narcissism which Ireland was fulsomely invested in. My secret was Ireland's enacted secret. Ireland's value orientation in the social structure was routinized in particular ways. I did not possess the critical insights to see through this. I was not on my own, but I felt as if I was in my own world. This kind of self-reliance is stressful and can burn people out. I could not let go of false ideas because I did not know they were false.

To be authentic in historic Ireland meant you could not be openly proud of being gay. In my youth and early adulthood, I did not realize how wrong this was. I did not even think the socially engineered prescriptions of Ireland's history were unreasonable. I learned to think I was the problem. I was a non-ideal citizen. It was my shame, not anyone else or society. My failure to grasp how wrong this was, was very limiting in adolescent transition, particularly as gay identity was thematized as an illness and disease by a deeply conservative and inward-looking society. Ireland's circular idea of critical self-scrutiny as self-abnegation cannot transcend itself. As a teenager, I was carrying the weight of Ireland's bad ideas. In order to build self-confidence, I needed a space of reasoning to think ahead. Instead, I was conditioned by a reactive feedback loop, where the direction of my own intentionality for making meaning of experience was damaged 'neither the life (or, we would say, the health) of an individual nor the history of a society can be understood without understanding both' (Mills 1959, cited by Keohane, Peterson and van den Bergh 2017, p. 1). These authors say that lived experiences need to be analysed in the broader context of occurrence. Individuals and stigmatized groups can be more easily shamed when the broader cultural context encourages concealment and secrecy, denying them a legitimate external reality. In my early development, what I could not grasp was how collective intentionality was performing its inverse magic on me. As emotions are crucial to self-understanding and context, helping us develop our interests and commitments, I was definitely not doing very well. When a person appropriates experience in a way where they act against their own best interests, for some, this can certainly mean that they have not grasped how their self-beliefs have been moulded for them. Social hierarchies are meant to aid to transitions, not obstruct them.

The next section describes a disastrous educational performance in secondary school where I was not up to the tasks of deep, focused and committed learning.

CHAPTER 9

Secondary School in St Mel's College, Longford, 1979–1984

After the disappointment of being ejected from De La Salle Castletown, I resumed my education in St Mel's College in Longford in 1979 for the second part of my first year in secondary school. At St Mel's, it was recommended that I repeat first year in 1979–80. I had not settled in well at St Mel's, after the first term at Castletown. During the early 1980s, my mother and I attended mass regularly, special novenas and went to religious faith meetings on a weekly basis. I was again sexually exploited and assaulted at thirteen to fourteen years old by an older man in a very crude way. He was one of the employees at the local golf club in Longford: 'The various forms of emotion regulation may produce symptoms or behaviours that may signal vulnerability to sexual predators, result in impairment of the ability to properly process danger cues, and impede successful defensive behaviour' (Marx, Heidt and Gold 2005: 67). I remember being on the tractor with this man at the golf course. I used to go to the golf club a lot, sometimes when I was skipping school. One day, this man exposed himself to me and defecated in front of me. I think he tried to grab my penis in a really hurtful way. I distinctly remember him holding his own penis and looking at me in a really menacing way.

I did not tell my mother about this ordeal because she did not know I was absenting myself from school. At this time, I began equating these sexual violations with the meaning of gay identity. It was all too easy to enact this stigmatic and shameful idea in a society that criminalized homosexuality. To think that these ideas in any way defined my gay sexuality was horrid, shaming and stressful. Stahl (2017) offers an analysis of collective responsibility for oppression:

> Even though dominant members of oppressive practice are not personally impli-
> cated in all particular instances of harm caused by these practices, by participating
> in a structure of mutual recognition that supports oppressive norms, they enable the
> harm being caused. It follows that when there is oppression, there almost always is a
> group that is collectively responsible for it, and there are often individuals that share
> in this responsibility. (p. 35)

Gallagher (2017) says that cognitive development is an interactive skill: 'Cognitive processes are in-the-world rather than in-the-head; they are situated in affordance spaces defined across evolutionary, developmental and individual histories, and are constrained by affective processes and normative dimensions of social and cultural practices'. This insight is highly relevant for how stigma is soaked up from social norms, imbibed onto affective modes of intelligibility, emotive ways of knowing. As Corbett (2009) says, 'culture and cultural symbols, society and social orders, what we might call "backstories," build a boy' (p. 11). In my youth, gay desire was constructed as criminal deviance, something to be overcome, and not worthy of inclusion. At the end of the 1970s and the early 1980s, it was more than reasonable to carry around ruminating self-criticism about my own self-worth as a gay teenager. I ultimately surmised that the violating events were telling me something about my own desire to be me. This pattern in my thinking made me feel deeply uneasy. This inflamed drama was alive inside my head. There were some boys at school I felt attracted to. I was so petrified that anyone might notice me being attracted to other boys. At school, I was always restless. I was watchful of my expressions, not letting myself go, just in case, anyone got any ideas about me. I was not consciously homophobic but I was afraid. It was too difficult to not interiorize oppressive concepts and ideals. All of this was so toxic and hard to deal with. We need an external social contract to validate our lives, baseline social protections to impress to us that we are lovable for who we are, so that we can be confident about who we are becoming. In my home town, fake appearances were encouraged for appearance sake. Rosenberg and McCullogh (1981) says 'the powerful needs to belong, to matter, and to be accepted can be exacerbated when unmet, and a child can engage in perfectionism strategies to attempt to have these needs met' (cited by

Hewitt, Flett and Mikail 2017: 11). Perfectionism was idealism and being gay was not construed as ideal.

At school, I did not achieve good results in my Intermediate exam (1982) and in my Leaving Cert (1984). These negative educational outcomes are well accounted for in child/adolescent trauma research (Chu 2011; Lanius, Vermetten and Pain 2010; Lisak & Luster 1994; Perez and Widom 1994; Eckenrode et al. 1993; Hibbard et al. 1990; Friedrich, et al. 1986). I started drinking alcohol in the latter years of my secondary schooling. I got expelled as a boarding pupil for disruptive behaviour, for setting off an alarm in the middle of the night in the school dorms. Children from disturbed family backgrounds in combination with sexual abuse experiences are more likely to turn to substances to cope with negative affects/stressors (Chu 2011; Grilo et al. 1999; Clark, et al. 1997; Van der Kolk, McFarlane and Weisaeth 1996; Rohsenow. et al. 1988). The development of formal/abstract reasoning is a critically important skill for adolescent learning and social development (Hauser-Cram et al. 2014; Schaffer 2004). I was failing badly in this regard.

I left St Mel's College in a shamed state because of my poor educational attainment. I remember the Vice Principal regularly saying in class that I was a disgrace to my family. My older brothers had performed so much better than me. In fact, my eldest brother received special recognition for the highest amount of honours in his Leaving Certificate. I got five passes in my final exam, the bare minimum to pass it. What characterized my early development was problem avoidance and drama rather than problem confrontation and problem solving. For my antics, I got streamed to the bottom pile. Some of my peers were so aggressive. I felt nervous around them. I got beat up, bullied and physically marked on several occasions.

When I look back at photos of this time period, I see someone who looks much older than his years. I did manage to put up a happy face and always got on well with older people. I felt really awkward around my peers. I had a talent for impersonation and acting the clown. Throughout my schooling, I regularly performed well in talent shows. It was easy for me to pretend to be somebody else, because I was profoundly uncomfortable in my own skin. My school peers egged me on in my quirky performances and very precise impersonation skills. Later on, my impersonation act was chosen from a local talent show. I performed my solo piece in a nationally televised competition. This was how I built my self-esteem. I got great attention and accolades for these performances.

Many of my teachers stood back as I performed. My sense is the school authorities may have pitied me because of our widely known family trauma. No one in school knew about the sexual violations. I kept all these to myself. Neither did they know how my self-esteem had been crushed when ejected from a school for developing a religious vocation. I did not share with anyone about my awareness of sexual orientation. That was concealed too. At this time, I had started to date girls to cover up. Just to fit in and be one of the boys. On finishing secondary school, I had brought a girl to the debutant ball. I had met her at a local religious group. The idea of bringing a boy to my debs was most definitely not an option. Back then, it was totally unheard of. Up to this point in my life, all I had witnessed in the town I grew up was bullying of a person who was supposed to be gay. I had heard how he got a terrible beating in the town. I remember how others talked about him behind his back. Some had tried to suggest he was mentally ill. These were depressing ideas which I soaked up.

I remember a teacher in school telling me that Catholicism stood apart from all other religions. It was along the lines that Catholicism was the one 'true' faith. He was a senior priest in secondary school. He was very popular, even among the left 'cool' thinkers at school. I remember thinking he must be right, even though I had half expected that he would not be so arrogant and self-righteous about his vocation. I never made any mention of my sexual orientation to him during secondary school. In my middle years at St Mel's College, the Bishop of Ardagh and Clonmacnoise Dr Daly departed our diocese for his next appointment. Fr Colm O'Reilly was installed as the new Bishop of Ardagh and Clonmacnoise in 1983. In 1990, our former Bishop Cahal B. Daly was promoted to Bishop of Armagh and Primate of All Ireland. In 1991, Pope John Paul II appointed Bishop Daly a cardinal (Daly 1998). Throughout my secondary schooling, I attended religious vocation weekends with the White Fathers, the Franciscans, the Pallottine Fathers and the Holy Ghost Fathers. Even after secondary school, I continued this process of religious discernment for many years. I went on weekends to the Legionnaires of Christ, the Divine Word

Missionaries and the Salesians in Maynooth, the Carmelites and the Sacred Heart Missionaries in Dublin. I never went beyond the exploratory stage of these weekend contacts and retreats with the religious orders.

Unconsciously, I learned to lie to myself. The good citizen was the straight citizen. To gain self-understanding, culture was clearly indicating to me 'you are on your own'. There was no contract suite of social protections for gay people and there was no sense that I possessed any inalienable right to such protection to anchor a gay identity. If anything, to fight against my own thoughts and feelings, and to not trust authority was very damaging. At this time, I needed good authority to know what was happening for me, someone whom I could trust to help me.

Even if someone knew, I am not sure this would have been sufficient, because of the way Irish society was organized. I was in a state of nervous panic about what other people thought of me. Traditional norms encouraged me to remain silent. Giving voice would have entailed even more panic and terror. In that state of anxiety, I could not re-interpret the wrongfulness of norms and traditions. My struggle was the interred feeling that it was only right and proper to think poorly of myself. To make sense of any personality disturbance, critical discourse has to interrogate how the tentacles of historic norms disempowers cognitive powers and the power to act in one's own best interests. What is unattractive about this formulation is how it may re-enliven stigma and fury, where gay people are viewed as less than optimal and deserving of sympathy. This disempowered position can easily invite new domination, where new redemptive prophets in the social order make a name for themselves and a financial fortune on the back of other people's sufferings and misery.

The next section lends further insight to the idea for how difficult it was to be gay when confronted with social oppression in 1970s/1980s/1990s Ireland. This is my attempt to ground my own personal story as historically contingent in 'the temporal locality of identity – the influence of time on issues of identity and understanding, its implications for legal interventions, social movement building, and paradigms of progressive change' (Knauer 2013: 362).

CHAPTER 10

Legal/Social Discrimination Against Gay Persons in Ireland

> The capacity to have control over one's life is an essential component
> of being a free, respected, and successful citizen, all of which in turns
> affects an individual's capacity for good health and wellbeing. (Allen
> and Allen 2015: 30)

In my younger life, I never fully grasped the reasons for the absence of gay
people in everyday settings, other than feel it would be unimaginable to
perform loving tenderness and care for someone of the same orientation
in everyday situations. Thus an elevated form of self-critique drove me to
fit in. That felt like a mode of resistance, a tool of survival where the external reality for being a gay is denied. I remember feeling my significance as
a gay person does not count and is not worthy of mention in the normal
scheme of things. Eribon (2004), citing a key tenet of Pierre Bourdieu's
writings, states, 'the way in which the social order, via a long 'apprentice-
ship by way of the body' that begins in infancy in the daily contact with
the world, comes to be inscribed in bodies and minds of individuals; the
way in which social or gender hierarchies are thus able to perpetuate themselves' (xxi). Much of this was unconscious but still had the power to shape
reflective capacities. What might be unconscious is how the collective
intentionality of social norms that is able to exert its influence by circulating ideas what those who do fit into its norms, must be deluded and need
to be treated with degrees of suspicion. One needs to be alert and smart
to dominating biases and how false ideas are easily transferred onto modes
of consciousness, exerting wilful pressure on people to conform. Expert
disciplines have had a bad reputation of conflating lack of conformity to

personal disorder taxonomies. In my young life, I saw up close and personal, how this power worked. Paranoid and delusional beliefs were construed as personality specific and family specific, without rigorous evaluation of the social mechanisms of domination. In some cases, the content of those paranoid states that I heard and witnessed, literally mimicked the messaging system of oppressive history. Psychosis as specific to personality often felt like a reductive level of explanation. In this scheme of things, our silent consciences were resigned to accepting the words of experts who were devoicing my family's lived experiences. I had bottled so much toxic fear in my family and I had no language for it. This kind of fear had a terrible impact on how I related to myself, other people and the world. I was moulded by the impressions of external routinization which claimed my fears were merely self-centred. These well-ingrained ideas were spell-like, narrowing the way I read situations.

As a young teen, I had no access to a more liberated narrative on gay orientation. There was no Internet. I had no other close friend who I knew was gay. I was always hoping that there were other gay people. I heard no talk of sexual rights or equality at this time. What I did hear were nuanced undertones of disrespect, insult and negative inferences of persons who were supposed to be gay. This footprint of stigma was so pervasive and colluded with in Irish society (Ferriter 2009). Esteemed Irish judges argued for retention of criminalizing homosexual acts, consistent with Catholic teaching and religion's 'sustained hope' that gays would 'overcome their personal difficulties and their inability to fit into society' (CDF 1975). This examples how religious leadership took little risk by simply aligning religious identity with dominant stakeholders and interests. However, religion was not relative to politics in Ireland. Historically, religion came first. In the foreground of social representations was the creationist narrative of biological complementarity and all the binary justifications and prescriptive like protocols that followed from it.

This reflection can sometimes generate earlier memories of the invisibility of gay couples in the rural town I grew up in. As a young boy, I did not realize how non-visible performance of identity shaped the meaning, value and worth of gay persons in Irish life. My perceptions of these practices, in the affordances of my socialization had the power to shape practical thoughts and feelings, suggestive that respect was only applicable to some relationships and legitimately withheld from others for good reasons.

When I had served as a boy at weddings and at funerals in St Mel's Cathedral, gay identity was never a cause for public celebration or mourning. Hegel's key idea of 'being-oneself-in-an-other' (Pippin 2015) was certainly not something that was visible in most everyday contexts of my young rural life. All the baptisms I had attended as a young boy server in St Mel's Cathedral were consistent with John Paul's II 1979 teaching to young people in Ireland 'marriage must include openness to the gift of children' (cited by Fuller 2002: 238). To live a good life, these social/ religious arrangements were clearly expressing an intention: a happy life deserving of celebration, or a noble life, deserving of a eulogy was certainly not a gay identified life. When God created the world, he did not create gay human beings in his own image. A desire for gay sexuality in religious ideation was described as an innately evil potential.

The 'ought' national standard was the heterosexual standard or abstinence standard. Anything else was sinful, impure and deserving of personal shame, arising from being unfortunate or defective, deserving of pity. Hammack et al. (2017) refers to the 'sickness script' of this time period, exampling the kind of social cruelty/exclusion that gay men were often confronted with. For me, social recognition for being an equal citizen was far from my imagination.

In 1977, a survey of social attitudes found considerable intolerance and prejudice towards homosexuals. In a study entitled 'Prejudice and Tolerance in Ireland' (MacGreil 1977) one of the study's key research findings reported that 39.9 per cent of respondents in Dublin supported the retention of the criminalization statute against homosexual relations (p. 410–14). Some politicians in mainstream politics tried to confront social prejudice. For example, a Fine Gael press release from Roy Dooney (1979) stated, 'Just as heterosexuality is a state of mind, so too is homosexuality' (cited by Ferriter 2009: 500). This politician is acknowledging how social representations are shaping social attitudes and beliefs for those who do not fit the undergone ideas on sexuality. Theologians promoted ideas that the child is governed by nature and has to undergo an educational process to overcome its nature to be truly free. The heterosexual adult person is then prepared to become a member of a self-governing community. Such preconditions in Irish history render dominant forms of life intelligible in a social and political sense. This was deemed essential to the fabric of a good and moral society. Irish Senator David Norris (2012) describes how constituting this template was in our history:

> It was an austere era, and I was an outsider in every way. I was Anglican in a deeply Roman Catholic society; I was half English in a narrow and negatively republican state defined more by hatred of England than love of Ireland; and I was homosexual when you could be jailed for being so. I knew I was an outlaw, and that my life wasn't real, which was the reason I didn't get into politics until much later. Politics was for the real people, and real people went to dances in cricket and tennis clubs, got married, bought houses and ran for election, while their wives sat on the platform beside them. Even as a child I was confronted with this unreality. All Irish schoolbooks concerned Daddy being at work and Mammy, as provided for in Mr. de Valera's Constitution, in the kitchen; and in fiction, the lucky hero and heroine overcame all obstacles and ended happily at the altar. (p. 78)

Hug (1999) says that during the period from 1940 to 1978, Irish Department of Justice figures indicate 'an average of six men per year were gaoled for "indecency with males", and an average of seven for "gross indecency"' (p. 207). Hug (1999) adds:

> What was particularly shocking to David Norris was the fact that out of 23 men sentenced in 1973, and 20 in 1974, respectively 18 (78 per cent) and 17 (85 per cent) were over 21 (i.e. the age of homosexual majority in Britain, the highest in Europe).
>
> Over the period of 1962–1972, he registered 455 convictions, including 342 involving men aged over 21. These 342 men would not have been prosecuted if Ireland had a legislation even as restrictive as Britain's. (p. 208)

Norris adds:

> Because of the public climate at the time, people were very ashamed of being discovered in these situations, and they would automatically plead guilty. They would be usually let off with a slap on the wrist, a suspended sentence, a fine or they would be directed to attend a psychiatrist. They would rarely be sentenced to jail. (Norris 1994, in Hug 1999: 210)

Norris also states that

> Because Garrett [Garrett Sheehan: Legal Counsel/a retired distinguished judge] and I started to appear in Court, I would be wearing a three-piece suit, a Trinity tie, a briefcase, look terribly respectable, and give character evidence .... When we started defending, and we had a string of successes, they realized it was not worth their while. And it went down to zero, they stopped prosecuting. (Cited by Hug 1999: 210)

Hug (1999) 'wonders whether it was because these men had been so well defended that the police lost all interest' (p. 210). Senator Norris (1999) says 'the Gardaí [police] were used to people coming in a state of collapse, saying I'm guilty' (cited by Hug 1999: 210). Legal academic and barrister Tom O'Malley (Gallagher 2016) offers a more benign view of Irish justice: 'Generally speaking, they [homosexuals] were dealt with fairly anonymously when they came before the courts.' Norris offers a very different view of Irish Justices up to the late 1970s and early 1980s:

> The court's' attitude was one of derision and contempt ... I remember on many occasions seeing people caught in those circumstances being subject to the most ignorant and personal questions of any judge. It was definitely viewed as a perversion and as an entertainment source for the ordinary decent criminals in court. These people were held up to ridicule. They were taken stage by stage through the sexual activities they engaged in and asked if they enjoyed it and all this kind of stuff. (Gallagher 2016)

Brian Sheehan, former Executive Director of Gay and Lesbian Equality Network (GLEN) says the historic laws were 'a huge weapon, a cudgel. It ensured lesbian and gay people never raised their head and become visible. The consequences of that are still felt by some people today who never got the chance to be who they were' (cited by Gallagher 2016). The Road to Equality Expo (2016a) states, 'Although Government rarely implemented the law, it tacitly exploited the aura of criminality around male homosexuality to avoid any meaningful, honest engagement with the needs, fears, and aspirations of an increasingly vocal, assertive and militant sexual minority.'

After leaving school, and living in country towns, I remember having a painfully hard time telling anybody. I remember a comment from an opposite sex partner where she said I was so distant in sexual intimacy. She was right. This was my attempt to fit in and be 'normal' in keeping up social appearances. On a couple of occasions, I tried to broach the subject of being gay with a couple of male friends. I remember feeling intense shame. I was always drunk on these occasions. I remember one of my friends could not handle my disclosure. Another friend was a little more accepting, but we never spoke about it again.

In an interview from this time period, Kieran Rose (1983) talked about gays having to flee rural towns to the Cities: 'The fact that so many gays flee to Dublin, and the big Cities of England, Europe and America, to escape the terrible fear, loneliness and oppression they experience here, saddens Kieran terribly' (Dolan 1983). Sangiovanni (2017) says 'when our sense of self maintains some minimum degree of reflective stability, consistency, internal coherence, and continuity across time and circumstance, we say it has integrity' (p. 79). The implications of dehumanizing social contexts is well captured by Ferriter (2009) when he says of the 180 callers to a national helpline in 1978 'whose 'problem' was homosexuality, 20 per cent were classified as suicidal' (p. 489). In later decades, as a helpline volunteer, I often took calls from older gays who felt trapped in heterosexual marriages. Some callers rang from other countries, having left Ireland in previous decades.

In a further recent commentary, *Irish Times* journalist Una Mullally (2017) poses questions which is a stark reminder of the Irish LGBT diaspora at the height of the AIDs/HIV crisis:

> Irish LGBT people left the country en masse in disproportionate numbers at the height of emigration in the 1980s. They left to live more open lives, leaving a country that was viscously sexually repressed, that criminalized their sex lives, that murdered and beat up their gay peers, and that refused to offer them a future. And in fleeing, they walked smack bang into the plague in the cities they gravitated towards for freedom. How many of those gay men in New York and San Francisco who were left for dead were Irish? How many sons and uncles and brothers and cousins never came home, dying mysteriously young, the cause of their deaths fabricated in country towns for the benefit of the neighbours? How many had their belongings dumped in the gutter? (*The Irish Times* 2017)

Croome (2014) says 'anti-gay criminal laws created the conditions for blackmail, social exclusion, hate crimes and suicide.' Concealment during this time was equivalent to the idea that the problem resides within the person. This is Ireland's ethics par exemplar, suppressing knowledge of how reality is informed by social modes of intelligibility, hoping that those dispossessed of a reality will learn to fit into the status quo. At this time, I did not have the required self-knowledge to know that an active mind in the world was shaped by 'the implicit norms that determine the social appropriateness of our linguistic practices including inferential reasonings' (Gallagher 2017), and 'that only communities, not individuals, can be interpreted as having original intentionality – The practices that institute the sort of normative status characteristic of intentional states must be social' (Brandon 1994 cited by Gallagher 2017). I did not understand that reduced self-confidence and esteem could be damaged by the external inputs of social repertoires and conventions. Unconscious absorption of normative regulation techniques by Church and state intensified stress and fear in significant ways. Significantly, hierarchical external inputs 'distorts and misshapes our cognitive capacity to see our world as cooperative, interdependent, and constituted by our actions' (Thompson, forthcoming). This kind of distortion can lead one to believe that any estrangement is about the core of one's own personality. Meyer (2007) referring to his 'minority stress concept' (1995) says 'ignoring the social environment would erroneously place the burden on the individual, suggesting that minority stress is only a personal problem' (p. 259). That said, his research points to the 'rich history of resistance and self-reliance that has characterized the history of LGB groups in the United States' (p. 260).

In Mullingar, I got to meet another gay man from responding to the Classified Ads in *Hot Press*. At the time, there was no online Grindr and Gaydar. In the town, I shared an apartment with another heterosexual man. He constantly bragged about his sexual prowess and conquests. I similarly kept up a façade. I will never forget the level of shame I felt in our apartment one night when my flatmate wondered who my *Hot Press* friend was. Despite his quizzing, I covered up who he really was. There was no way I could let him know. I had great sex with this guy. It was one of the best things that had happened for me at this time, just to enjoy desire. I met one other guy at a straight disco. He was from Australia. He was very attractive but deeply secretive. Like me, he kept up a front that he was not gay in public. Livingstone (2010) says 'society polices sex, sexuality, and gender with such rigidity that people who appear to flout heteronormative constructs confound to the extent that they are viewed at best sceptically and often with fear. Those who appear to transgress these norms in any way are persistently deemed defective, disordered and dangerous by the most powerful regulatory triad – religious, secular and medical discourse' (p. 7).

In the latter part of the 1980s, I started to break away from socializing with my heterosexual friends and acquaintances. I felt the pressure of their expectations too much for me to cope with, so I avoided them. I started to drink in different pubs, mostly on my own. I remember an older lady commenting to me in the same bar that she had never seen a woman by my side. At the time, drink for me was my refuge. Walking home after nights of heavy and relentless drinking, I often collapsed at the side of road, and would wake up in the ditch, near to where I lived. At the time, I worked long hours, drank every night and smoked heavily. I got comfort from drinking and smoking. But I knew I could not sustain this pattern. I was very disconnected, caught in an inflamed feedback loop of fear, dread and terror. The next section highlights the continuing difficulties for gay people living in Ireland. While some progress had been made in the 1970s, much of that good work was undermined in the 1980s. This was a period when frightening and terrifying ideas about gay people were consistently foregrounded in the public domain.

CHAPTER 11

Further Key Themes in 1970s/1980s Ireland

In this section, it is worth spending some time analysing the ideological arguments put forward in Ireland for restricting people's right to contraception. For example, in 1971, clearly buoyed by Pope Paul VI's *Humanae Vitae*, the Archbishop of Dublin, John Charles McQuaid stated his outright opposition to contraception:

> Any contraceptive act is always wrong in itself. To speak, then, of the right of contraception, on the part of an individual, be he Christian or non-Christian or Atheist, or on the part of a minority or of a majority, is to speak of a right that cannot even exist ... Any change in legislation that would allow the sale of contraceptives would be an insult to the faith, gravely damaging to public and private morality and would remain a curse upon our country. (Hug 1999: 93)

Social deference for these pronouncements dulled the imagination and impeded social reform. The extraneous social demand for contraception is constructed as a curse. While many feminists openly challenged and protested this coercive logic, their struggles in 1970s Ireland did not gain normative traction to erode the binding force of old traditions. Citing Irish research, historian Mary E. Daly (2016) says 'In 1971, 63% of those surveyed opposed the sale of contraceptives' (p. 150). Feminist activist, Neil McCafferty (1985/2010) say

> The IWLM (Irish Women's Liberation Movement) in 1970 demand for legalisation for contraception had met with popular support, but opposition from State and Church. The sale or advertisement of contraceptives was illegal and punishable by penal servitude.

Throughout the 1970s, feminist activism managed to shift the discourse on the sale of contraceptives along the continuum of moral sin, a crime, toward a limited civil right (Robinson 2012). Despite the risks of criminal prosecution, the IWLM imported contraceptives from Northern Ireland that were banned in the Republic (Ferriter 2012). Mary Robinson's bill to change the status quo did not manage to secure a hearing on her first attempt in the Senate. She did succeed in producing a bill on a second attempt in late 1972 (Robinson 2012). The measurement of conservative traditions in Irish attitudes enabled Liam Cosgrave as Taoiseach (Prime Minister) to feel confident in 1974 when he voted against a restrictive contraception availability in Ireland. While Cosgrave gave the members of the FG party a free vote on the legislation, his own high profile vote helped defeat it. Like his father before him, Liam Cosgrave was a Catholic first, which determined how both father and son voted. The Fine Gael leader in the 1970s was of the view that faith principles were above culture, where the ethos of religious faith is superordinate to the workings of national legislature. The fundamental premise for such a position is that moral conscience as personal faith beliefs is the holding container for a nation's character and identity. The job of politics is not to get ahead of itself in dismantling immutable truths preordained by religious revelation. The inalienable right of conscience is God given where God acts through conscience. Saying no to the sale of contraceptives is an expression of this moral imperative, consistent with the unexpected position adopted by Pope VI's *Humanae Vitae* encyclical in 1968. In this scenario, the duty of the conservative politician is to express resistance to immorality.

While Cosgrave, in partnership with the Labour Party from 1973 to 1977, pragmatically pursued social justice in large government spending on public housing and increased social protection for those who needed it most, on the issue of enhanced civil liberties that required constitutional change, the FG leader was firmly embedded in status quo deference to the teachings of the Roman Catholic Church. Interestingly, Cosgrave never seems to reflect that the freedom to practice religion is just one civil liberty among many. Somehow, like many other figures in the FG party, and in the main opposition Fianna Fáil party, both parties adopt the same persona that religious conscience is a right that ought to have superordinate reach to regulate the moral fabric of a society. Any other civil right is viewed as a relative and subjective whim of intellectuals and feminists. Cosgrave saw his religious faith as intrinsic, a constitutive first order principle, rather than something that is socially learned in routinized ritual and indoctrination. Cosgrave also sees himself as fighting off liberal influences in his own party. Cosgrave was renowned for his hyperbole speeches in the 1970s, creating suspicion, vowing to 'blow out' the 'blow ins' in the FG party (Meehan 2013; Ferriter 2009).

What is particularly striking about the Catholic domination of modern historic Ireland is how its justification for no inalienable right to contraception is passed down through the generations, based on divine revelations and infallible papal teachings (Kitcher 2011). Many senior clerical and political figures in Ireland used their offices to resist social change and as a smokescreen to uncover unsettling truths about the fiction of moral puritanism. Alcoff (2017) in reference to history says this dynamic 'perpetuates the sort of epistemic injustices that came to be consolidated in many European intellectual trends, during its extended efforts to colonize the globe' (p. 406). In Ireland, those intellectual trends were not remote or aloof, rather the manifolds of religious tenets were pragmatically felt in key domains of Irish life for much of the twentieth century. Reflecting on the projection of idealism as a perfectionistic persona, the following insight from Hewitt, Flett and Mikail (2017) may be useful:

> The trepidation and anxiety that the perfectionistic individual experiences can be exacerbated in particular clinical situations, particularly during the initial encounter with the clinician and office staff. It has been our experience that perfectionistic people are acutely uncomfortable in clinicians' waiting rooms. Such individuals' subjective experience is that they are announcing to everyone there that they are having personal difficulties. Therefore, perfectionists often prefer not to be seen in or associated with a clinical office in any way. (p. 173)

Perhaps perfectionism conceals deep levels of hypocrisy in the social order. In Ireland's history, the façade and projection of perfectionism within the social and political hierarchies often acted as a cover for concealment of crimes. It is unlikely any 'trepidation and anxiety' was felt by those who abused power. Rather, many people have to carry the weight for conditions not of their own choosing or making.

In the late 1970s, restrictive legislation on contraception was introduced by the Minister for Health Charles J. Haughey in the FF government that replaced the Cosgrave's FG/Labour coalition in 1977. Haughey's 1979 legislation was in response to a 1973 court case, McGee v. The Attorney General (Hug 1999). In this case, the Irish Supreme Court ruled that a constitutional right to marital privacy was been contravened in the national bans and criminalization of sale of contraceptives (Ferriter 2009).

In 1977, when I was a young teenager, Dr Noël Browne asked the Minister for Justice to reform the law on homosexuality. As Kieran Rose remarked, Browne's proposal was 'literally laughed out of the Dáil' (cited by Lacey 2008: 247). In the same year, Sweeney (2010) highlights a significant incident of homophobia in Ireland where FF members of Dublin City Council (DCC) drew attention to the staging of 'obscene plays' (p. 115). Establishment logic succeeded, as DCC withdrew its funding from the Project Arts Centre. The plays had been performed at the Project by the London-based group Gay Sweatshop. Councillor Patrick Cummins (FF) had warned in his contribution at the Dublin council meeting that 'The whole fabric of our society was being threatened by works of this type ... There should be a greater concentration on good plays and good music. They would bring in the crowds and then they would not need to come to the Corporation looking for a grant' (cited by Sweeney 2010: 115). Another FF party colleague on the council, Gerard Brady, who went on to serve as a member of Parliament, was demanding 'an apology' for the staging of the plays (p. 115). However, the rationale which was given for ceasing funding was proven false. Kevin Byrne an independent member of DCC revealed

> that the Olympia Theatre, which operated on a similar lease and from the same landlord, had received £200,000 from the City Council. Two small right-wing organizations, the Irish League of Decency and Parent Concern, were mentioned as having influenced the decision. With the centre's future in danger, Gay Sweatshop returned to stage repeat performances of the two offending plays, Mister X and Any Woman Can, at the Eblana Theatre, playing to full houses, the £700 raised going towards the Project. (Sweeney 2010: 115)

The Irish Arts Council Chairperson described the decision as 'the worst thing that had happened in in the Irish art world in the last twenty years,' with the Labour Party group on the council decrying 'the spurious arguments put forward' (cited by Sweeney 2010: 115). Later that year, the Council began funding the Project Arts Centre to the tune of £4,000. Sweeney (2010) cites Councillor Jim Mitchell (FG) who said that 'the Council was not a censorship board and if anybody was offended they could go to the Department of Justice' (p. 115). Many critical analysts highlight the myriad ways in which unjust group relations are reproduced in social norms. Elizabeth Anderson (2011) says:

> The central cause of categorical inequality is the exclusion of one social group from equal access to critical resources controlled by another. Segregation – social closure – is the linchpin of categorical inequality, since it is needed to keep critical goods preferentially circulating within the dominant social group and out of the hands of the subordinate group, except on disadvantageous terms. (p. 16)

This is an important critical insight which is backed up by Irish gay advocate Kieran Rose. He acknowledges that while religious mores/values were on the decline in late 1980s/early 1990s Ireland, Rose (1994) says the power of dominating perspectives in the social order had the effect of slowing down the pace of the social reform agenda. Apart from censorship, Rose cited further examples: 'AIDS initiatives, progress for young people and direct public funding for our community services. This resistance consumed much of the scarce resources of the gay movement' (Rose 1994: 41). For myself, moving to Dublin from country towns certainly removed a great deal of fear of others knowing I was gay. Yet the 1980s/early 1990s context of Ireland showed no significant sign of let-up in social stigma. Juster, Vencill and Johnson (2017) define stress in the following terms:

> Stress is broadly defined as a real or interpreted threat to an individual that results in biological and behavioural responses. The stress-disease literature includes three broad perspectives with regard to measurement of stress and subsequent coping: environmental, psychological, and biological. As a multidimensional construct, stress involves interactions among inputs (environmental stressors), processes (subjective psychological distress), and outputs (objective biological stress responses). (p. 36)

The presence of macro-level HIV/AIDS stigma in 1980s Ireland and elsewhere were stressful contexts for many gay men. As outlined in my own young life situation, social stigma certainly added to the weight of an already stressed equilibrium arising from earlier adversities and trauma. Hug (1999) says as the AIDS epidemic was 'beginning to rage' (p. 205) dominant political/religious discourses and understandings had the effect of contributing to 'the allusion to AIDS as the gay plague' (p. 205). Hug (1999) cites the writings of Cardinal Josef Ratzinger as Leader of the Congregation of the Doctrine of the Faith (CDF) in Rome from 1986. On the death of Pope John Paul II, Cardinal Ratzinger succeeded him as Pope Benedict XVI from 2005–13. The following quote from Cardinal Ratzinger, as prefect for the CDF, gives a flavour of the Vatican response to HIV/AIDS: 'Even when the practice of homosexuality may seriously threaten the lives and well-being of a large number of people, its advocates remain undeterred and refuse to consider the magnitude of the risks involved. The Church can never be so callous' (p. 205).

Here, Cardinal Ratzinger is impressing the idea that gay men are bringing calamity onto themselves and society. Cardinal Ratzinger's position was consistent with 1980s right-wing hysteria in the UK, Europe, and the USA which equated gay identity with innate disorder and pathology (Robson 1995: 56–7). At the same time, a Catholic Church document from 1986 also authored by Cardinal Josef Ratzinger declared that being homosexual is not itself a sin, rather 'it is more or less a strong tendency ordered toward an intrinsic moral evil; and thus the inclination itself must be seen as an objective disorder' (CDF 1986). Citing the CDF document, Hug (1999) observes how the Vatican Prefect takes his argument a stage further: 'When civil legislation is introduced to protect behaviour to which no one has any conceivable right, neither the church or society at large should be surprised when other distorted notions and practices gain ground, and irrational and violent reactions increase' (p. 205). Not unlike Archbishop McQuaid of Dublin in 1971, who remained steadfastly opposed to contraceptives, Cardinal Ratzinger is also suggesting gay people have no conceivable right to condoms for what he terms as 'an intrinsic moral evil.' Ratzinger is clearly inferring that HIV/AIDS is the vital proof of homosexual sexuality. Thus, the Prefect of the CDF is recommending against the state advancing civil legislation to protect gay people.

Cardinal Ratzinger argues Church dogma is above the state and accuses the latter as implicit in engineering legislation that violates the collective moral conscience. Reflecting on Irish history and elsewhere, such formulations were deeply embedded in powerful constitutive spheres which informed so many practices, attitudes and beliefs. The cardinal's arid positions undermined many in the Church who were providers of care during the HIV/AIDs crisis. Ratzinger is following through on JPII speeches from his trip to Ireland in 1979, advising no complacency against the tide of freedom which the Polish Pontiff equated to the 'moral sickness that stalked society.' Cardinal Ratzinger held Augustinian theological positions, where true redemption/purity narrative recommends restraint, self-denial as conversion from sin. In a very insightful historical quote from *From Shame to Sin*, Harper's (2013) study captures how the state/religious complex is interwoven through the centuries:

> It is one of history's true paradoxes that such a model of freedom was harnessed to a movement that was anti-erotic to its very foundations, and that this concept of freedom enabled a model of responsibility that would promote unprecedented accumulations of power in the regulation of sexual acts. These paradoxes are part of our cultural history .... (Harper 2013: 257)

Referring to philosophical systems, Vogelmann (2018) says:

> Philosophy is fascinated by a self-explication based on a deeply rooted 'concept of responsibility,' and thus goes on to discover everywhere this 'responsibility' with which it has furnished every corner of itself, without ever noticing the consequences of its own devotion to this discursive operator. The blind fury with which philosophy labours to legitimize the concept of 'responsibility' conceals both what 'responsibility' inflicts on the individuals to whom it is ascribed, as well as the very walls of the theoretical cell in which a philosophy under the spell of responsibility imprisons itself. (p. 2)

From where I was situated in historic repertoires, the idea of imprisoning myself is an easy idea for me to grasp. The denial of external reality for gay people was binding and enjoyed normative force. I interpreted Ireland's idea of responsible citizenship as explicitly inferring that if you choose to be gay, you must live with the testing consequences of this decision. The recommended ideas from the social hierarchy, in combination with interpersonal signs and experiences amounted to disapproval. These were the motivating scenes where I was in a state of thinking that I must be wilful and sinful. Shame affects alone do not capture the violating impact on a gay teenager's self-esteem. It is the routinized thought-insertions from the social hierarchy that damaged my capacity to think clearly. Feeling I had brought this unease upon myself, made me feel suspicious of my own motives. At the time, I did not possess a confident voice to articulate how the mechanisms of external thought forms had distorted my capacities to make meaning of our own experiences. My personality had literally been shaped to put up a front, as my authentic motivations were construed as my downfall. To be in control of oneself, a fake appearance was externally endorsed in Irish culture. With reference to the murders of gay men in Ireland in the 1980s, Una Mullally (2014) writes:

> In 1982, three separate killings had a profound impact on the gay community. On 21 January 1982, Charles Self, an RTE set designer, left a pub on Duke Street and returned to his home in South Dublin. There, he was stabbed to death. He was 33. His killer was never identified. On 8 September, John Roche, 29, was stabbed to death in room twenty-six at the Munster Hotel in Cork. The hotel porter who killed him, Michael O'Connor, 26, said, 'Your gay days are over.' As he stabbed him, he told Gardaí, 'He would have ruined my life. He wanted me to become a gay. I said no way, and I killed him.' The jury found O'Connor not guilty of murder, but guilty of manslaughter. (Mullally 2014: 168)

Furthermore, Ferriter (2009) writes Declan Flynn was murdered 'by young men who had grown up playing in the same Park' (p. 499). Max Krzyzanowski of LGBT Noise (2014) talked about this incident on the promo footage of a documentary film *From Ireland to Alabama* (Merriman 2014). He states, 'one of these youths admitted to approaching Declan Flynn and subsequently being joined by a gang, brutally beating him to death as he tried to escape. These young men also admitted to the systematic robberies and beatings of other men in the Park that summer' (Krzyzanowski 2014). The documentary says that prior to this murder, a local Catholic prelate in Fairview had warned 'that something horrible would happen if the attacks continued' (*Capital Gay* 1983, cited by Merriman 2014). On sentencing the youths, Judge Gannon gave suspended sentences for manslaughter. His ruling stated 'this could never be considered murder,' and that these 'vigilantes were cleaning up the area' (*Capital Gay* 1983, cited by

Merriman 2014). Judge Gannon, who died in 2011, had said in 1983 'While I must demonstrate the abhorrence of the community by imposing sentences, I don't think it necessary to be served immediately by detention' (Carswell 2018). His ruling was consistent with the prevailing juridical and moral norms. Regarding the Fairview murder in 1982, Maggie O'Kane (1983) recounts how the young men she interviewed had tried to justify his murder (Ferriter 2009, p. 499):

> The night they killed Declan Flynn the girls had gone home. The girls always went home when they went queer bashing or bashing people they thought were queer. Sometimes it didn't really matter if they were or not but it was better if they were because queers used to molest young kids and stuff like that in the park ... one of the lads thought it would be a good way of getting a few bob – robbing a few queers ... Steamers they called them. (Cited by Ferriter 2009: 499)

These self-radicalized youths had been on a rampage for some time, administering 'a series of homophobic beatings in the park during the summer of 1982' (Carswell 2018). The leniency of the sentences led to a significant public outcry (Mullally 2014). Carswell gives a flavour to the political reactions that followed the five-year suspended sentences for the youths:

> Mary Harney, then a Fianna Fáil TD, challenged the Minister for Justice at the time, Fine Gael's Michael Noonan, to seek the judge's resignation. She reminded the Dáil of its agonising over the right to life of the unborn in debates leading up to the 1983 abortion referendum, when people who had taken away life were now roaming the streets. The outcome horrified the Flynn family. 'I had expected that justice would be done and be seen to be done' said Declan's father, Christopher Flynn. The family described the judge's decision as 'an insult.' (Carswell 2018)

Carswell (2018) further recounts how Declan Flynn's family want to remember him 'a kind, gentle man who loved his family and who 'came into his own at Christmas, decorating the family home from top to toe and giving everybody gifts.' This journalist interviewed Declan's nephew Niall Behan who remembered his 'grandfather rallying around the family 'trying to support them, but his grandmother was "absolutely devastated". He heard stories of her crying endlessly in the house over Declan's death' (Carswell

2018). Niall Behan, the former head of DCU Student Union, attended and spoke at the twenty-fifth anniversary event at Dublin Castle to mark the decriminalization of homosexuality in Ireland, where the Taoiseach Leo Varadkar issued a formal apology and talked about how the national Parliament (Dáil) played its part by providing a buffering rationale, extending a 'licence to punish those whom they believe are committing it.' In essence, the Taoiseach is saying these instances of social harm against gay people in Irish history was intricately woven by the prevailing moral and legal logic of this time period. Senator David Norris knew Declan Flynn personally; he recalled 'that his fear of being seen by work colleagues led him to avoid established gay venues in favour of meeting spots that were potentially dangerous' (Carswell 2018).

The age composition of the perpetrators were from 18-14 years old (Buchanan 2016). Ferriter (2009) adds:

> One of the 16-year old peers of the killers thought 'they went too far' with Flynn, 'but he's not against bashing queers. But that's pervert queers, not ordinary gay people who go to their friends' houses … a pervert is a person who has a mental disorder and you can't fix mental disorders, you have to do something physical to them. (p. 499)

After the court case, Buchanan (2016) says 'Bonfires were lit and street parties were held in celebration in Fairview as the five returned home to heroes' welcomes.' In a radio interview with Declan Flynn's family on RTÉ Radio One, Declan's brother Chris spoke with Miriam O'Callaghan about the decades of hurt endured by the family after Declan's death in 1982. Chris Flynn described how sensitive, kind and caring his brother Declan was (O'Callaghan 2018). Declan Flynn's murder is a particularly strong example of how the manifold messages from the social order extended moral licence for psychotic levels of violence and murders of gay people. As previously stated, one of these youths used psychiatric terminology to justify the murder of an innocent gay man. As Sugarman (2015) states in reference to the work of Nikolas Rose, 'The language of moral pathology infiltrated political reasoning because it made certain features of persons intelligible as objects of government' (p. 175). Ferriter (2009) refers to the Irish Queer Archive describing the 'story of a man who went to the Garda station complaining about queer bashing, months before the Flynn killing: "he was jeered and laughed out of the station"' (p. 499). Regarding the broader issues of gay rights in the 1980s, the Irish High Court and Supreme Court continued to uphold criminalization of gay sexual desire and intimacy in various rulings. In the Irish High Court (1980), Judge McWilliam confirms how the judiciary and religion ethos were strongly cross-pollinated in their ways of thinking. This judge's ruling is explicit in how he objectifies homosexuality onto the social imagination:

> Although I accept that the traditional attitudes of the Churches and of the general body of citizens towards homosexuality are being challenged and may be success-fully challenged in the future, it is reasonably clear that current Christian morality in this country does not approve of buggery or of any sexual activity between persons of the same sex ...
>
> Individual cases of hardship cannot invalidate statutes which can reasonably be considered by the legislature to be desirable for the true social order and the pres-ervation of the public order and morality mentioned in the Constitution. (Cited in Hug 1999: 212–13)

Referring to religious fundamentalist narratives in Ireland, Chris Robson (1995) says 'Politicians' offices were flooded with such stuff. In a country where most view gays and lesbians as peculiar or simply different, the objec-tive was to make us appear loathsome and riddled with disease' (p. 56). For the equality struggle, Robson (1995) says it was 'boasted that Ireland, on paper at least, was the worst legal regime in Western Europe for lesbians and gay men' (p. 47). The Catholic Hierarchy remained resolute in their disagreement on the availability of contraception. In 1985, the Irish govern-ment went against Catholic doctrines and legislated for wider availability of contraceptives. Robson (1995) says up to the beginning of 1988, 'there was restricted access to non-medical contraceptives' (p. 47). The Irish Bishops' Conference recommended abstinence and monogamy as the surest solution against contracting HIV (Fuller 2002: 246). Regarding a change towards more progressive social attitudes since the 1970s, the 1980s was 'a time of great concern about HIV/AIDS' (Park, et al. 2013). In the 1980s, 'it was common for many bars to refuse entry and service to any men or women perceived as homosexual' (Road to Equality 2016a). As the 'Road to Equality Exhibition' (2016b) states: 'A combination of cultural and political factors, not least the illegality of contraceptives, criminalization of gay male sex, censorship of sexual health information and a rigid Catholic morality, informed official attitudes to the disease throughout most of the 1980s & 1990s'. Robson (1995) says even though the campaign of Senator Norris had started to gain traction in the 1970s, the continuing sluggishness of social legislation in eroding social discrimination and prejudice against gay people 'insulted and marginalized tens of thousands of gay men and, by association, lesbians as well' (p. 47). Olson (2016) terms this 'the existential force of the political imagination' (p. 170), which captures the prevailing atmospheres of social oppression. At this time, transgender rights had limited visibility in Irish advocacy.

The Oireachtas (Parliament) did not even debate the AIDS crisis until 1989, 'five years after the first cases of AIDS were reported in Ireland' (Road to Equality Exhibition 2016b). When I received my own HIV positive results in the 1990s, it became another source of fear and shame. I felt marked and interiorized the stigma from external cues and judgement (London and Rosenthal 2013). When drunk, I told my mother that I was gay and HIV at the same time. At the time, I was very depressed. I had a strong feeling that I was not going to live much longer. Director of AidsWise, Ger Philpott had been highly critical of the Irish government's historic response to the AIDS crisis: 'It wasn't until 1993 that an Irish Minister for Health had the balls to launch the first media campaign unequivocally urging people to practice safer sex and wear a condom. Brendan Howlin was responsible for this. He got a lot of praise for the campaign. It was seen to be significant. Indeed it was, but only in terms of what hadn't happened before' (Hug 1999: 234). In the next section, I outline the speed of my decision-making on suicide intent. This was a time of panic. From my younger years, such panic was more than familiar to me. Life in my mid-twenties felt like it was escalating out of control. No one could really get close to me in this state. Neuberg and Kenrick (2018) capture this pattern reasonably well: 'discrimination processes can create desperate environments for stigmatized individuals and groups, thereby eliciting fast strategies that potentially have significant downstream implications for health' (p. 130).

Self-Injury and Active Suicidal Intent

From the last section, the emphasis was to shine a light on historic prejudices that secured normative force in Ireland. Respected institutions set the terms for what was considered normal and deviant, proper and improper. My own autobiographical narrative cannot be separated from how I developed my assumptions about the world, assumptions that cut me off from opening up about my reality to others. Being open to ourselves, with others, in the world are critically important skills for realizing and maximizing our human potential. In my history, my own psychology had been actively primed to work against my best interests, to repress what was important. In my formation as a human being, historic Ireland did not love, respect and esteem the development of my uniqueness. As a gay child and adolescent, historic norms in Ireland did not treat me as an equal citizen in a non-discriminatory rule of law. I did not feel esteemed in the pursuance of my talents and abilities. Christman (2018) says:

> Nonalienated appropriation requires the extension of the self into the world in ways that make the ongoing process of self-formation intelligible to the person ... Additionally, this is by no means a solitary endeavour, in that appropriation takes place within self-defining social roles. (p. 76–7)

In the latter end of the 1980s, at nineteen/twenty years old, I collapsed outside a doctor's surgery and was subsequently hospitalized in Mullingar General Hospital. After a number of weeks, I was transferred to Baggot St Hospital in Dublin. I was diagnosed with coronary artery spasm, a diagnosis not consistent with the health profile of a twenty-year-old. Like so many other researchers in the research literature, Juster, Vencill and Johnson (2017) suggest 'Social inequalities have health consequences' (p. 44).

In 1993, at twenty-six years old, some years after my hospital admission in Mullingar, I failed in an attempt on my own life. I took an overdose of pills. I drank all of the pills down with a bottle of gin. I remember dropping one of the pills on kitchen floor and desperately rummaging in the dark to find it. I was fearful of turning on a light. A number of my friends were trying to contact me out of concern for my wellbeing. I had heard the doorbell ring and saw a friend in the driveway. Throughout the day, I had spent the day attending three different medical doctors, gathering and collecting prescriptions for Valium from each one. I consumed all three prescriptions at once. I had been drinking all day. I was extremely depressed. I felt useless, burdensome and hopeless.

I remember taking a bus from Camden Street up to Leinster Road, where I lived in Dublin. It was raining heavily. On the bus, I remember thinking this is the last time I will ever see people. A number of friends had raised the alarm when I had not turned in for work that day. I thought I had covered my tracks by telling my closest friend that I was going away for a few days. Later that evening, I was discovered in the house by the landlady. When she received a call from a friend, she happened to be in the upstairs part of the house. She had rented the downstairs part of her home to me. When she came downstairs to investigate, she initially thought I was not there and was about to leave. My apartment was in complete darkness. She went further into my apartment and discovered I had collapsed by the side of the bed. She was speaking on the phone to my friend at the same time. My friend surmised that I was drunk. When the landlady took a closer look at me, she did not like my skin colour and determined it was necessary to call medical emergency. I was then taken to Accident and Emergency in Meath Street, Dublin 8. When I woke up from the overdose, I was so unhappy to be alive. I was subsequently hospitalized for three weeks.

At the psychiatric hospital, I was psychologically diagnosed with a profound grief reaction to the loss of my gay male partner to AIDS. Stephen was twenty-seven years old when he died at the end of 1992. When he died, I drank heavily. I had vivid hallucinations of his presence in the house I rented. While my relationship to Stephen was not long-term, the loss of his life sealed what I thought was to be my own fate. We had been seeing each other for two years. Stephen was the first gay man I had dated. His deceased mother, family and longer-term friends were devastated. I remember the night Stephen was buried, one of his friends said particularly cruel things to me. He accused me of wallowing in self-pity for being HIV positive. Some of my other friends were dying from AIDS-related symptoms at the time. The topic had been a constant theme in the media. In this context, I felt hopeless and unable to sustain myself. My failing performance in work was also evident. Overall, my emotional reactions to experiences were extreme and overwhelming. I could not cope with the world: 'the capacity for regulating and modulating affect is severely impaired in a suicidal state ... there is no hope, no connectedness, and no time' (Goldblatt 2014: 258; Shneidman 1985). No time, is exactly what I felt. I just wanted out now. O'Gorman (2011) says the historic pattern of concealing minor sexual exploitation in Ireland had implications in adult life. He says these experiences 'Pushed many to the edge of the margins, effectively "othering" them, deeming them unworthy of social inclusion and rightful legal protection. They were made invisible, turned into outsiders by their own society' (p. 8). At the time, all of this felt like a self-induced personal conflict. I had learned to be silent, consistent with the valorization of suffering I had witnessed in my early development. Furthermore, as a gay adult survivor, integrating and speaking about my childhood traumatic experience was something that was not widely discussed. Some definitions and vocabularies added insult to injury. Silence can be so corrosive and damaging to wellbeing and bad ideas that equate 'same-sex child abuse with homosexuality are shamefully wrong' (Lew 2000: xvii). The predation of a child by a senior and respected authority figure is bad enough. As an adult, to be confronted with toxic ideas about the meaning of childhood violation was a horridly shaming and silencing experience. The experience of childhood sexual abuse was something I experienced in secret and to be expected to keep it a secret as an adult was very burdensome.

I had grown up in a society that expressed its national discourse in characterological and moralistic terms without knowing this theological objectification was a social and political construction. Renault (2017) says 'the concept of social suffering does designate a complex interweaving of the psychic and the social, of life history and context, of structural and situational factors. It is only in light of this interweaving that the idea of social factors in suffering takes on meaning' (p. 152). My psychological modes of expression were enacted and internalized in naive socialization. Tightened modes of understanding felt like a psychological dissociation, encouraged by social devaluation and stigma for gay identity. A lack of social reality can result in a form of invisibilization. I was not used to being free in a vital sense where I could create sufficiently reasoned space for evaluating life on life's terms. I had not robustly internalized conscious practices of self-control to inspire confident self-prediction for dealing with psycho-social problems. I was clinically depressed and overwhelmed where my sense of self had generated a false equivalence with stigmatic prophecies. This reinforced pattern was dominating in how I made meaning of life's experiences. Consistent with this interpretation, critical social science theorists credit Hegel with the broad idea that 'self-definition is something that comes in degrees depending on the scope that is available historically for the fulfilment of human needs and the expression of human capacities' (Smith and O'Neill 2012: 9). More crisply stated, Renault (2017) favours the conception of 'an idea of a clinical social psychology that designates a specific approach chiefly on the ways in which the social is inscribed in the individual psyche and on the dynamic relations which exist between psychic structures and social systems' (p. 154). This definition captures how the power of the social order obstructs people from making meaningful connections about their own experiences. O'Neill (2010) says:

> A distinctive feature of any critical theory of society is that it aims not only to explain or to interpret key aspects of the social world but also to engage in a project of eman-cipation. This involves an obligation to connect theory with practice by focusing on the ways in which the causes of unnecessary suffering in the world, and the structures of injustice associated with such suffering, might best be dismantled. (p. 127)

Over a decade and a half after childhood family trauma and adolescent sexual abuses, the early social context of HIV simply added more fuel to the logic of shame. No matter how well I dressed up, the speed of a self-obsessed critic had the upper hand on my personality. I was never at ease or at peace with myself. I drank alcohol every single day. I did not have the capacity to grasp: 'the individual's experience of identity and self fits within a larger society, its rules and standards' (Davis-Siegel, Gottman and

Siegel 2015: 218). Consistent with the theory of recognition as formulated by Honneth (2012a) it is important to 'take into consideration the requirement of basic relations of mutual recognition and the permanent possibility of individual or collective resistance against the already established forms of recognition'. In extending these insights to my own suicide intent, Renault's (2017) formulation can be applied:

> This biographical condition must be complemented by a contextual condition, that is, the existence of a disadvantageous or unstable social environment, in which the individual is placed in a position of structural vulnerability. It is on this triple condition (life history, contextual, structural) that an event can tip individuals over into a trajectory characterized by the progressive undermining of their different horizons of expectation, of their models for interpreting themselves and others, by the disappearance of all forms of trust in social relationships and, consequently, by the destruction of their last relational supports and by a social incapacity which reinforces their suffering. (p. 155)

At this stage of my life, I never opened up to anyone about my early life experiences. My relational capacity was mired in a negative spiral of post-trauma symptoms from my youth, meaning 'no individual is culture free' (Arnett-Jensen 2015: 5). Often, psychological and medical disciplines and recovery programmes collectively formulate this trait as a personality disorder, and/or as a defect of character. Clinical author Shahar (2015) describes how 'Self-critics actively create the social-interpersonal conditions that generate their distress, and their distress itself exacerbates self-criticism'. I did not like feeling burdensome. I felt pathetic. I thought my attempt on my own life would put an end to feeling like a tainted scumbag inside. I felt my death from AIDs was going to happen at some stage in the future.

In 1993, my attempt on my own life was not attention seeking or an attempt to transcend. It was my active attempt to erase myself from the planet. Even apart from the stigma of HIV diagnosis, I felt so persecuted. Researchers report higher rates of depression and suicide attempts among persons with a history of CSA (e.g. Heilbron et al. 2014; Chu 2011; Teunis and Herdt 2007; Rosenberg et al. 2005; Johnson et al. 2002; Brown et al. 1999; Fergusson et al. 1996; Herman 1992; Bryer et al. 1987; Roberts and Hawton 1990). Heilbron, et al. (2014) say 'There remains a crucial gap in knowledge about social influences that are specific to SITBs (Self

Injury – Thoughts and Behaviours) and how they transact with other aspects of SITBs (e.g., biological, cognitive and behavioural factors)' (p. 219). Renault (2017), while recognizing the deeply ingrained trajectory of social humiliation and violence, states that 'not all individuals react in the same way to violence and humiliation' (p. 156). Thus, 'the analysis of the specific social context and of the life history must, moreover, be completed by taking into account other social constraints weighing on the individual and other difficulties encountered in the course of the social trajectory' (p. 156). In sum, 'being at the wrong end of inequality is disempowering, it can deprive people of control over their lives' (Marmot 2015: 7). In my own case, while there were bright spots and buffers – caring friends and a caring therapist – yet I was so disconnected. I wanted out of my hellish life experiences. To my shame, I never once thought how my suicidal action would have impacted on my mother or those close to me.

In the early 1990s, through my employment, I had been able to raise substantial funds for AidsWise to assist families impacted by HIV in Ireland. Shortly after, with a change of management, I had started to run up against some discrimination in work where very unpleasant inferences were aired by some of the new management. Some of my subordinates were warned about my 'lifestyle'. I stayed silent and did not confront this. Silence has always been pivotal to how I dealt with public distress. I learned to bottle things up, where I learned that what I subjectively felt really did not matter (Hewitt, Flett and Mikail 2017). An incident in my work life that stands out was around the time of the release of *Philadelphia* starring Tom Hanks, a movie focusing on the theme of AIDS. As purchasing and product marketing manager, I had been able to procure funds for advertising with the movie's release as a video. Subsequently, the new management queried the overrun for studio production costs. I had authorized the increased costs for the national TV promo to accompany its release. I made this extra spend to make the TV promo better and more context-sensitive. This explanation for the overrun was not accepted. At this time, talking to a good friend, he advised I was not reading the writing on the wall. He had been listening to me for some time. Shortly after, my friend died of an AIDs related illness. For a six-month period after my departure from the company, I worked for the old company as an external consultant.

During this period of my life, self-pity and shame were definite factors in a declining ability to adapt to my life circumstances. At this time, I felt there was nothing in my social context where I could find hope to push through tough times. The smart skills of deepened awareness and self-confidence were not in my possession at this time. I could not muster a resilient pathway out of my situation. Jose Medina (2017) states in his essay 'Varieties of Hermeneutical Injustice' that 'injuries can go very deep, indeed to the core of one's humanity' (p. 41). In a similar vein, Koopman (2013) says 'genealogies articulate problems' suggesting those problems: 'condition us without our fully understanding why or how. They are depth problems in that they are lodged deep inside of us all'. Nussbaum (2001) adds that 'Emotions shape the landscape of our mental and social lives'. Kohut (1971) describes acute anxiety as 'an intense and pervasive anxiety that accompanies a patient's dawning awareness that his self is disintegrating and experiences of severe fragmentation, serious loss of initiative, profound drop in self-esteem, sense of utter meaninglessness' (p. 103). Hewitt, Flett and Mikail (2017) research on perfectionism also resonates with a failed ideal, 'at a broader level, perfectionists who are overly concerned about being stigmatized for coping in less than optimal or ideal manner, can become extremely isolated from other people' (p. 146). The social noise of negative self-criticism was a well-ingrained developmental pattern. At this time, this socially learned pattern was winning out in my psychology.

In my young life, esteemed office-holders were arguing that any suffering arising from legal inequality was not consequential enough to change the status quo. Some theorists might view the main hypotheses in the book as overly invested in social determinants to the exclusion of psychological resistance. I did not engineer Ireland's repressive ideas on sexuality. I was not responsible for the laws, customs and traditions of Ireland that silenced people and naturalized secretiveness. I did not create the social menu which influenced attitudes and beliefs that often caused stress and trauma. I did my level best to cope in these situations. Persecutory self-beliefs are hard to redirect toward hope in oppressive social contexts. When social contexts become less oppressive, they encourage more people to grow in authentic self-esteem.

In a recent critique of Roman Catholic Church doctrines, Mary McAleese (2018) describes how her 'church's teaching on homosexuality is, in my view, evil. It conduces to homophobia; homophobia is evil. It ruins people's lives. It has ruined families' lives. It has caused people to commit suicide. It has caused people to live in dark shadows' (Humphreys 2018). Mrs McAleese added her son Justin 'loved the church' and then discovered 'that same church has a view of him that is inimical to the way God made him'. It directed him 'to retreat into the shadows of self-doubt, of misery of being really frightened' (Humphreys 2018). McAleese (2018) develops her own critical analysis for how this happens, whereby 'infant conscripts are held to lifelong obligations of obedience' (cited by McGarry 2018). She contends that these rituals are a fundamental breach of human rights: 'You can't impose, really, obligations on people who are only two weeks old and you can't say to them at seven or eight or 14 or 19 "here is what you contracted, here is what you signed up to" because the truth is they didn't' (cited by McGarry 2018). The former president says, 'My human right to inform my own conscience, my human right to express my conscience even if it is the case that it contradicts the magisterium [teaching authority of the Church], that right to conscience is supreme' (cited by McGarry 2018).

Feeling that we as individuals have induced a conflict in our own conscience is profoundly shaming. For some, like myself, it can take time to get greater emotional purchase on the experiences we have come through. What is there to come through? Stating the most obvious, the objective reasoning of my early socialization imputed that gay sexuality was objectively disordered. Gay sex was deemed not normal by supreme theological and legal thinking. Ireland's historic laws were designed to create suspicion and reduce the freedom of gay people in the public sphere. In this way, according to someone else's group conscience in history, gay intimacy was appropriated as illegal and immoral. In this way, society actively structured a context that recommended gay and trans people be alienated from a desire to be oneself, with others in the world. My society actively emboldened prejudice, ignorance and silenced significant moral harm. Many have twisted the truth. I appropriated far too many bad ideas from my experience of Irish culture, one that subordinated my conscience to other people's ideas. If you distrusted yourself, historic society endorsed this position. Unless psychological solutions are invested in trying to uncover the social sources of oppression, expert disciplines will continue in a very truncated view of lifespan development. In reorganizing our attitudes, behaviours, feelings and ideas, it is important to recognize and understand what repressed and oppresses us, so that we can change the appropriated self-beliefs that lowered our self-esteem and self-confidence to begin with.

The final section in the first part of this book examples how 1990s Ireland witnessed significant changes in social discourse that are more enabling to love, respect and esteem.

CHAPTER 13

Reconfiguring Guilt/Shame in 1990s Ireland: Struggles for Social Freedom/Equality

The mid- to late 1990s was a critical period when the Catholic ethos started to lose its normative grip on the polity and juridical/legal frameworks. The right to adult homosexual relations were decriminalized in 1993. Ireland fulfilled its obligation to the EU Court of Human Rights judgement from 1988 (Fuller 2002: 246–7). In 1992, the controversial X case of a pregnant fourteen-year-old girl received significant attention in Ireland. The teenage girl was 'raped ... and prevented by court injunction from traveling to Britain for an abortion' (p. 246). The Irish Supreme Court then overturned a High Court judgement and found in favour of abortion in limited circumstances with due regard to the equal right to life and welfare of the mother. Fuller (2002) says:

> In a referendum held on the 25th November 1992, the electorate voted in favour of the right to travel, and the right to information on abortion services, but rejected the wording of the substantive issue relating to the circumstances under which abortion is permissible ... In 1992 also, further liberalization of the law in relation to family planning meant that contraceptive devices became freely available throughout the country. (p. 246)

By the late 1980s and early 1990s, with the support of the trade union movement and other social justice advocacy movements, LGBT equality initiatives were starting to achieve notable successes in legislation. After the success of the 1988 EU decision in favour of Norris vs Ireland in the EU Court in Strasbourg, Christopher Robson (1995) briefly summarizes those achievements in his essay 'Anatomy of a Campaign':

- The abolition of all previous laws criminalizing gay activity, and their replacement by a new gender-neutral law with a common age of consent of seventeen, and no special privacy conditions. [June 1993]
- No exceptions from this law for the armed forces or for the merchant marine. [June 1993]
- A prohibition of incitement to Hatred Act, which includes in its title the category 'sexual orientation'. [November 1989]
- Specific protection for every category of worker from 'unfair dismissal' because of sexual orientation. [April 1993]
- Work codes in all government and local government employment statutes which include the sentence 'Discrimination on the basis of sexual orientation will not be tolerated.' The same codes also specifically protect those with HIV/AIDs [First code implemented July 1988]. (Robson 1995, p. 47–8)

Robson also refers to further developments in 1994 where the government were discussing adding new categories to an Expanded Employment Equality Act 'to cover all forms of workplace discrimination' (1995: 48) including a broad commitment for an agency charged with oversight of 'a radical new Equal Status Act prohibiting discrimination in non-work areas from housing, education to social services' (Robson 1995: 48). The Catholic Church, as a key employer in various sectors in Ireland still managed to secure opt outs from the equality initiatives based on its ethos. In 1994, a year after decriminalization of homosexuality in Ireland, Pope John Paul II referred to homosexuality among other issues such as divorce, contraception and abortion. His teaching was 'to coincide with the UN International Year of the Family' (Hug 1999: 206). Consistent with previous teachings on homosexuality (CDF 1975, 1986, 1992), the Pope stated that

> Marriage forms the basis of the institution of the family and is constituted by the covenant whereby a man and a woman establish between themselves a partnership for their whole life ... Only such a union can be recognized and ratified as a marriage by society. Other interpersonal unions which do not fill the above conditions cannot be recognized, despite certain growing trends which represent a serious threat to the future of the family and society itself. (Hug 1999: 206)

Hug (1999) said the Pope's letter was published after a EU Parliament recommendation to grant equal rights to homosexual couples in the union. Some EU member countries were already recognizing gay and lesbian unions, 'in particular the right to marry and to adopt children' (p. 206). The Pope described the EU resolution as 'asking that a moral disorder be legitimated .... A relationship between two men and two women cannot make up a real family and, more to the point, you cannot grant such a union the right to adopt children' (Hug 1999: 206).

In 1995, a referendum in Ireland removed the constitutional ban on divorce in Ireland. It was a narrow win at the polls. Cardinal Cahal B. Daly (1998) in his autobiographical reflections believed that the criticisms often levelled against the conservatism of Pope John Paul II sprang from 'manifest prejudice ... Pope John Paul towers intellectually and, above all, spiritually above all the criticisms' (p. 213). He further advised 'A major pre-occupation with some theologians nowadays seems to be to resist "papal centralism" One and Universal' (p. 213). What was further evident in Dr Cahal B. Daly's autobiography is how St Thérèse of Lisieux's idea of 'everything is grace' (p. 432) was a source of comfort for the Church even in their darkest hours. These darkest hours, were the subject of recent critique by the UN Committee for Human Rights in 2014. Its chairman, Sir Nigel Rodley (d. 2017), in his closing statement to the committee, addressed the record of human rights abuses/violations in Ireland. In the presence of the Minister for Justice, Frances Fitzgerald, Rodley (2014) said Ireland's 'collection is some collection and was hard imagining any state party tolerating it.' The chairman added that he could not help but note 'that these abuses were connected to the institutional belief system, one that occasionally dominated the state party' (Rodley 2014). On hearing these remarks, Minister Fitzgerald appeared uncomfortable, perhaps knowing how key figures within her own political party had historically propped up and defended right-wing religious understandings. Many Fine Gael deputies fought against the secularism trend of new human rights (Meehan 2013). Frances Fitzgerald had never aligned herself to these less progressive elements within her own party, and clearly embraced the social pluralism advocated by Dr Garret FitzGerald, leader of Fine Gael in the 1980s. From the 1970s, the Irish Labour Party as a socially progressive coalition partner were always key players in pushing the agenda forward for amending the conservative nature of the Irish constitution (Ferriter 2009). During the 1960s, the Labour Party stayed out of coalition which allowed Fianna Fáil to dominate political life in Ireland (Meehan 2013).

A sign of cultural change in the 1990s was when my mother eventually stopped letting religious sisters into her home. My mum said they were saying things that really crossed her boundaries. Society was changing, and my mother could feel the power of saying 'enough is enough' to the old order. Up to the mid- to late 1990s, my mother had thought I was thinking of pursuing religious life. My mother had good solid friends who called regularly to her. She was great company. Even her psychiatrists loved her. That said, she had a very hard time with her health. There was a long period where she was in and out of mental hospitals. She often said she was admitted seventeen times to mental hospitals. It was terrible to see her and hear her on the phone and visit her when she was so unwell. She had so many depressive episodes of highs and lows. As a woman, life in Ireland had been so cruel on her for a very long period.

As my mother aged, the nature of her health problems did change. Within that, I believe the chronic physical conditions which eventually immobilized her were not just related to ageing. The stressful strains of her early life trajectory, on low income supports in Ireland, had weakened her. My sisters and the local family were part of her life. My mother went to Australia on a regular basis to see my sister and her family. This sister, her husband and daughters came to see our mother in Ireland at least once and sometimes twice a year. Another sibling, partner and daughter came on a regular basis too. In the last years of my mother's life, one of my sisters cared for my mother at home. My mother then moved into the nursing home. She had started to fall a lot and then lost confidence to walk. She put on a significant amount of weight. In her later years, suffering with chronic pain in the Accident and Emergency Department in Mullingar, most of the medical professionals who cared for her were totally unaware of my mother's history. A critical appreciation of how her chronic overlapping health issues were shaped by her early life history were not up for consideration. Kirkengen et al. (2016) of the Norwegian General Practice Research Unit says:

> Medical knowledge ignores central tenets of human existence, notably the physiological impact of subjective experience, relationships, history and sociocultural contexts. Biomedicine will not succeed in resolving today's poorly understood health problems by doing 'more of the same'. We must acknowledge that health, sickness and bodily functioning are interwoven with human meaning-production, fundamentally personal and biographical. (p. 1)

My mother's vocabulary would have exampled significant dissociation, just to survive. She was selective in who she spoke to. She was not too inclined to speak up. Even though, she would often say she stood her corner, she was more often silent. My mother continued to suffer from physical ailments in the last decades of her life. She was in and out to hospital all the time. For her doctors, her presenting health issues were the immediate concern. Like many others, her socio-economic class meant she had to suffer the indignity of long overnight waits in our over-stretched Accident and Emergency public health system in Ireland. Within the Accident and Emergency Department in Mullingar, and also in my mother's nursing home, I recognized a couple of women who had suffered poor mental health from earlier stages in their lives. The social and economic obstacles they faced throughout their lives were significant.

With the continuing dominance of neuroscience in psychology and psychiatry, there has been much less focus on understanding the social metrics of health. Increasingly, many in the field are now arguing that health inequities need to be analysed. Allen et al. (2014) say health inequities 'are shaped by various social, economic, and physical environments operating at different stages of life. Risk factors for many common mental disorders are heavily associated with social inequalities, whereby the greater the inequality the higher the inequality in risk' (p. 392).

In understanding social determinants of health, it is also important to grasp the political and historical contexts of experience. Enlarged understandings are needed 'to continue our examination of pervasive contexts by considering the direct and indirect impacts of political and economic systems on motivations and need satisfactions' (Ryan and Deci 2017: 591). To my knowledge, mental health leadership have not addressed social injustices in a substantive way. For example, there is little critical inquiry into how 'individuals cognize and legitimate the social world and their place within it' (Thompson 2013a: 301). Thus, psychological disciplines need a vocabulary 'that fundamentally calls into question prevailing norms, values and social institutions that govern society' (Thompson 2013: ix). The job of critical social analysis is to evaluate the impact of social conditions which may give rise to disparities in health outcomes from gender inequalities (McNay 2016).

Since the 1970s, the women's/feminist movements made a significant contribution to the negative health impact of rape, domestic violence and child abuse. Many of the key gender and trauma/PTSD theorists were women who strongly embraced feminist ideas and a commitment to an ethics of care (Warner 2009). Feminist theory analysed the systemic impact of male patriarchy and privilege which often sustained gender inequality and silenced victims of injustices (Kidd, Medina and Pohlhaus 2017; Kelly 2015; Disch and Hawkesworth 2016; Stringer 2014; Butler 2004; O'Connor 1998).

Regarding sexual violation of minors, in-house debates raged on the accuracy of recovered adult memories of childhood abuses. These debates slowed down progress in research, questioning the credibility of negative impact of sexual violation and any inferred or causal/correlative relationship to adult health inequity (Schwartz 2000; Chu 2011). Bernstein (2015) suggests the concept of moral injury in societies is in: 'the first instance about degrading or diminishing the value of others, how their worth or standing is shown to be less than that of the perpetrator through his actions … all wrongful actions express the idea of there being a moral inequality between doer and victim' (p. 134).

From my own experience, to find effective ways to express the logic of moral harm/marginalization as a method of empowerment has proved difficult. To be open as a male was complicated by cultural misogyny, where expressing vulnerability was discouraged, internalizing the idea that the male is the oppressor and is never the victim. To be anything less than an empowered male was viewed as a weak and fragile victim performance. A nationalistic version of being an Irish male is about robustness and strength (Beatty 2016). Stepien (2017) captures this nicely: 'It is not that shame is informed by the politics of gender alone; however, the politics of shame is shaped by religious, national and cultural ideologies, too' (p. 55). Toxic stress exposure can alter a life trajectory in concrete ways. Some psychiatrists in Ireland are recommending the necessity of social/political advocacy to address social injustices (Kelly 2016a). Medina (2017) believes injustices 'can radically constrain one's hermeneutical capacities and agency … This is something that oppressed groups have denounced for a long time' (p. 41).

At the time of writing this book, the campaign for reproductive services, including the right to an abortion in Ireland, in line with best medical practice, was centre stage in Ireland. The Citizens Assembly in 2017 recommended significant change to the status quo. A national referendum was recommended to change Article 40.3.3 (The Eighth Amendment) in the Irish Constitution. Having received clarification from a recent Irish Supreme Court judgement, Ireland's Health Minister Simon Harris had stated the constitution is not the best place to "'regulate access to healthcare for women" – and launched an impassioned argument for the repeal of the Eighth Amendment' (Staines 2018). Meehan (2013) gives a good account of the recent precursors exampling how restrictive Ireland's current abortion laws have been. She says despite the impulse for social change in Irish society, the topic of abortion remained divisive in a historic context. Meehan says:

> On 28 October 2012, Savita Halappanavar, who was seventeen weeks pregnant, died at University Hospital Galway after suffering a miscarriage. Her husband maintained that she had requested an abortion, which had been denied as a foetal heartbeat was detectable. Although initially denying the remark, Ann Maria Burke, midwife manager at Galway University Hospital, admitted telling the Halappanavar family that Savita could not have an abortion because 'Ireland is a Catholic Country'. (Meehan 2013)

There was significant outcry on the death of Savita Halappanavar. Independent TD (member of Parliament) Claire Daly had also raised the issue of abortion in the national Parliament on the twentieth anniversary of the X case from 1992. Following public pressure, Meehan (2013) outlines how the Fine Gael-Labour coalition had little option to introduce 'a limited measure' entitled 'The Protection of Life in Pregnancy Bill' which passed comfortably by 127 votes to 31 in the Dáil and also passed the Seanad (Lower House) in July 2013. Meehan (2013) says 'Claire Daly had earlier accused the Government of framing legislation so restrictive that "most women who will be affected will not bother and, instead, they will continue to make the journey to Britain, so that the Government can pretend that there is no Irish abortion"' (p. 197). President Michael D. Higgins after convening the Council of State exercised his right to not refer the government legislation to the Supreme Court 'to test its constitutionality' (p. 197). The government did impose the whip, which resulted in a government minister, Lucinda Creighton, losing her seat at Cabinet and losing her membership of the FG party. Meehan (2013) adds 'She was one of only five government party members to vote against the legislation as some TDs who had previously expressed doubts or concerns followed the official government line'.

Independent TD Claire Daly (2018) in a recent foreword to a book entitled *The Adoption Machine* by Paul Redmond says Ireland's history examples the

> worst manifestation of the repression of women, the collusion of Church and State to restrict reproductive rights. Fear of women's sexuality created an entrenchment and an over-reaction that led to intrusive levels of supervision on a parish basis into the lives of young women and men. Irish women, especially those from the working classes and rural poor, who became pregnant outside of marriage during the greater part of the twentieth century, were considered a great shame; they were castigated as sinners, shunned, tainted and ultimately cornered. (Daly 2018)

On 25 May 2018, the Irish electorate went to the polls and repealed the Eighth Amendment with a landslide majority. Out of a total poll of 2,159,655 and a valid poll of 2,153,613, the result in favour of repeal was 1,429,981 and 723,632 No votes were cast, with a majority in favour of repeal 706,349 (*Sunday Business Post* 2018). In the space of thirty-five years, the change in Ireland from the moral conservatism of the 1980s examples how Ireland has 'wrestled with its past and voted to define its future' where 'young, old, women, men, urban, rural, liberal and conservative' voted in the affirmative for repeal of the 1983 Eighth Amendment (*Sunday Business Post* 2018). The Taoiseach Leo Varadkar (2018) greeted the referendum result saying 'Everyone deserves a second chance, and this is Ireland's second chance' (*Sunday Business Post* 2018).

The first half of the book positioned historic lives in the context of social stigma/adversity. The impact of stigma has been reduced in Ireland, extending opportunity to explore historic experiences in greater depth, from recognizing 'many of our gay teenagers are our sons, brothers, nephews, cousins, friends, and boys next door' (Savin-Williams 1998, p. xii). Before moving to the second part, I want to take up a concept I previously mentioned, that is, the minority stress concept (Meyer 2007). For example, I often had to stomach derogatory statements about the meaning of gay identity, consistent with the national ideology of stigma. The pain of being told by a relative that because I was HIV positive, my nephews and nieces should avoid me. Over a long period of time, this hatred was aired behind my back. I was also harassed by a relative when they equated my internet browsing on Gaydar to searching for child pornography. In 2007, I responded to this person by providing them with a link to the site I visited on a relative's computer. In the response to my email, they persisted with damning conflations, which amounted to nothing short of pernicious homophobic hate mail. In this email, they go on to make a comparison to one of my brothers, saying I was not 'a fraction of the man' (10 March 2007). They then promised to copy this email to a relative who is not well, instructing that this person should 'ask for nun's prayers to conquer his dangerous Internet compulsion' (10 March 2007).

Subsequently, I heard how this person had been very excited by the elevation of Cardinal Josef Ratzinger as Pope Benedict XVI in 2005. This person was a big fan of the deceased Pontiff John Paul II, stating this Pope had rescued the Church from the liberal decline. This person also transmitted the idea that Pope Benedict XVI would put a stop to what they considered vulgar pay-outs to adult survivors of clerical child sexual abuse. This person was saying victims of clerical childhood sexual abuse should not be trusted. Furthermore, my recently deceased brother told me how incensed he became when it was communicated to him, that 'wasn't it a pity that one could not choose one's siblings.'

In academic writings, LGBT persons have experienced this pernicious toxicity within families (Carastathis et al. 2016). In recent reports of the murders of gay men in the Muslim region of Chechnya, the authorities reportedly invited parents to kill their gay children (*Attitude* 2017). It is worth noting the Russians continue to minimize the implications of violations of human rights. In the Russian Parliament in 2013, pernicious legislation gained 'quasi-unanimous' support by the Duma and was signed by President Vladimir Putin. David Crary (2013) of the Associated Press says this legislation banned the 'propaganda of non-traditional sexual relations' imposing 'fines for providing information about the gay community to minors,' where some gay parents felt they had to flee Russia for their safety (*The Guardian* 2013). Rensmann (2017) describes the aftermath in Russia at the time:

> Violence against gays subsequently erupted in Russia, and the authorities began arresting and detaining Russian human rights and gay activists. The human rights conditions of gays in Russia instantaneously deteriorated. But the Russian antigay laws and politics also immediately became subject to a multifaceted international human rights campaign that involved a variety of local groups and actors operating under great peril. The global public was further mobilized by many transnational human rights activists opposing the antigay propaganda law for violating basic human rights. Human rights and gay rights thus became the focal point of political attention and conflict before, during, and after the Sochi Olympic Winter Games, a global political event hosted by Russia.

On a more positive note, on Tuesday, 20 June 2018, the Irish government officially recognized and apologized for the historical criminalization of gay men in Ireland in response to a motion tabled by the Irish Labour Party (Senator Ged Nash) which was accepted by all the political parties. Bardon (2018) reporting for *The Irish Times* first cites how Charlie Flanagan, Minister for Justice, addressed the issue of apology in the Irish Senate. The minister acknowledged how the historic laws had the 'effect of denying sexual and gender minorities 'the right to live without fear arising from the failure of tolerance in Irish society' (*Eile* 2018). For this, Flanagan (2018) offered 'a sincere apology ... I apologize to any person who felt the hurt and isolation created by those laws, and particularly to those who were criminally convicted by the existence of such laws' (O'Halloran and O'Regan 2018). Like so many other public representatives, the Minister for Justice mentioned the brave stance of Senator David Norris, who from the early 1970s had fought hard to reform the discriminatory laws in Ireland before he went on to secure a historic victory in the European courts. As

David says regarding the 1988 victory, only 'winning by one vote, with the Irish member of the court voting against us' (Norris 2018). In the Dáil, the Taoiseach Leo Varadkar conceded the apology 'could not erase the wrong that was done but said society had learned ...' (Bardon 2018). On Tuesday, 19 June 2018, the Taoiseach began his address by stating

> Twenty-five years ago this week, President Mary Robinson signed into law an historic Act that brought an end to decades of cruelty and injustice. The Fianna Fáil-Labour Party coalition at the time deserves recognition for its courage in driving this change, and a special mention should be made of the then Minister for Justice, Ms Máire Geoghegan-Quinn, who piloted the legislation through this House and the Seanad. (*Eile* 2018)

The Taoiseach then moved that:

> Dáil Eireann acknowledges that the laws repealed in the Criminal Law (Sexual Offences) Act 1993 that criminalized consensual sexual activity between men were improperly discriminatory, contrary to human dignity and an infringement of personal privacy and autonomy; caused multiple harms to those directly and indirectly affected, namely men who engaged in consensual same-sex activities and their families and friends; and had a significant chilling effect on progress towards equality for the Lesbian, Gay, Bisexual, Transgender and Intersex (LGBTI) community, acknowledging in particular the legacy of HIV/AIDS within the context of criminalization; further acknowledges the hurt and the harm caused to those who were deterred by those laws from being open and honest about their identity with their family and in society and that this prevented citizens from engaging in civil and political life and deprived society of their full contribution; offers a sincere apology to individuals convicted of same-sex sexual activity which is now legal. (*Eile* 2018)

The Taoiseach added that he

> was born in 1979, and in the three years before that, there were 44 prosecutions in this country. It is not all that long ago, and it is very much in living memory. Homosexuality was seen as a perversion .... Others saw it as a mental illness, including the medical profession at the time. For every one conviction, there were a hundred other people who lived under the stigma of prosecution, who feared having their sexual orientation made public and their lives and careers destroyed as a result. (*Eile* 2018)

Leo Varadkar also paid special tribute to the unknown heroes and the 'number of patriots who were involved in the founding of the state' who were homosexual (O'Halloran and O'Regan 2018). Flanked by his minister Katherine Zappone, the Taoiseach gave special praise to Ann Louise Gilligan, Katherine's recently deceased wife, who had fought for many years for marriage equality in Ireland. With that acknowledgement from the Taoiseach, Minister for Children and Youth Affairs Dr Katherine Zappone 'could not hold back the tears' in the Dáil (Lord 2018).

Senator Norris reflecting on his fifty years of spirited advocacy wrote 'a couple of months ago I saw two young men walking across O'Connell Bridge hand in hand and I thought, that is what it is all about. Now there is a generation of young men released from the guilt and shame experienced by men of my generation' (Norris 2018). Former president Mary McAleese welcomed the Irish government apology, saying 'it was an evil visited upon this country by homophobia being translated into law' (Bardon 2018). Mary McAleese proudly marched with her gay son Justin and his husband in Dublin's Gay Pride Parade at the end of June 2018 (Duffy 2018). Mrs McAleese also spoke at the Pride event.

Finally, to return to Mary McAleese's comments on the notion of evil as preordained in historical Ireland. Her analysis takes aim at how legal repertoires endorsed religious moralism in the construction of homophobia in Irish history. This is a significant critique as it examples how social norms generates a social pathology of reasoning as a first-order principle of social regulation. It is significant because we are not just talking about the outcomes of stigma as incidences of negative affect (e.g. shame). Rather, state and religion converged in a normative discourse for sundering the meaningfulness of gay people's lives in historic time. My sense is the impact is often not fully grasped by those on the receiving end of state sanctioned homophobia.

The next part of the book deals with the responses I have received over two decades from esteemed institutions, regarding historical injustices. The second part of the book illustrates the current difficulty in pursuing social justice for past harms in my own life journey. Even though the broader context of social change is positively transformative, closer engagement with personal life stories clearly suggest that a pursuit of justice for historic harm is still hampered by social and political contexts. The following sections also shine a light on how psychological theory can often remain at an ivory tower like remove from how historical experiences of oppression and exploitation constrain emancipatory potentials. The former president of the Psychological Society of Ireland in a recent set of guidelines for LGBT clients (PSI 2015) acknowledges, 'We have a history of treating people who did not comply to dominant social norms punitively, or at the very least with cold indifference. Psychology itself has often been silent on these abuses and in some cases even complicit' (D'Alton 2015, Foreword in PSI 2015). The charge is that the realities of individuals in history are more complex than currently described in the literature. I further highlight how psychiatry, from my own experience emboldens stigma through its ideas and practices. King (2000) says, 'Given the trauma inherent in a cultural context which stigmatizes, devalues, pathologizes and punishes homosexuality, the added trauma of childhood sexual abuse in effect exponentially intensifies the trauma and the task of healing' (p. 19). In my own historical circumstances the feeling of fear was 'precisely the impossibility of appropriating the world as the product of one's own activity that constitutes alienation' (Jaeggi 2014: xxi). As I have shown in the first half of this book, an individualist theory of narrative lifespan development completely misses interrelations of self-development to 'various dimensions of the world' (Allen and Mendieta 2018, p. xxi).

PART II

Enlightening Our Potential:
Looking Back to Move Forward

CHAPTER 14

The Journey of Personal Recovery in a Changing Ireland

In 1995, I started attending Alcoholics Anonymous for addiction recovery. Sometime afterwards, I started attending psychotherapy. Researchers have reported high rates of alcoholism and drug dependencies in adult survivors of CSA (Han et al. 2013; Teunis and Herdt 2007; Widom, Weiter & Cottler 1999). Indeed, an inordinate percentage of 'addicts' who are admitted to professional treatment centres exhibit PTSD symptoms (Najavits 2002). These findings suggest one of the key features of addiction is its relationship to early adversity/trauma. The suggestion is micro-regulative skills are in some way inflamed through adversity and trauma, where our neural architecture compensates in stressed out environments.

In my own experience, shaming the core of a young person's self-worth and identity was a negative tariff from the social order. I was socialized into a powerful belief system where I was encouraged to think that any unease I felt, emanated from, an unruly and sinful self, a wilful state of being. The seductive power of this normative thought system played havoc with how I understood my position in the world. If I was to try and distil how I carried this, it would be to say silence and and then feeling punished for trying to lift the lid on this normative veil of ignorance. Secrets is a key feature of Irish history. If I had lost my mother in my young life and my partner Paul in my adult life, I do not think I would be writing this. This is a measure of how poorly I felt inside, how I carried experience, how unmanageable my life really felt.

Recent clinical authors formulate social adversity/suffering in a younger person's life. Teicher et al. (2010) in a paper entitled 'Neurobiology of Childhood Trauma and Adversity':

Exposure to childhood adversity leads to the early initiation of drug, alcohol and
nicotine use and risky sexual behaviours and accounts for 50–75% of the population
attributable risk for alcoholism, drug abuse, depression and suicide. It also substan-
tially increases risk for ischemic heart disease, chronic obstructive pulmonary disease,
liver disease and obesity. This powerful adverse relationship is best understood as a
cascade. Exposure to early adversity alters trajectories of brain development, which,
in turn, leads to emotional and cognitive impairment, followed by the adoption of
health-risk behaviours. (p. 112)

However, as Renault (2017) articulates, this view of suffering is not a uni-
versally held view in the academy:

'Suffering' as based on a vision of individuals reduced to the status of powerless victims, a view that supposedly keeps the excluded trapped in their role of those who
need help instead of encouraging their efforts at integration. As for the supporters
of political liberalism, they condemn the paternalism of a state that under the guise
of fighting against suffering claims to take responsibility for individual happiness –
a confusion of morality and law that supposedly replaces a politics of social justice
with a mixture of paternalism and utilitarianism. (p. 5)

I believe social suffering should play a role in social critique as a key method
for improving social science knowledge and mental health interventions.
This is also well captured by Thompson (2017):

Defective forms of reasoning lead to the re-creation and sedimentation of the prevailing, existent reality and to the continued endorsement by members of that society of
its irrational and dominating relations and forces. The key insight of a critical theory
of society is therefore not meant to impose some set of a priori values and ideals onto
the social world, but to unravel the contradictions that already exist within it; to
make evident an emancipatory insight into the very fabric of what we take as given,
as basic to our social world.

Going back to my experience in Ireland, in 1995–6, the progress of anti-
retroviral therapies significantly changed the life expectancy for persons
with HIV (Road to Equality Exhibition 2016b). I gained fresh hope that
HIV was no longer an immediate threat to my health. This was a huge
weight off my shoulders. On a deeper level, I was still moving very fast
inside. I was very wound up and reaction sensitive. I kept up a front, with
plenty of activity. At this time, I possessed very little critical insight into

my ingrained restlessness and noisy state of mind. I did not possess an attention span for figuring out how my life experiences were so strongly influenced by historic social conventions, how my early development of self-worth had been shaped through stigma, silence, and shame. I was so used of thinking in certain ways about myself. I found myself gravitating toward cues and triggers that reinforced low self-confidence and self-worth. Deep down I distrusted others. Sugarman (2015) captures the limitations of psychological theory which he says struggles to incorporate the tenets of history in its formulation of human development:

> A significant implication of historical ontology is that by neglecting the constitutive influence of historical, social, cultural, and political institutions, psychologists frequently have attributed features of persons to human nature rather than to characteristics of institutions within which we become persons. (p. 180)

Aspects of this quote captures how normative frames of historic thought are naively picked up, imbibed onto intentional modes of consciousness. A stigmatized person must be conscious of how this works, otherwise this reduces one's imaginative capacity to resist dominating knowledge which can lower self-confidence. To liberate people from oppressive ideologies and practices, my book is aiming to show how social ideation can undermine psychological resistance, motivation, relationality and social solidarity. Clinicians seldom ask their clients to reflect and consider what has shaped a worldview. Instead, our lens truncates the world and imposes ideological checklists to follow that amputate core characteristics of historical and present contexts of life experience. In this sense, operational definitions deal with symptoms but strip such symptoms of their meaning. A life well lived requires meaning and truth. Hulatt (2016) says 'truth is, ideally, knowledge of something external to us' (p. 13). When historic societies reasoned that gay life was a pathological form of life, it aimed to prescribe for control purposes, to define what lay outside its ideal normative framework.

Within the recovery process of Alcoholics Anonymous, my purpose was to stop alcoholic drinking one day at a time. At the outset, I was more than happy not to be drinking. I needed to not drink, to bring about a greater degree of stability and focus in my life. In the opening section of their book, Miller and Plants (2014) state the purpose of twelve-step recovery as:

To question deeply ingrained assumptions on which we habitually rely and deeply ingrained habits that we assume. Each can radically enhance our self-awareness and profoundly broaden the horizon of meaning in which we operate. The process of philosophizing and the process of practicing Twelve Step spirituality do not just have the potential to change some part of ourselves or some part of our lives. They have the potential to change how we experience and think about everything.

I immersed myself in AA and started to feel part of something. The task was to live by spiritual principles and actions, and to grow in experience, strength and hope (AA 2002). I am not quoting the AA literature directly because it was written in America in 1939. The language used in AA parlance is fairly old-fashioned and dated. That said, the benign premise of AA is the 'only' requirement of AA membership is 'a desire to stop drinking/ using' is very pragmatic. The problematic 'addicted' drinker is being asked to consider how alcohol creates unmanageability, constraining individual and relational freedom and mature responsibility. AA suggests that stopping alcoholic drinking a day at a time in solidarity with others will result in a better quality of life. Step Two offers fellowship as a mechanism for its pragmatic aims. This is a step involving social solidarity with others in promoting change. Step Three promotes a discourse of submission to God's Will, a loving God as we understand him. Step Four suggests a moral psychological approach to taking personal inventory, a self-critique of weaknesses and strengths and admission of this pattern with another person in Step Five. How did my own instincts for survival go astray and how did my behaviour negatively impact on other people, on work, etc. This type of analysis requires open and willing self-examination, honesty and balance. In this, it was relatively obvious how my own engagement with the world lacked direction, purpose and meaning. My methods of self-regulation were dysfunctional. In addressing the issues of addiction and self-harm, Pickard and Ahmed (2015) say that

> Some addicts may not care about themselves enough to care about the negative consequences of their drug use – indeed, they may, both consciously and unconsciously, embrace these consequences, in keeping with their sense of self as a person who is bad or worthless, and so deserving of them. In such cases, the costs of drug use in effect count as benefits from their perspective. Fundamentally, the problem lies less in the choice to use, than in the self-destructive mind-set than this choice serves. (p. 33–4)

In my life experience, I did not possess enough critical insight or resistance to dominant ideas for building self-confidence with others. When I came to AA, I had deeply internalized assumptions, learned from my social environs and religious traditions. In AA, I had no real reservation about the mention of God within the recovery programme. At the time, I wanted to embark on change. I was so familiar with AA ideas from religious traditions. However, I did feel God centred ideas had placed too heavy a burden of responsibility in my thinking, but I did not question it, because I genuinely started to feel better about myself. I met so many decent people whom I call friends to this day. We supported each other. A genuine kindness and warmth existed, shown to me over many decades, to this very day. I did stop drinking from my participation in AA. I like that choice to say no to a drink. I have also witnessed how so many people's lives have gotten better by stopping problematic drinking. Solidarity with others has helped reduce shame and increase my self-esteem. Stepien (2017) says in her analysis of male characters in movies/books that deal with the theme of shame that 'Avoiding revisiting or sharing the shame, he protects it, which results in the self being cut off from others in a prison, which is the self-paralysed by shame' (p. 167). From the movies and books she analysed, the characters 'address shame that is suppressing, shame which relates to their gender, class and ethnicity and turn it into a potentially liberating' narrative (p. 167–8).

At the beginning of this century, with the help of a gay therapist, I prepared myself to report the crimes of sexual abuse I had experienced as a minor. My main focus during the 1990s was getting my emotional life straightened out. I kept going to AA meetings and doing service. From 2004, I began a decade of volunteering for Gay Switchboard Ireland. These safe spaces and being involved in these activities were stabilizing and enriching. Meeting my eldest sister for the first time in 1995 was a great source of strength. She had a recovery vocabulary. In this way, her love and warmth proved important.

Working through the past in AA recovery, personal therapy and clinical trainings were important to me. In the security of a private space, I was able to put words to feelings for what had happened. In personal therapy, the presence and support of the therapist and knowing I had somewhere safe to go was a good experience. There were times when I did not want to go. I was always watching for external cues of judgement. At times, this was very testing on the therapeutic relationship.

What is significantly absent in existing mental health research is how dominant social ideologies exact a tariff on human persons and their modes of functioning. Rarely, when I read theory in the discipline of psychotherapy, do I come away with the feeling that the historical and political nexus of human experience has been accounted for and critically unpacked. A historically informed analysis of regional ideologies that create script patterns of disempowerment towards enlightenment is important. In the book, I have gone to significant lengths to situate how the moral tentacles of a religious ideology, as foregrounded in Ireland's history, had demoralizing impacts on people's lives, altering what people thought and felt, reducing their power to act, silencing their awareness, cutting off options, which added insult to injury in many cases. Such ideologies can significantly limit self-understanding, self-determination and relational wellbeing, and how the 'idea of social pathology designates the effects of institutions upon the forms of individual existence' (Renault 2017: 201). There is very little work in psychology that explores how regional historical ideologies shape subject formation. This leaves citizens in a position where they may not grasp how they have been regulated to think and feel about their lives. It suggests that persons may not know how disempowerment is housed. This has knock on implications for some persons, when the normative logics of the social order, preordain a low horizon of expectation.

As a young traumatized person I simply did not have the tools to work this out. The expectation of disrespect was in some way expected. Fear is very natural for me. Butler (2018) says that 'when we think about how history works on us, setting the stage for our own action, we are confronted with the fact that we are acted upon as we act, and that if we were not acted upon, we could not act' (p. 214).

Psychologists may think they have no ethical obligation to explore the effects of historical ideologies on modes of self-understanding. A key aim of my book is to try to connect theory with the particulars of lived experience, to unearth what was previously imbibed, identified with, censored and carried as a deserved tariff in lifespan development. Fuchs (2017) refers to the current dominance of neuroscience saying 'all subjective and qualitative elements have been practically excluded from science's reinterpretation of the world'. In sum, psychological theory ought to be more proactive in grasping how historical scenes of life are enacted on human psychologies: how history has law-like effects on identity and action and inaction.

The next section example my own persistence in pressing for transparency and institutional accountability for silenced moral harms in historic Ireland.

CHAPTER 15

The Challenges of Confronting Childhood Sexual Abuse in Adulthood

Bernstein (2015) describes the moral injury of torture and rape:

> To say to these individuals that their intrinsic worth is perfectly intact, that nothing in their essential standing as a human being has been harmed or injured, that everything in their moral personhood is exactly as it should be, sounds like a form of vicious cruelty. It denies the possibility that degradation, humiliation, and devastation might be actual in the lives of sufferers. (p. 136)

Stated less philosophically, and more empirically, in exploring the relationship between childhood adversity and adult physical health 'a consensus in the developmental psychopathology literature is that the experience of chronic, uncontrollable stress – is a risk factor for a diverse set of poor outcomes across development' (Ehrlich, Miller and Chen 2016, p. 1). Thinking in a less deterministic/reductive way, changing social dynamics has extended me greater critical scope and purchase to upend traditional self-beliefs enacted in historical time. Much has been denaturalized in Irish life about what constitutes good moral authority. Loosening self-identity out of grip of old ideology is an ongoing work of maturity.

Making a decision to report the sexual crimes to the police authorities in 2001/2 was important. It was one of the first overt signs I showed of confronting historical injustice. Up to this point, I was only at the beginning of seeing how a moralistic ideology left its mark on me – moulding quietude and silence as noble virtues. Self-restraint is mental reservation and normative dissociation.

Regarding my own case, the entanglement of old deference within legal frameworks can still be a feature of High Court justices' rulings. Many of our senior judges received their early education within religious ethos settings of Ireland. Daly and Hickey (2015) capture the dynamic of prevailing norms, 'the fact that Judges in constitutional courts so routinely reach different conclusions on the balancing of rights in particular cases suggests that legal disagreements about the nature of rights hinge on precisely the same kind of disagreements that exist in the political community generally' (p. 116). On the morning of the High Court motion in 2012, my senior legal counsel said it could all come down to the personality and gender of the presiding judge. The presiding judge hearing the motion was the President of the High Court the Honourable Mr. Justice Kearns (Record No. 2010/2789P). From the outset, the cards were stacked against me.

Within the advocacy section of the counselling service I attended, the medico/legal representation offered, conceptualized my case in demeaning terminology. The psychiatrist's formulation stated my sexual abuse had a 'fixating impact in terms of my psychosexual orientation.' Nowhere in his assessment did the psychiatrist once refer to Irish society's repressive and infantilizing 'fixation' on homosexuality. It did not appear to dawn on the psychiatrist how historic norms created a further obstacle for gay adult survivors of childhood sexual abuse. Much of traditional psychiatry operates from a biomedical/psychoanalytic frame of reference. This type of knowledge is reductive, potentially homophobic, stigmatizing and injurious. The historic bias for psychoanalytic formulation on sexuality in psychiatry are now discounted as 'malignant prejudices' (Fonagy and Higgit 2007: 213). These ideas defined 'homosexual pleasures as an illness' (Fonagy and Allison 2015: 129). Frankowski (2004) states 'there is no scientific evidence that abnormal parenting, sexual abuse, or other adverse life events influence sexual orientation' (p. 1828).

As part of my case, the psychiatrist concluded the report by stating that 'post-traumatic stress disorder is part of his presentation profile in the general context of Personality Disorder and Homosexuality' (McDDD 2006: 7). The psychiatrist's conclusions strongly resonated with the stigmatic ideas that were so frequently aired on homosexuality. In his assessment, the psychiatrist is largely choosing to efface the impact of discrimination, prejudice and social exclusion of gay people in Ireland and resultant stigma. Instead, he foregrounds the dysfunctionality of my home environment without positioning my home as a subset narrative of social oppression in historic Ireland. He makes little effort to confront state logics that were conducive to the expression of patriarchal violence against women.

In my case, the psychiatrist is decontextualizing these scenes of disempowerment. His truncated lens of understanding felt wounding. There is a clear inference that I am abnormal. He gives no sense that the absence of joy in my presentation style may well be related to the moribund and repressive state logics prevalent in my youth. He does not position how upset, grief, and deep depression nearly succeeded in toppling me. He does not articulate that the 'ultimate success of all forms of oppression is our self-oppression' (*With Downcast Gays* 1974, cited by Duberman 2018).

The broader history of psychoanalysis within psychiatry from the early to mid-twentieth century illuminates its 'deeply disturbing psychiatric effort to reorient homosexual persons to heterosexual preferences' (Kelly 2016: 1). In a further study, Kelly (2016b) says 'there is a paucity of primary evidence' of such practices in Ireland. In this book study, Kelly 'canvassed the opinions and memories of 10 prominent psychiatrists and clinical directors who practiced during the 1950s up to the 2000s and none recalled hearing of ECT being used for the treatment of homosexuality in Ireland, although psychological and aversion therapies were provided' (Kelly 2016b, Chapter 6).

However, pathologizing ideas, particularly in the social context of legal criminalization and moral stigma were the signature fault-lines for understanding homosexuality in Ireland (Mullally 2014; Ferriter 2009; Lacey 2008). The global prescription of heterosexist ideas and the historic pathologization of homosexuality often 'weighed heavily on the mind, spirits, or senses; causing physical or mental distress' (McKechnie 1971: 1256). Many gay men were confronted with social presuppositions which foregrounded innate pathology and criminality arising from discriminatory laws, psychiatry and social/religious customs. For example, Mukherjee (2016) cites the psychiatrist Sandor Lorand's 1956 writings on the topic: 'it is the consensus of many contemporary psychoanalytic workers that permanent homosexuals, like all perverts, are neurotics' (p. 370). The premise of these psychiatric writings was to impress to gay men that there was nothing natural about homosexual desire. These psychiatrists became the secular versions of dark theological prophets. Religious discourses were well anchored in Ireland's imagination, giving rise to deep seated prejudices and incidences of violence against gay men in Ireland. Rather than religious ideas being viewed as social distortions of reasoning, gay men were encouraged to think of themselves as intrinsically disordered.

The re-orienting practices of aversion and conversion therapies appears to have had a significant level of traction in the UK, Europe and North America (Kelly 2016b; Clarke et al. 2010; LeVay 1996; Tatchell 1972). The UK and American Psychoanalytic Association's openly dissuaded gay and lesbian therapists from training as psychoanalysts (LeVay 1996). Richard Isay, a gay psychoanalyst of Cornell Medical College, led the campaign to persuade 'the psychoanalytic association to admit gays and lesbians … Isay had seen many gay men in his practice, including some who had been severely traumatized by earlier efforts at conversion to heterosexuality' (Le Vay 1996: 82–3; Isay 2009). I myself never experienced conversion/reparative therapy. However, I was well immersed in the regulatory thought control of Ireland's disrespecting norms all through the 1970s, 1980s and early to mid-1990s.

Given the early conditions of my youth, combined with social stigma, what did take hold was diminished self-esteem, self-confidence and shame. Stepien (2017), in a chapter entitled 'Social and Historical Conditions of Shame', says that

> Shaming Jews in Nazi Germany as a part of their social exclusion, shaming women in patriarchal society as a way of denying their rights to fully participate in social and political life, or shaming gays by labelling homosexuality as a pathology or a disease, all these practices stem from the shamer's vision of society where no place can be given to those shamed and thus, creating ostracized and marginalized groups. (p. 33)

Acknowledging these societal prejudices in 1970s Ireland, Senator David Norris (1999), reflecting on his fears to run for national Parliament, said it was important 'not to make a meal out of that [being gay], because I was afraid they'd turn me into a freak' (cited by Hug 1999: 217). His election put 'a human face on gay people' (p. 217), confronting the idea that gays 'were child molesters, monsters roving about in the dark, giving Smartie sweets to kids, ready to prance on them … it defused that one, a little bit' (Hug 1999: 217). More recently, Panti's Noble Call at the Abbey Theatre in

2014 referred to the oppressive feel of social bigotry, aired along the lines 'about whether you are safe around children' (O'Neill 2014a). These ideas were enacted within the broader denial of civil, legal and political rights for equal and inclusive citizenship for gay citizens. These prejudicial and stigmatic contexts can and do impair the assertive development of key psychological resources of self-trust, self-respect and self-esteem.

In my case, the psychiatrist conflated my sexual desire with the concept of the arrested homosexual. This is how he objectified my nature. When I received my psychiatric report, I was very angry about his conclusions. However, the advocacy service were paying the bulk of the psychiatrist's consultation fees. Again, the psychiatrist made no real attempt to account for how social silence and homophobia were the social-cultural factors that enacted so much pain and devastation in my young life. Without a critically nuanced analysis of social determinants, the pursuit of justice is distorted. In this, the psychiatrist was putting me at an 'unfair disadvantage when it comes to making sense of "my" social experience' (Fricker 2007, cited by Medina 2017: 41). Furthermore, it is the absence of critical account of Ireland's stigma that makes his account of my experience, truncated, reductive and pathologizing.

My central criticism of psychiatry relates to how it downplays the impact of early social domination and stigma. In my later experience of suicidal intent, the psychiatrist completely evades the religiosity of 1970s Ireland and the further negative impact of HIV in the 1980s for stigmatizing gay identity. In general, international psychiatry has been coming to terms with its past, how it has been slow to implement a changed curricular, reflecting social change and progress (WPA 2016; AAMC 2014; Institute of Medicine 2011). Further research highlights how some gays and lesbians who experienced childhood adversity and abuses are more vulnerable to adult assault, particularly if early stressors led to PTSD, alcohol/drug misuse (Han, et al. 2013) and dissociative strategies for coping with such adversity (Chu 2011). These subsets of experience are in need of recognition, evaluative analysis, refined formulation, conceptualization, intervention and prevention. In measuring health inequalities, the term syndemic is defined 'as a set of closely intertwined and mutually enhancing health problems that significantly affect the overall health status of a population within the context of perpetuating configuration of noxious social conditions' (Singer 1996: 99). Risk is understood as proximate exposure to structural stigma, dysregulating and undermining to the pursuance of self-confidence potentials.

In a Report for the Irish Rape Crisis Network (RCNI 2016) the research findings disclose how LGBTI+ adult persons took twice as long to report sexual crimes than the majority heterosexual population (cited by McGrath 2016). At the launch of the report, Children and Youth Affairs Minister Katherine Zappone said the findings 'demonstrate the fear, the hurt and the isolation felt by LGBT people who are survivors of rape and sexual assault' (McGrath 2016). In effect, the socially woven pattern of historic disrespect, shame and legal exclusion, impeded persons to come forward and report crimes. For some, shame is a factor in disclosing sexual violation. This can even extend to guilt where LGBT persons are left carrying as elevated sense of blame for crimes committed against them.

In March 2016, the World Psychiatric Association stressed the imperative of addressing social discrimination: 'Psychiatrists have a social responsibility to advocate for a reduction in social inequalities for all individuals, including inequalities related to gender identity and sexual orientation' (WPA 2016). Regarding my own diagnosis of personality disorder, it is difficult to ascertain how the psychiatrist arrived at this conclusion from the very few sessions I attended. This type of language is not conducive to opening up the socially woven patterns of psychological stress, as rooted in historic stigmatic norms of Ireland. The psychiatrist needed to be much clearer in situating PTSD, Personality Disorder and HIV in its historical context. Rather than characterize my personality as disordered, he should have been able to articulate the causal historical root of Ireland's oppressive ideology. He chose not to. It is the way he formulates my history that is so wrongheaded. He does not make intelligible, the scenes of my disempowerment. Bromet et al. (2018) say PTSD is 'a chronic, under-detected and untreated psychiatric consequence of trauma that is often linked to new-onset medical and psychological conditions, impaired quality of life and long-term disability across the globe'. What is absent from this perspective is the discourse of human rights violations and health inequity. This would require the lens of psychiatry to confront how social traumas were enacted within historical ideological contexts, the transferences enacted onto consciousness. Martinez and Hinshaw (2017) recognize stigma as 'inseparable from social hierarchies' (p. 999). Kirmayer and Gold (2012) add 'ultimately neurobiological reductionism in psychiatry serves a larger ideology that locates human problems in our brains and bodies rather than in our histories and social predicaments' (p. 308). In agreement, Rose and Abi-Rached (2013) inform us of how 'Conceptions of sociality in social neuroscience are frequently impoverished, reducing social relations to those of interactions between individuals, and ignore decades of research from the social sciences on the social shaping and distributed character of human cognitive, affective, and volitional capacities' (p. 57). The next section further contextualizes my pursuit of justice in the Irish court system.

CHAPTER 16

Further Backdrop to the High Court Action in 2012

In 2004, I commenced a legal case against the De La Salle Order. The case extended to the Diocese of Ardagh and Clonmacnoise in 2009. A motion to dismiss came up for hearing in the Irish High Court in 2012. I lost. The De La Salle Order argued they were not responsible for the inordinate delay. However, CSA (Childhood Sexual Abuse) studies continue to emphasize the length of time it has taken adult survivors of CSA to come forward. In one study, David Finkelhor et al. (1990) have reported a thirty-year time gap from a relatively large sample of 2,626 American men and women. Furthermore, arising from socio-cultural factors, males were more likely than females to conceal childhood sexual abuses (Riggs 2015; Spiegel 2003; Gries et al. 1996; Lamb & Edgar-Smith 1994; Lynch, Stern, Oates & O'Toole 1993; Gordon 1990). Terry et al. (2011), in their executive summary of a research report prepared for the US Conference of Catholic Bishops, state that 'Minors who were abused typically did not disclose their victimization; the signs of abuse were not detected by those close to them. This silence, typical of the period of the 1950s through the 1990s, is one reason why the abusive behaviour persisted' (p. 12). Regarding delay, I would also contend that the theory of religion suggests the experience of suffering is normal. The background logics of Irish history certainly sustained concealment of moral injury. Reductive logics are like that, until other social factors are able to demonstrate that the dogmatic reach of certain hierarchies of knowledge are not always appropriate: 'It is when a whole constellation changes that a specific moral institution can become peculiar, weird, repugnant, or even outlandish and can be thematised, rejected, and denounced by social actors or social movements' (Jaeggi 2018: 40).

The main CSA findings suggest that the reporting of historic cases of childhood abuse were not handled appropriately. Often, sexual predators were protected, their crimes covered up in Ireland and elsewhere (Holohan

2011). The Irish Bishops' Committee on Child Abuse published a report entitled *Time to Listen: Confronting Child Sexual Abuse by Catholic Clergy in Ireland*. The authors of this report conceded that the systemic concealment of historic CSA in Ireland was the dominant response pattern (Goode, McGee & O'Boyle 2003). For many survivors, stories of abuse were disbelieved, and a pursuit of justice by victims ended in defeat through heavy handed legalistic approaches adopted by religious and state authorities (Holohan 2011).

One of the pleas of the De La Salle Order in the Irish High Court in their motion to dismiss in 2012 was that the order would be prejudiced from the outset. The accused, Bro. Bernard, died suddenly in 1985. The De La Salle Order said no other person had come forward with a sexual abuse allegation against him. The order claimed that Bro. Bernard was a man in good standing in the order. At the motion hearing in 2012, both the Diocese of Ardagh and Clonmacnoise and the De La Salle Brothers had not shown much evidence of trying to ascertain if there were other claims of sexual abuse against Bro. Bernard. The presiding judge, Nicholas Kearns maintained that further discovery of abuses was more the responsibility of the plaintiff, not the defendants.

Prior to court, attempts at a fair resolution regarding payment of fees for my education were rejected by the Diocese of Ardagh and Clonmacnoise and the De La Salle Order. Even though the Church in Ireland is in a strong position to know that 'academic problems in childhood persist through adulthood as a history of abuse correlates with a record of undermined educational goals and sub-standard academic outcomes, both incongruent with their potential' (MacMillan 2000, cited by Spiegel 2003: 85). As Ingram (2017) highlights, 'In 1986 the United Nations General Assembly declared the Right to Development (RTD), which affirms that "every human person and all peoples are entitled to participate in, contribute to, and enjoy economic, social, cultural and political development, in which all human rights and fundamental freedoms can be realized"'. Kreide's (2016) formulation is worth noting as an alternative conception of human rights. This theory stresses how political self-determinations are socially configured:

A political conception of human rights, one can say, assumes that human rights are the product of struggles for recognition as political equals. They are placeholders for the political conflict over the correct interpretation and the fair value of human rights. All varieties of oppression, humiliation, and arbitrariness can in principle be thematised in public discourse as violations of human rights – where the outcome is completely open. The realization that we speak of human rights violations when they were committed by agencies of the state enabled us to demarcate them from 'regular' crimes. However, the demarcation is itself in turn a political issue. At the same time, it becomes clear that human rights claims aim to change or create new institutions. Human rights claims are always a political matter. For, however, diverse they may be, they are understood everywhere because they speak the language of the oppressed and emphasize political self-determination. (p. 23)

Formal political discourse needs to be complimented by personal experiences of oppression, to illustrate how social devaluation and stigma is toxic to human potential. The concept of pathology in this study is best thought of as historically induced, a space of reasoning, where many human beings were significantly pained through structural violence and exploitation. Such persons may not grasp how social arrangements have undermined self-determination potentials. Experts can often recreate stigma/shame by not approaching or theorizing this dynamic appropriately. The main reason for this is that the psychological disciplines truncate and occlude how personal narratives as deficit symptoms (e.g. PTSD) are strongly influenced by oppressive ideologies and traumatic situations. Many declarations of human rights are so high sounding regarding inalienable rights, inherent dignity and that people are born free and equal.

As in the previous section, I argued that the diagnosis of PTSD and personality disorder felt stigmatizing. To have particularized my home environment and clerical sexual exploitation as the main causal inference for cognitive atrophy, stress and trauma certainly did not enlighten or emancipate me, with little effort made to 'document the links between social structure, individual subjectivity and well-being' (Hammack 2018).

A key influencer in sustaining this truncated position is through social ignorance, where the purveyors of meaning in the social hierarchy make a determination that damaged persons will simply fade away. My writing of this book is my expression of political self-determination. This is how I choose to practise care for self and others. My writing is oriented toward self-transformation and social transformation. For long periods of time, awful fear has kept me stuck and sick. As a boy and teenager, finding ways to numbing emotional pain was crucial to coping with repetitively shaming adversity. As an adult, understanding these patterns has taken effortful self-critique, education and time. I concur with Slaby and Choudury (2018) on their proposal for a critical neuroscience:

> it is crucial to penetrate beneath the surface of emerging practices, relations and styles into the dynamics of power that may shape or stabilise surface phenomena, facilitate or hinder effective alliances or actions. It is important to reckon with pathological developments and render explicit interest-driven biases, hegemonic schemes of judging, templates of knowing and classifying, dangerous blind spots in interpretations, unquestioned narrative patterns and various unholy material alliances. (p. 351)

The De La Salle Order did make a private minuscule offer with no public admission of responsibility. I felt cheapened on their terms. This offer would not have covered post-graduate part-time education fees, small solicitor fees, and counselling costs for one calendar year. In terms of how this order evaluated the moral injury done to me, I was originally offered a sum of 15,000 euro and this climbed to 25,000 euro closer to the time of the court motion. I rejected these offers. The order were keen to stress my claim against Br. Bernard should be treated with suspicion. I walked away from the hearing downbeat and shamed by the tone of my own senior counsel. He put the blame full square on me, for my lack of gratitude for the work of the solicitor firm working on my behalf. Furthermore, this legal firm forwarded me bills for extra psychiatrist's fees.

As further context to my own adult education, the State subsidizes full-time post-graduate conversion psychological degrees and then underwrites doctoral studies in counselling/clinical psychology for the lucky candidates who succeed in obtaining a place on these courses. On completion, state employment is guaranteed. Because of the highly pressured time constraints of these courses, I had to drop out of this full-time process. It was too stressful for me. At a slower pace in part-time university courses, I was able to pursue my education up to doctoral level. I had to fund the entirety of this long education process through privately raised funds. The part-time route was time-consuming and very isolating.

Prior to the motion hearing in 2012, I had approximated my projected educational costs for these trainings. I forwarded this information through my solicitors to the De La Salle Order and the Diocese of Ardagh and Clonmacnoise. Given that the orders and dioceses had monolithic patronage of Irish education, I thought they would have been open to my education proposal. Instead, I was advised by my solicitor that the De La Salle Order had warned that if I managed to get beyond their motion to dismiss, the De La Salle Brothers said they would appeal such an outcome. They knew I could not afford the costs of same. The religious orders and dioceses can afford the top legal firms to represent them in court. The same legal firms act in their interests for the furtherance of their international investment portfolios (Cision Newsletter 2017; Phelan 2017; Bloomberg 2016; Carswell 2009). Smart power cannot be sustained in a social vacuum. This financial power relates to old religious ethos and its future development. The tentacles of these investments aim to calibrate religious symbolism to key domains of life.

The next section examines how the Diocese of Ardagh and Clonmacnoise have responded to me, since the motion to dismiss my case in 2012.

CHAPTER 17

The Diocese of Ardagh and Clonmacnoise

The Diocese of Ardagh and Clonmacnoise had always stated it had no case to answer. The diocese asked to be excused from having any responsibility arising from these matters at the High Court in 2012. On hearing their rationale, the presiding judge acceded to this request. A year after, in 2013, I informed the Diocese of Ardagh and Clonmacnoise that Bro. Doyle enjoyed systemic access for at least a decade to the schools within the diocese. In 2013, the serving bishop, Dr Colm O'Reilly maintained that no other boys had come forward with claims of sexual abuse by Bro. Bernard. To my knowledge, many boys from Longford were recruited for the De La Salle School in Castletown, Portlaoise. Some of these boys, were also taken away to France by Bro. Bernard Doyle to the birthplace of St Thérèse of Lisieux during the 1970s and early 1980s as part of the preparatory recruitment for the De La Salle school at Castletown.

In the submissions to the High Court, the De La Salle Order did acknowledge that Bro. Bernard organized trips to the continent. Before I entered the Junior Novitiate in Castletown for my first year term in 1978, I was taken to Lisieux by Bro. Bernard. This was during Dr Cahal B. Daly's tenure when Colm O'Reilly was a high-profile priest in the diocese. Colm O'Reilly succeeded Dr Cahal Daly as bishop of the diocese in 1983. For the first time in 2013, a year after the court motion, Bishop O'Reilly made mention that he had been in receipt of a letter from a former teacher at St Michael's Boys National School in Longford. This letter written by Sean Moran stated that external vocational directors did come to St Michael's Boys Primary School in Longford. However, the former teacher had no memory of these religious vocational directors been introduced to the national school by local clerics. Bishop O'Reilly stated in 2013, that if he had been aware of these historic practices and had been bishop, he would not have facilitated recruitment of junior religious vocations. He expressed the view that to inculcate the idea of religious vocation at such a young age was something he was not in favour of. However, this line of thinking raises questions about the legitimacy of the foregrounded right to religious patronage of schools. If, as the bishop suggests, it is too soon to expose a child to ideas relating to religious vocation, is it also not too soon to expose children to religious indoctrination? For example, what pre-ordained right had I to think that my religious faith was privileged over other faith systems (Kitcher 2011). In a state of naive socialization, it was so easy to absorb this view in historic Ireland, given the sheer scale of Catholic symbolism over the social imaginary of Ireland. At the time, I did not have the critical skills to know any different. I believed Church dogma and propaganda as immutable truths, and that I had no inalienable right to question this system of religious patronage. Regarding Bro. Bernard specifically, the bishop said in 2013 that he had no recollection of ever having met Bro. Doyle personally. To be sure, I had never stated that Fr O'Reilly knew that Bro. Bernard sexually molested me at the time. I had simply stated that Fr O'Reilly was the senior cleric who introduced Bro. Bernard to St Michael's Boys National school. Bishop O'Reilly in 2013 said he did not introduce him to the school as I had stated.

Dr Colm O'Reilly as Bishop of Ardagh and Clonmacnoise was first informed of my abuse allegation in 2009. Yet, it took his diocese over four years to bring forward a letter acknowledging that vocational recruitment was a practice in my primary school in the late 1970s and early 80s. Even with this admittance, Bishop O'Reilly still refuted the idea that his diocese had facilitated systemic access for the De La Salle Order to recruit young boys from the national schools in Longford and elsewhere. The bishop said he had consulted other clerics in the diocese, and none of them had any recollection of any diocesan facilitation of these initiatives. This lack of recollection among the clerics is simply not plausible. The De La Salle Order and other religious orders used the dioceses as a supply chain for recruitment for their orders. De La Salle Castletown opened in 1880/1 (Towey 1980). In reference to the De La Salle Order, Bro. Towey's book study of his own order is replete with examples of how the Irish Bishops and the political establishment facilitated the order all over Ireland.

However, Bishop O'Reilly stated that any person with a collar in the late 1970s could have walked into the national schools of religious patronage. He said these visits would not have required prior authorization from the diocese. Once again, I wish to refer to the words of Bro. Bernard Doyle in 1970 when he was school principal at De La Salle College in Churchtown, Dublin. In his writings, this is how Bro. Bernard (1970) accounted for the links between the dioceses and the religious orders. It examples how the educational architecture was most definitely a site for fostering religious vocations: 'Our Parish Priest, his curates and our devoted Jesuit Retreat Masters help our boys in a way we cannot repay. The services they render is sincerely appreciated by all the boys, particularly the seniors. We are happy that four of our Leaving Cert students of last year are now in Arch-Diocesan and other Seminaries. They have our prayers ...'

Furthermore, in 1965, the year before I was born, 'ordinations peaked in Ireland, when 447 priests, including priests from religious orders, those ordained for overseas missions, and approximately 90 diocesan priests, were ordained ... The number ordained in 1965 exceeded the places to be filled in parishes so that some priests had to emigrate on a temporary basis to parishes oversees until places could be found for them at home' (Kennedy 2011: 8). Daly (2016) says 'there was no anti-clerical party in Irish politics ... leading politicians mingled on a regular basis with religious leaders' (p. 195); 'priests were commonly regarded as some combination of political fixer, fundraiser, social worker and entrepreneur' (Daly 2016: 196).

The suggestion by Bishop O'Reilly that the school system was not a mechanism for religious recruitment for both the dioceses and the religious orders is simply not plausible in the context of Ireland's history. Furthermore, at such a young age, there was no other way for Bro. Bernard to gain access to me. This level of access for the De La Salle Order to my national school in Longford had been in place for a very long time. Professor Emeritus of Modern Irish History, Mary E. Daly (2016) succinctly captures the historic pattern: 'Many poor and academically talented students in the past only received secondary or university education by joining a seminary' (p. 198). In reference to homes run by religious in Ireland, Ferriter (2012) refers to how John Bruton had noted in a letter to Liam Cosgrave in the mid-1970s that 'the decline in vocations for religious orders has resulted in a preponderance of lay staff in homes; these will not be satisfied with the conditions of service (including the absence of salary scale) under which the religious have worked' (p. 376). Despite calls for reform of these arrangements, the Minister for Education Richard Burke said his 'department is of the view that nothing should be done which would detract from the voluntary character of all these homes ... and that the state should not interfere in this sensitive area any more than is necessary' (Ferriter 2012: 376). At this time, Fine Gael were very much a right of centre party, consistent with the party's history since the foundation of the Irish state (Meehan 2010; 2013; McGarry 2014). The main opposition party, Fianna Fáil came back into power in 1977 under Jack Lynch with a landslide majority. The Fianna Fáil party were instrumental in forging a close alignment between Church and state since the foundation of the Irish state in the early twentieth century.

My secondary schooling in the early 1980s in Longford involved a number of school retreats given by religious order figures. Indeed, the purpose of Pope John Paul II trip to Ireland in 1979 was to try to reverse the downward trend in religious vocations and faith practices. Ireland was the first port of call for the new Pontiff. There is little doubt in my mind that one of the purposes of the association of religious priests and brothers for spiritual retreats in religious patronage schools contained a wish for vocational discernment and recruitment. This did not have to be explicitly stated or actively sought for by religion. For me and others, the coherence of this social phenomenon was grounded in the assimilation and accommodation of religious tenets in self and national identity (Jaspal and Breakwell 2014). On the question of national school patronage, the Church still defends its right to patronage (Humphreys 2014). Up to 2015, the Church had successfully sought exemption based on its religious ethos from national equality and anti-discrimination legislation.

The position taken by the Diocese of Ardagh and Clonmacnoise to my case feels inconsistent with the exhortation of Pope Benedict XVI (2010) pastoral letter to Irish Catholics. In this letter, the Pope instructed his Irish bishops to desist from their historic practice of a 'misplaced concern for the reputation of the Church and the avoidance of scandal'. In the opening paragraph, the current Emeritus Pontiff gives voice to these concerns:

> I am deeply disturbed by the information which has come to light regarding the abuse of children and vulnerable young people by members of the Church in Ireland, particularly by Priests and Religious. I can only share in the dismay and the sense of betrayal that so many of you have experienced on learning of these sinful and criminal acts and the way the Church authorities in Ireland dealt with them. (Pope Benedict 2010)

In a further section of his unique pastoral letter to Irish Catholics, the Pope states 'I am confident that ... the Bishops will now be in a strong position to carry forward the work of repairing of past injustices and confronting the broader issues associated with the abuse of minors in a way consonant with the demands of Justice and the teachings of the Gospel' (Pastoral Letter 2010).

My call in 2018 is for a full investigation of Bro. Bernard's activities in the Diocese of Ardagh and Clonmacnoise during the 1970s and 1980s. Bro. Bernard visited many schools in Longford. As Kilkelly and O'Mahony (2015) say the culture of secrecy allowed sexual predators 'to operate with impunity for extended periods of time' in the Irish school system (p. 4). Before my mother passed away in 2014, she informed me of another victim of Bro. Bernard in Longford. My mother had been told by the boy's mother of an incident where Bro. Bernard had indecently exposed himself to two boys in Stone Park National School in Longford. This boy's mother is also deceased. When I contacted her son, he said my mother's recollections were untrue. I subsequently discovered Bro. Bernard had visited another boy in my local area. Recently, a brother of this boy reacted in a very angry way when he heard the De La Salle Order's name being referred to. He specifically remembered Bro. Bernard calling to his home for his brother. His tone was very negative.

When I asked Bishop O'Reilly to investigate these matters in 2013, he said he felt under no such obligation to conduct any investigation. He said these matters were the responsibility of the police (Gardaí). Bishop O'Reilly said he was willing to offer pastoral sympathy to potential victims, whenever such incidents had occurred in his diocese. When I met Dr O'Reilly in 2013, he did not directly acknowledge the plausibility of my own account. He offered no formal acknowledgement and no written apology. Neither, did he address the substantive issues I had raised in my prior communications to him. Initially, it took him considerable time to respond to my communication. In 2013, I felt Dr O'Reilly was merely going through an exercise. The bishop's immediate and pressing concerns was focused on the rebuilding of St Mel's Cathedral which had been significantly damaged by fire. I had expected to meet a different person from my recollections of him as a young boy. However, at my request, Bishop O'Reilly did visit my mother in her nursing home. The visit from the bishop was a positive experience for her and my sister. At my request, Bishop O'Reilly also attended her funeral in 2014.

During my meeting in 2013, Bishop O'Reilly never indicated to me that he was prepared to offer a public apology for the alleged abuse incident. Since that time, the newly elected Bishop of Ardagh and Clonmacnoise, Dr Francis Duffy has offered a public apology for historic crimes committed by another diocesan cleric (Shannonside 2015). Thus, it seems reasonable to conclude that the Diocese of Ardagh and Clonmacnoise pick and choose which sexual abuses to be open about in the public domain. Undoubtedly, the Diocese of Ardagh and Clonmacnoise is aware of the large number of local boys who were recruited from the local schools for the De La Salle school in Castletown, Portlaoise. Bro. Towey's historic study of the De La Salle Brothers (1980) continually refers to how his order managed to secure its identity in Ireland. Without bishops, politicians and societal deference, the legitimacy of this order would not have gotten off the ground in Ireland. The order's growth in Ireland was entirely dependent on forging such alliances. The recently published audit of the De La Salle Order in Ireland says: 'Since the De La Salle Brothers came to Ireland in 1880, they have been involved in 64 schools, both Primary and Secondary, as well as three children's residential centres, a teacher training college and three pastoral centres' (NBSCCCI 2017: 6).

These audits are carried out by the National Board for Safeguarding Children for the Catholic Church in Ireland (NBSCCCI 2017). The De La Salle Order gained the trust of Irish people over a long time period (Biancalana 2009). Without question, the Brothers availed of this opportunity to position itself with an oppressed Catholic majority in nineteenth- and early to mid-twentieth-century Ireland. This order could not have achieved this social capital without co-operation from the bishops of the dioceses who are the majority patrons of the school system in Ireland (Towey 1980). Despite requiring the approval of bishops to situate in their dioceses, they are keen to impress that there is no accountability mechanism between the bishops and the religious orders in Ireland. Rather, the religious orders are said to receive their imprimatur from the Vatican in Rome. This explanation is not substantive, considering how the orders created their social identity in Ireland.

The diocese's and the order's choices of deciding not to offer me an apology in the public domain certainly isolated me as the sole complainant of sexual abuse. This strategy may well example how the De La Salle Order and the dioceses are merely protecting each other's interests. The stagecraft of concern by Pope Benedict XVI in his unique pastoral letter to Irish Catholics in 2010 feels more resonant with what the philosopher Charles Taylor (1989) views as 'Trite formulae [that] may combine with the historical sham to weave a cocoon of moral assurance around us which actually insulates us from the energy of true moral sources' (cited by Cooke 2006: 156). Cooke (2006) is referring here to questions of 'how articulation of moral sources can be evaluated rationally' (p. 156). Cooke adds that Taylor: 'seems prepared to admit that articulations may be "propaganda" rather than "words of power": they may insulate us from the power of moral sources rather than bring us closer to them, feed our self-conceit rather than empower us, and serve sinister purposes such as reinforcing a discreditable status quo' (Cooke 2006: 156).

As I mentioned in previous sections, Irish life in 1979 came to a standstill for the visit to Ireland of a newly elected Pope. John Paul II knew the developmental possibilities for religious faith in Ireland. Catholic ethos was a significant influencer in becoming a member of a self-governing social/political community. The Church had a foregrounded institutional status and its key tenets have always been substantively aligned with majoritarian intent. John Paul II knew that religious aims could not be achieved in a social vacuum. It required ongoing political and social capital. My own conscience was shaped to observe a repressive silence, where I had internalized oppressive concepts that distorted my abilities and capabilities to meaningfully deal with life on life's terms. Accompanied by my friend, when I met with the bishop in 2013, I felt I was breaking through walls of silence. I did not feel truly received at this meeting. I thought Bishop O'Reilly would have been keener to learn more and discover more about how this Vocations Director had recruited boys through diocesan schools in historic time. This was naïve on my part. I needed to subvert my own certainties, rather than being seduced by own deferential modes of subjection. In other words, I needed to be better prepared for understanding how power is exercised in all its depth and complexity. This dynamic is so more transparent to me than it once was, where I walk into situations, ill-prepared for grasping how a 'cocoon of moral assurance' still envelopes modes of my thinking. By maturely recognizing how my own history is enacted, I can take responsibility for it. I can say this is who I am. Repressing this reality, creates blindsides, one-sidedness and can give rise to resentment and dangerous fury. I want to decentre from this pattern. I do not want to be infected by vengeful states of mind, because I have enough autobiographical experience to know the total misery and suffering that fury perpetuates. The next section looks at the history of the De La Salle in Dublin where Bro. Bernard resided at HQ in Churchtown when I first met him in 1977.

CHAPTER 18

The Dublin Archdiocese and the Early History of De La Salle Brothers

The Dublin Archdiocesan website provides continuing recognition and legitimacy for the work of the De La Salle Order in Dublin. The De La Salle Provincialate (HQ) was based in Dublin. As a further backdrop to my own story, the Dublin Archdiocese had been aware how the De La Salle Order were prepared to positively defend the reputation of Bro. Bernard Doyle at the High Court motion in 2012. This is despite knowing that Bro. Bernard had been referred to as a 'dubious figure' and a 'figure of loathing.' This character reference came from within the Dublin Archdiocese itself. This information related to Bro. Bernard's tenure as a School principal in Churchtown, Dublin. However, just like the Diocese of Ardagh and Clonmacnoise, the Dublin Archdiocese claimed it had not received any other child sexual abuse allegation against Bro. Bernard Doyle.

Bro. Bernard was headmaster of De La Salle College in Churchtown from 1968 to 1972. He served as principal for a number of schools in Dublin and surrounding environs. As school principal at Churchtown, Bro. Doyle turned up at an official school function, drunk, missing his seat, falling down where parents and students were present. During this historic period, a former student of De La Salle Churchtown informed me how Bro. Bernard secured the nickname 'Bubbles' because of his well-known drinking. This former De La Salle student referred to his own school trip to Lisieux in France. In the hostel, in the company of his school friend, he remembered out of nowhere, Bro. Bernard started punching him in the back. He later reported this incident to the De La Salle Order in 1995. The student stated how his own father was a devout Catholic and was never inclined to speak ill of a religious person. From his memory of his father, the former student said the exception to this rule was Bro. Bernard, the principal of the De La Salle School Churchtown in Dublin.

On the same school trip to Lisieux, the former student recalled how he had little choice to sit with Bro. Bernard for much of the train journey between Germany and France. Bro. Bernard had nominated himself to care for him. The student had sustained a leg injury. He recalled that Bernard's talk was puritan and confusing. He recalled how Bro. Bernard praised German youth as moral exemplars of discipline and control. Regarding his own experience, this student could only speculate on the reasons for Bro. Bernard's violence toward him. He said his older brother had previously attended the De La Salle Schools in Churchtown. On his way to Lisieux, the former De La Salle student mentioned that he met his older brother at a stop off in the UK en route to Europe. He thought Bro. Bernard may have caught sight of his older brother's flower power appearance.

Referring to this generation who had emigrated to the UK after schooling, Prof. Tom Inglis (2012) also a former pupil at De La Salle Churchtown in the 1950s and 1960s, says 'We could see and hear the Sixties from across the water in Britain. We headed there as soon and as often as we could. It was the promised land of freedom, pleasure, music, sex and drugs' (p. 58). Taking this background into account, it is more than plausible that Bro. Bernard saw his role in authority where he should fight against these trends. Back then, religious persons were always speaking about the ills of the modern world. In previous decades, I have no doubt a greater percentage of persons had to listen to these evil warnings. Bro. Bernard was not violent towards me. He chose a much more seductive method to wean a young boy into his world.

In the order's affidavit to the High Court, the De La Salle Brothers viewed my allegation against Bro. Bernard with 'shock and scepticism.' In 2012, I informed the former De La Salle Churchtown student, how the order provided a glowing character reference for Bro. Bernard. This man said the order's claim of no prior complaint against Bro. Bernard was incorrect. This pupil said he had made his complaint to the De La Salle Order in 1995. He had stated that Bro. Bernard had physically assaulted him in Lisieux in France. He said he made this complaint at the same time he was reporting another De La Salle Brother for sexual abusing him as a minor. Thus, in relation to Bro. Bernard, he felt the order were creating a misleading impression. While the De La Salle Order acknowledged Bro. Bernard had frequently organized trips to the continent for school pupils, the order claimed that they did not make the connection from their records (19 January 1995; Personal communication 2009) that this historic complaint of physical assault in France was referring to the Vocational Director Bro. Bernard. This strategy enabled the De La Salle Order to stand over their prior affidavit of never having received any other complaint against Bro. Bernard.

Further context is provided by Professor Tom Inglis (2012) of cruel discipline and violence meted out on young pupils at De La Salle Churchtown. As a former pupil, Inglis recalls how he ended up severely punished for a note he had written and circulated in class. The written message was 'Don't kiss your girlfriend tonight, there is danger under her lips' (p. 52). On discovery, Tom was 'fingered' (p. 52) as the culprit. The enraged reaction of his teacher was then to take out his 'leather and he started to wallop my hands' (p. 52). As to what was written was beyond the 'normal offense' (p. 52) Bro. Bernard, his primary teacher called in the headmaster. Just to point out this is not same Bro. Bernard I have been talking about in this book. This is another Bro. Bernard who was Tom's sole teacher for the duration of primary (preparatory) school. Inglis says this brother engaged the same ritual every morning where 'he paraded up and down the rows as we sang out the morning rosary. He loved to hear the classroom resonate with the devotion of young boys in full prayer. He had a simple strategy: if you did not pray loud enough, he beat you' (p. 51). Bernard, tired from his morning exertions would sometimes snooze in class in the afternoons. It was rumoured that this brother's private parts could be seen, while he slept in class. Regarding the specific incident of circulating the note, described as 'such filth' (p. 52) by his teacher, Inglis (2012) describes what happened next, when his primary teacher came back into class with the headmaster:

> They both stormed back into the classroom. Flory (Florence) grabbed me by the ear and pulled me down the stairs into his office. He was ranting. He could not contain his rage. He fumbled for the cane behind the door. He was a small, fat man. He lashed into me. He was sweating heavily. The lashing and running up and down the stairs had taken their toll. After a number of lashes, he stopped for a breather. It was

my moment of salvation. He gasped: 'How could you write such a thing?' 'A boy from High School told me,' I said. I had played the Protestant Card. It worked like magic. It was a complete lie, but he believed me. (p. 52–3)

This religious context of sectarianism and the close alignment of religious brothers and priests with Irish Republicanism is well documented in historical sources (Daly 2016; Biancalana 2009; Coldrey 1988). Further evidence of this violent pattern was confirmed by the former student I earlier referred to. Apart from experiencing violence and sexual abuse himself, he also witnessed extreme violence in Churchtown. The former De La Salle pupil says the following incident was above the 'cultural norm of chastisement.' He says 'I recall one incident, for example, where one boy came to school with bandages on his hands due to a beating he had received from a brother. This brother flew into a rage and ripped the bandages off. All of these experiences were seen through the eyes of a child' (Affidavit communication 2009). This is the same brother who the former pupil reported to the order in 1995 for sexual abuse. The use of corporal punishment of children in schools was banned in the early 1980s in Ireland.

I subsequently discovered from another person when Bro. Doyle was principal of Beneavin De La Salle College in Finglas in North Dublin, Bernard did not report a priest from the Passionist religious order who sexually assaulted a pupil at the school. This incident occurred in 1967/8 in the context of religious confession which formed part of a day retreat at the De La Salle school in Finglas. This young boy was in a shocked state when he came back to his friends after the experience. After telling his peers what had happened, his classmates supported him by bringing him to the principal's office. As principal, Bro. Bernard dealt with the incident by halting the retreat and banishing the priest from the school. Bro. Bernard then gave the boys the remainder of the day off. No promised follow-up investigation occurred after the incident. The boy or his parents heard no more about it.

Despite all the above regarding Bro. Bernard's behaviour, Bro. Pius McCarthy of the De La Salle Brothers in an affidavit on 27 July 2011 still maintained Bro. Bernard was correct in his behaviour and this is the universal view of others in the Order with whom I have spoken with who knew him. I find it very difficult to believe that the allegations made could be true but of course, it is now impossible to investigate these allegations as Bro. Bernard was long dead when the allegations were first made to the Order.

These positive appraisals of Bro. Bernard are not plausible. However, the order's defence is consistent with the overall pattern of systemic avoidance of responsibility, effacement and erasure. Thus, after this dubious tenure as school principal, the De La Salle Order have a case to answer for why they propelled Bro. Bernard into the position of National Vocations Director for the De La Salle Order. Surely, Bernard's previous behaviour and deportment could not have gone unnoticed by his peers in his order? Bro. Bernard's behaviour is simply not consistent with how an esteemed school principal would behave with pupils and parents in school settings. Given the systemic pattern, it seems to me the order are consistent in downplaying the significance of important contextual information for one of their most senior deceased brothers.

Referring to the history of the Irish Christian Brothers, Coldrey (1993) maintains a crossover with the De La Salle Order in Paris by the 1820s resulted in a significant change of direction in school discipline. In 1802, the Irish Christian Brothers were founded by Edmund Ignatius Rice, a wealthy merchant in Waterford City (Wall 2013). In Coldrey's account, he explains the historical roots of corporal punishment, highlighting the negative influence of the De La Salle Brothers on the Christian Brothers. As a response to the anticlericalism of the French Revolution, a further broader trend in Church politics was the Vatican teaching of papal infallibility at the First Vatican Council (1869–70) by Pope Pius IX (r. 1846–1878). Pius IX was also responsible for creating a truth dogma for Blessed Virgin Mary's Immaculate Conception in 1854, making him one of the most controversial popes in Church history (Howard 2017). Nearly twenty-five years later in Ireland, the Virgin Mary was said to have appeared to locals in Knock, Co. Mayo in 1879 after Mary had appeared in Lourdes in 1858 and afterward again in Fatima in 1917. These ideas were moulded into public consciousness by senior Irish clerics trained in Rome. Cardinal Cullen, Cardinal Logue and Archbishop McQuaid were most notable in this regard. In reference to the Christian Brothers, Coldrey (1993) says,

> By 1814 the Brothers could claim that they had managed their pupils more through love than fear and had removed 'as much as possible, everything like corporal punishment from their schools, a plan which is found to answer the best purpose in the formation of youth.' By the 1820s the Irish Brothers were in touch with the headquarters of the French Brothers of the Christian Schools in Paris (De La Salle Brothers). It was from this source that they received an important disciplinary instrument, the leather strap. This leather slapper – 13 inches long, 1.25 inches wide and .25 inches thick' used only on the hand, was a mild instrument of discipline in terms of contemporary schools in the British Isles. In fact, use of the strap did not qualify as corporal punishment at the time. (p. 345)

By the late twentieth century, Wall (2013) says the reputation of the Irish Christian Brothers was

> blackened by a series of scandals that exposed widespread sexual, physical and emotional abuse of children in the Order's care, stretching back over decades. Ireland was not the only country of widespread physical abuse, as such crimes occurred in every country the Order had a presence, including Canada, the United States and Australia. Ireland was in fact the last country to deal with these scandals as they were ignored and were covered up for so long. Sex abuse was rife in the Industrial Schools that the Christian Brothers ran.

Towey (1980) adds further context to the founding name and governing structure of the De La Salle Order itself:

> The proper title of the De La Salle Congregation (Order or Institute) is Fratres Scholarium Christianarum (F.S.C.), that is, Brothers of the Christian Schools, their crest, a five-pointed star, and motto, 'Signum Fedei'. The Superior of each house, or community, of the Order is called 'Director'. Houses are grouped into 'Provinces' and at the head of each 'Province' is a 'Visitor or 'Provincial', who has a Provincial Council, or District Council, to advise him. The District Chapter, the legislative and pastoral assembly of the brothers, is a means for all the brothers to share in the government of the Province. The head of the Institute is the Superior General, now usually called 'the Superior' who, to assist him has a group of Councillors and together they make up the General Council, or the 'Council.' (p. 9–10)

My aim in writing is to extend a stronger picture of how the normative impulse of historical secrecy ends up calibrated at deep levels of self-organization, where the self is often moulded to believe or leans into believing that putting up with bad behaviour is par for the course. Howard (2017) thinks of historical analysis as follows:

> To understand, to achieve historical insight, one must seek to enter the mind-set, the mentality, of the historical actor, in all its vexing complexity and in its difference from the assumptions and convictions of subsequent generations. This fundamental task of historical inquiry, as difficult as it is necessary, always proceeds through a tangled web of motivations, beliefs, ideas, impersonal forces, individuals and institutions. Nonetheless, the historian's proper business is fidelity to the past in all its messiness and stubborn otherness, understanding the past qua past, not insofar as it measures up or fails to meet present-day sensibilities. (Howard 2017: 10)

Emeritus Professor of Politics at UCD, Tom Garvin (1986) has stated that 'Irish political culture is secretive, and the public and private faces of political actors are often very different'. To make good on Garvin's observation, it is important to further excavate the social-political scenes of Irish history and its evolvement in the present. Such issues are significant and often relate to an equitable and just society. Some members of minority groups are often targeted because they are perceived as easy to exploit and silence. In this sense, the issues raised in the book have wider resonance, because of how powerful constellations in Irish society get to reproduce certain notions of objectivity and regulation. Some academic questions are actively discouraged over others. A culture committed for so long to certain ways of knowing over others takes time to change. Some of us may not grasp how normative ideals were learned and intensively reinforced in self-beliefs. These levels of denial/subjugation means that academic knowledge may not be as socially transformative as it ought to be. Very seldom do we consider that some subset patterns of mental illness are the outcomes of structural violence in Irish history. Ingrained patterns of denial from a dark past can hurt minds in significant ways in the present, potentially destroying life opportunities and even shortening lives. Fossilized practices and ingrained policy habits in modern social/neuroscience research do not capture denial states as biosocial imprints. Instead, the pressure is placed on individuals to reconfigure the ill effects of history. Alternatively, Bernstein (2015) in his essay on moral injury says that

> If devastation is loss of trust in the world, and trust in the world is what allows us to forget our existential helplessness, then trust must be both deep, connected to our most fundamental conceptions of who we are as persons, and pervasive, contouring and underwriting all our everyday social interactions (or explicitly not so doing when conditions to trust are palpably absent). (p. 17)

The following section tracks how the De La Salle Order developed their presence as a teaching order in Dublin. Prior to the installation of Dr John Charles McQuaid as Archbishop of Dublin, the De La Salle Brothers had not managed to gain a presence as a teaching order in Dublin. This all changed with Dr McQuaid's elevation to the most important Church position in Ireland.

The De La Salle Order in Dublin under Archbishop John Charles McQuaid and After

In 1940, when John Charles McQuaid became Archbishop of Dublin, there were 370 priests in the Archdiocese and 99 students in the diocesan seminary; by 1965, the year of his golden jubilee, there were 550 priests and 140 seminarians .... A further 141 men were ordained for foreign dioceses .... Half of all priests ordained in the early 1960s left Ireland for service overseas. (Daly 2016: 192)

Cooney (1999) says there was a strong link between the De La Salle Order and the Archbishop of Dublin, Dr John Charles McQuaid. During his tenure in Dublin, Dr McQuaid was keen to translate his respect for the De La Salle Brothers by extending to them a presence in his diocese. He wanted the brothers to be part of educating his flock. Prior to his appointment as Dublin Archbishop, Fr McQuaid, as a Holy Ghost Father, studied in Rome. Cooney (1999) says at the beginning of the twentieth century, Rome was a 'highpoint of his career to date' (p. 51). In Rome, Fr McQuaid got the opportunity to 'meet "the Pope of the Missions," Pope Pius XI, Christ's Representative on Earth' (p. 51). Cooney (1999) adds this time period for Fr McQuaid in the papal city also marked the Holy Year of Jubilee, when

1,500,000 came to the eternal city as pilgrims ... with the prestige of the papacy reaching new heights, Pope Pius staged a number of impressive canonization ceremonies in St Peter's Square, including those of a number of saints to whom McQuaid was devoted, like St Therese of Lisieux, St John Baptist Vianney, more popularly known as the Curé d'Ars, St John Baptist de la Salle and St John Eudes. (p. 51)

As previously stated, Cooney (1999) says when Fr McQuaid was installed as the Archbishop of Dublin, the bishop was instrumental in progressing the work of the De La Salle Brothers in education in the 1950s. Cooney (1999) states: 'As a result of his admiration for the seventeenth century French educationalist John Baptist De La Salle, McQuaid lifted the veto on the participation of the De La Salle teaching order in Dublin' (p. 236). De La Salle Brother, Dr John Towey (1980) concurs with Cooney's analysis:

> For more than half a century, the De La Salle Brothers felt a certain frustration that they had not been able to establish themselves in any of the major Cities and especially in the Capital .... All this changed, however, with the appointment of John Charles McQuaid as Archbishop of Dublin ... He had received part of his early training as a Holy Ghost Father in France where he had met and admired the De La Salle Brothers and had made a study of their founder. (p. 533)

In his historical study of the De La Salle Order in Ireland, Bro. Towey (1980) says Archbishop McQuaid officiated at the openings of the De La Salle schools across Dublin. In his personal memoir, Inglis (2012) says it was during the 1950s that Dublin's boundaries began to expand with 'myriads of young married couples producing young children who had to be educated. The De La Salle Brothers moved in to provide their services' (p. 51). In 1952, De La Salle Churchtown was 'blessed and officially inaugurated by Dr. McQuaid' (Towey 1980: 537). Tom Inglis, now Associate Professor of Sociology at UCD, has written extensively on the history of Catholicism in Ireland (Inglis 2005; 1998). Inglis (2012) describes his schooling at De La Salle Churchtown in the 1950s and 1960s:

> I detested most of my school days. I was inspired by some of my teachers but there was too much emphasis on discipline and control. Most of what remains of those days is a feeling of fear. We were beaten regularly for small misdemeanours and minor mistakes. Often, the beatings were simply routine. You were asked a question, and if you got it wrong, you had to leave your desk, and when the questioning was over, you lined up to be beaten. Some days the teachers were bored and they did not put much effort into the beatings; they might even yawn in between each one. Other days they were very angry and they took it out on us. (p. 55)

On further reflection, Inglis (2012) says his experience and that of his friends in their private fee-paying section of the De La Salle school in Churchtown turned out to be a 'faint test' (p. 56). Here, Inglis is situating his experience with what had happened in other public schools run by the religious orders in Ireland. He adds, 'I know that while I was being beaten, boys of my own age were not just being beaten by religious brothers and priests, but terrorized, brutalized and raped' (Inglis 2012, p. 57). However, faint the experience, Inglis (2012) still mentions where the elderly De La Salle Brothers retire to. He then poses the question to himself 'Maybe I should go to Castletown to forgive and forget, but I can't' (p. 57). His reluctance is best understood from the sheer scale of violence/abuses which have subsequently come to light (e.g. Wall 2013; Tyrrell 2007; Raftery and O'Sullivan 1999). Ferriter (2014) says many children from

> the 1920s-1960s in particular, were failed by the contract between the dependent generations, had no rights recognized, and were burdened with responsibilities that should not have been theirs, often as result of institutionalization. The harrowing treatment afforded to unmarried mothers and the abuse of children was an illustration of collaboration between state, church, and society in refusing to deal humanely with the deprived, or the so-called 'fallen' of Irish society and a determination to contain them out of sight. (Citing the critical tenor of historian Joe Lee's analysis, Ferriter 2014: 680)

Adding further context to his own schooling, Inglis (2012) said the pattern in Churchtown had a wounding impact on adult lives (p. 50–8). He mentions a Bro. Thomas as the 'most cruel' (p. 56). This De La Salle Brother taught physics, a subject that the author said he did not excel at (p. 56). Inglis (2012) states that 'the beatings were brutal and ritualistic' (p. 56). He adds, 'I never really liked or trusted the brothers, but soon, like many others, I began to despise and laugh at them' (p. 57). That said, Inglis (2012) says, 'Even though I might have left the Church, it had not left me. No matter how much I tried to change, there were continual deep feelings of shame, guilt, awkwardness and embarrassment, not just about sex, but any form of desire or self-indulgence' (p. 55).

Inglis (2012) gives further context to his school experience, and how his love for his now deceased wife in 2005, enabled deep healing from the negative effects of early socialization:

The years of sexual repression into which I had been born, which had been inculcated by my parents and the De La Salle Brothers, were cast off like old skin. I was with this warm, loving woman who showed me how to play without fear of losing, who encouraged me to make new moves, who took my hand and led me through fields of love and sex ... I was willing and able to put myself on the line with a woman without any fear of shame or embarrassment. (p. 90)

Even during the latter part of his tenure as Dublin Archbishop, Dr McQuaid still held firm against the more progressive intent of Pope John XXIII Second Vatican Council (1962–5). As part of his resistance, Dr McQuaid lobbied and received Vatican approval for a resonant theology in the formation of his clerical seminarians and Catholic educators at Clonliffe College Dublin and at the Mater Dei Institute of Education respectively (Cooney 1999).

During the 1960s, Archbishop McQuaid felt vindicated in his right-wing positions when Pope Paul VI succeeded John XXIII. In 1968, Archbishop McQuaid interpreted *Humanae Vitae* [*On Human Life*] (1968) as 'infallible' even though the teaching had not been presented as infallible by Pope Paul VI himself. Archbishop McQuaid tried to ensure the outright ban of contraception in the vast social/medical care architecture under his control (Cooney 1999: 393). Even though the 1960s is often viewed as a period of change in the context of 'Vatican II, the arrival of television and the potential of EEC membership' (Meehan 2013) substantive social and economic transformations were slow to evolve. Meehan (2013) gives a flavour of the appetite for change from some members of Fine Gael in the 1960s. Citing the social mindedness of Declan Costello, a politician/jurist and social reformer, Declan was a son of John A. Costello, a member of Cumann na nGaelheal. John A. Costello had served two terms as Taoiseach for two inter-party governments from 1948 to 1951 and 1954 to 1957. Meehan (2013) says that in 1964, Declan Costello (1927–2011)

put before Fine Gael a set of proposals designed to transform the party and which offered a blueprint for a new Ireland through greater state involvement. They represented a significant break with traditional Fine Gael policy .... and caused considerable unease within the party, especially its rural members ... Although he was never party leader and the 'Just Society' effectively remained an un-tested document, he effected change by encouraging a new generation of politicians into the party, most notably Garret FitzGerald.

Meehan's book (2013) traces the 'discontinuities between Costello's Just Society policy document of 1964/65 and Fitzgerald's Constitutional Crusade in the 1980s' (p. 1), highlighting how on 'issues of a moral nature' there was still a lack of 'willingness to embrace change.' Meehan highlights some paradoxes in Costello's career. Having served as Attorney General in the 1973–77 Fine Gael-Labour coalition, Declan Costello went on to become a High Court judge and President of the High Court. Recognizing Costello's distinguished career 'if at times controversial,' (p. 18) Meehan (2013) says:

> Some of the more controversial cases in which he was involved appear to draw into question his commitment to social justice. Eileen Flynn, a teacher at a Catholic convent school, was dismissed from her post because she lived openly with a married man whose wife had left him and with whom she had had a child. Her case challenging the dismissal was heard in the High Court by Costello in March 1985; she had already lost appeals in the Employment Appeals Tribunal and in the Circuit Court. Costello also found that her dismissal was not unfair. Noting that Flynn was employed by a religious, not a lay, school, he remarked, 'I do not think that the respondents over-emphasised the power of example on the lives of the pupils in the school. ... More controversially, he was the High Court judge in the 1992 X case who granted the request of the Attorney General Harry Whelehan for a temporary injunction to prevent a fourteen-year-old girl, pregnant as a result of rape, from traveling to Britain for an abortion. (p. 19)

Meehan (2013) outlines distinctions that Costello offered for the different functions of politicians and judges and while conceding the point on different functions, Meehan presses her argument that even Declan Costello's Just Society proposals 'did not touch on or recommend reform on matters of a moral nature' (p. 19). A persistent theme in her book is that all through the history of Fine Gael, while acknowledging different positions among party members, Meehan maintains there has been a significant tendency in the party to be morally conservative.

Consistent with this interpretation, it is worth noting that when Enda Kenny declared his support for marriage equality in November 2013, Fine Gael were the last major political party in Ireland to declare that it would canvas for a Yes vote in support of marriage equality (O'Regan 2014). With the notable exceptions of the smaller parties, namely Labour, Sinn Fein and the Greens, most of the mainstream political parties in Ireland's history have been mostly deferential to the normative impulse of the status quo. However, in 2017, the FG party were the first political party to elect a gay man as its party leader. Leo Varadkar won, despite a significant challenge from Simon Coveney, a senior FG minister. Varadkar was also replacing a serving FG Taoiseach, Enda Kenny when he became Taoiseach himself. Leo Varadkar, in coming out as gay in 2015, went on to play an important role in support of the referendum for marriage equality. As Minister for Health, he advanced progressive policies for minority sexual and gender persons and groups. Since becoming Taoiseach, he has visibly supported local LGBT initiatives, including attendance at annual Pride Parades in North and South Ireland. In October 2017, Taoiseach Leo Varadkar and Minister for Children Katherine Zappone were among the award winners at a Ceremony in Dublin. The GALAS Awards, are co-organized by GCN and the National LGBT Federation (Independent Newsdesk 2017). The next section deals with recent developments for the De La Salle Brothers.

CHAPTER 20

Recent Developments for the De La Salle Order and Revelations of Concealed Historic Abuses

A childhood memory that comes to mind was the time when I was brought by Bro. Bernard to the birthplace of St Thérèse of Lisieux in France. The Vocations Director referred to St Thérèse as 'petite' and 'little' in her saintly ways of being. St Thérèse had a short life. Bro. Doyle said St Thérèse had endured great suffering but still managed to become a saint. Thérèse is also referred to as 'The Little Flower of Jesus.' Bernard in 1977/8 was comparing her situation to mine. I was all ears. To me as a young boy, these teachings on St Thérèse were consistent with how Dr McQuaid and my local bishop Dr Cahal B. Daly positively interacted with her legacy (Cooney 1999; Daly 1998). Within this theological discourse, spiritual formation is built through the notion of sacrifice for a greater good. In this scheme, developmental modes of self-confidence are not encouraged. Rather, to doubt oneself is prudent and virtuous. To be small and know one's place in the overall scheme of things and to abnegate self to a higher cause is recommended. To confront the social order is a vice.

As a young boy, this dynamic is a story of Ireland's legislative history which had a tentacle like grip of my modes of understanding. What I am saying is that a stressed young boy, found it difficult to decentre and not be constituted by these thought insertions from the normative order. Bro. Bernard provided proximate reinforcement for the national prescription to overcome sin and redeem oneself in the eyes of God. While there was more radical ideas circulating across the world – not so, in my relatively enclosed home town of 1970s Ireland. Over a century later, the impulse of the First Vatican Council (1869–1870) was still all too evident. This veil of ignorance and dogma still enjoyed significant anchorage in social traditions in 1970s, 1980s and 1990s Ireland.

Since 1996, the bones of St Thérèse had been touring the globe (*Independent* 2001). In 1997, Pope John Paul II made St Thérèse a Doctor of the Church (Vatican Info. Service 2011). The Relics of St Thérèse of Lisieux toured chapels and churches throughout Ireland during April and May 2001 (*Independent* 2001). In 2011, Pope Benedict XVI in a general audience at St Peter's Square 'dedicated his catechesis to St. Therese of Lisieux' referring to her as 'Little Therese' (Vatican Info. Service 2011). Pope Benedict continued, 'she never failed to help the most simple souls, the little ones, the poor and the suffering who prayed to her' (Vatican Info. Service 2011). Dr Joseph Schmidt of the De La Salle Brothers has written a book on Theresa's life entitled *Walking the Little Way of Thérèse of Lisieux* (2012). He frequently delivers talks on her life, available on YouTube (Schmidt 2013). As I have emphasized in earlier sections, these discourses were part and parcel of my early development. Critical to the success of imbibing these ideas is where the child feels they are at the centre of the prophecy. Being enveloped in this way, is key to understanding systemic concealment of moral injury. It is also key to grasping why deep social transformation is often so slow to emerge. The De La Salle ideas merge with the emphasis that is placed on the quieted self on the way to sainthood. For example, Pope John Paul II encouraged popular piety and dogma while Cardinal Ratzinger saw the theology of the Church as a stoic counter-cultural force to the emergent trends of modernity (Fuller 2002; Hug 1999). Without question, these 'distinct forms of historical selfhood' (Toews 2004) were significant cultural repertoires in the imaginary of historic Ireland.

Regarding the legacy of historical abuses, Ireland's former Minister for Education Ruairi Quinn met with the religious orders in 2011 (Dept of Education 2011). The De La Salle Order were represented at this meeting. Minister Quinn was trying to impress upon the religious orders to make good on their financial commitments of 50:50 contributions from an earlier agreement in 2002. A financial correspondent for *The Irish Times*, Simon Carswell (2009) says:

> The De La Salle Brothers were one of 18 religious orders that signed up to the 2002 redress claims made by abuse victims in exchange for payments and property capped at 127 million Euro. The total bill for the redress scheme is estimated at about 1.3 billion (euro) and the religious orders have come under pressure to reduce the cost to the State

A section of the transcript from the meeting, illustrates how the De La Salle representative interacted with the minister in 2011. Bro. Manning said, 'The essential role of congregations was to carry out a mission, if they are prevented from doing so they will no longer have a reason to exist' (Dept of Education 2011). Bro. Manning said he was struggling to understand what 'fair and reasonable' meant. In this, he wondered how small congregations could be treated on the same basis as the government in terms of assets? Bro. Manning was the named defendant for the De La Salle Order in the High Court in 2012. After much delay responding to my written communications since the court hearing, Bro. Manning (2015) at the De La Salle Provincialate finally replied regarding my request for an investigation into Bro. Bernard's tenure. Bro. Manning's response was brief and to the point:

> I now write to you to let you know that, having considered your request, I am not in a position to carry out a meaningful inquiry/investigation into the life of Bro. Bernard Doyle because he is thirty years deceased and we have no other complaint of sexual abuse against him. I wish you every blessing and success.

In 2017, the first audit of the De La Salle Order in the Republic of Ireland was published by the National Board for Safeguarding Children in the Catholic Church (NBSCCC 2017). In an overview, the auditors 'highlight concerns relating to weak or, on occasion, poor practice which require urgent corrective action' (p. 1). The report said the order's 'records were not well maintained, making the work of the reviewers difficult' (p. 1). The publication of the audit on the De La Salle Brothers in the Republic of Ireland was delayed because of the HIA 2017 (Historical Institutional Abuse Inquiry). This inquiry contained a module on the work of the De La Salle Brothers in Northern Ireland. Both the Southern and Northern Provinces are accountable to the same De La Salle Provincial/Superior General based in Dublin. The HQ has more recently moved to the UK.

The Northern Inquiry published its findings in January 2017. Sir Anthony Hart's QC report contained twenty-seven bulleted points of systemic failures in the protection of children under the care of the De La Salle Order at Rubane House. The Diocese of Down and Conor had invited the Brothers to run this home from the 1950s. The NI inquiry examined allegations of physical and sexual abuse at Rubane House, Kircubbin, in

Northern Ireland between 1951 and 1986. Sir Anthony Hart's QC HIA Inquiry (2017) says the scale of the incidences of abuse and maltreatment at the Northern Ireland De La Salle home were systemic in nature, whereby a culture existed that served to undermine the welfare of children.

The HIA Inquiry also found the diocese were negligent and not proactive in the protection of children. Dr Cahal Daly was in charge of this diocese during the 1980s after he left Longford in 1981/2. The report by Sir Anthony states:

> We consider that the chaplains should have found a means of alerting the bishop in a more general way to concerns about sexual abuse in Rubane and that as far as we are aware this failure to do so contributed to the continuance of that abuse in Rubane. We consider this to be a systemic failure by the Diocese to ensure that children were kept free from abuse and a systemic failure to ensure the institution provided proper care. (HIA 2017, 405: 106)

Previously the BBC reported on the systemic concealment of crimes in 2014:

> The inquiry heard that in a letter to the brother against whom the allegations were made, the senior cleric referred to one boy's accusations and assured him: 'Don't think for a moment that I am accepting his word against yours.' He added: 'I advise that no reference is to be made at any time or to anyone regarding the inquiry, it is best forgotten and I have told some brothers that no reference is to be made to it among themselves or the boys. 'The whole affair is best dropped'. (BBC 2014)

A transcript example from the HIA Inquiry is the Witness Testimony of No. 56, a former resident of Rubane House, reads:

> I have gone through life feeling sad and empty. I feel drained. I feel I have no worth, no value. I am lonely. I feel excluded and isolated. I wonder why I am different. I question 'is there something wrong with me?' I am clamped to the past. I have no qualifications, no employment prospects. I feel completely and utterly contaminated by abuse. I am sexually disorientated. I have prostituted my body and my mind – I feel destroyed and worthless. I avoid people where possible. I always try to please and pretend there is nothing wrong. I can't take the risk of letting people get too close. I feel afraid to trust. I am aware of the loneliness and isolation this creates. It is despairing but I feel safer. I have no motivation to make progress in anything. I have

never loved or been loved. Simmering beneath the surface I feel dangerously full of unexpressed rage and anger with a dreadful sense of hopelessness. (HIA 2017: 111)

In a society so committed to secrecy, it is understandable how people find it difficult to transcend such injury. When responsibility is not placed, the person feels utterly worthless and burdensome. The pattern from the key findings for both North and South provinces of the De La Salle Order converge in themes of sexual exploitation; physical violation and emotional abuse and neglect of vulnerable children; non-reporting and delays in reporting to state authorities; no canonical disciplinary hearings recorded; external agency failures in proceeding with criminal investigations; over-crowding just to secure increased state subsidy; opportunities were missed to prevent further harm/neglect; transfer of problem clerics to another district; two senior authority figures remaining in place despite serious complaints against them; untimely death of two abuse claimants prior to giving evidence to the HIA inquiry itself; legalistic approaches which secured the defeat of claimants in court proceedings and the absence of substantive pastoral solutions or outreach (HIA 2017).

The NBSCCCI (2017) for the Republic of Ireland reported that seventy-six De La Salle Brothers had received 213 allegations of sexual, physical and emotional abuses during the period from 1975–2015. The majority of abuse related to sexual abuse by the De La Salle Brothers, 'even if another type of abuse was also alleged' (p. 3). The Dublin auditors were hampered in their efforts, as records were: 'incomplete, and therefore did not contain full information regarding complaints received, either directly by them, through their legal representatives, or through the statutory authorities' (p. 3).

A recent report by Tusla (The Child and Family Agency) identified the De La Salle Brothers as one of the five religious orders where they had identified 'significant [child] safeguarding weaknesses' out of a total 135 religious orders in Ireland (Little 2018). The RTÉ Religious and Social Affairs Correspondent adds:

> The report censures the Christian Brothers, De La Salle Brothers, the Irish Norbertines, the Missionaries of the Sacred Heart and the Holy Spirit Congregation for weak-nesses ... They include failures to adequately alert Tusla to measures being adopted to protect children from members who had sexually abused minors. The audit team,

which finished its work last year, says it helped the orders concerned by establish-
ing links between them and relevant Tusla areas to share concerns about potential
risks. (Little 2018)

The Royal Commission into Institutional Responses to Child Sex Abuse
in Australia report the same statistical pattern. Varying estimates range
from 13–22 per cent of De La Salle Brothers in Australia who have been
accused of historic sexual abuses. This figure is for a thirty-five period up to
2010. The quantitative total of abuse claims against the Catholic Church in
Australia is 4,444 incidences (Knaus 2017). It is worth noting, one of the
purposes in setting up the novitiate at De La Salle in Castletown, Portlaoise
in 1880/1 was in response to a formal request for postulants to the De La
Salle HQ in Paris. As Ireland was religiously devout and English-speaking,
the Irish arm of the De La Salle Order were strongly positioned to meet
this demand and provided many Irish De La Salle missionaries over many
decades to Australia. Up to the early 1900s, the Australian region of the De
La Salle Order was predominantly staffed by missionaries of Irish heritage
and descent (BRA 2015; Towey 1980).

Despite the significant obstacles and limitations of the NBSCCCI
(2017) on the De La Salle Brothers in Ireland, the authors conclude:
'Certainly, something has gone badly wrong in relation to how some members of the De La Salle Brothers in Ireland have interpreted their mission
to teach and witness to children and so to lead them to God' (p. 33).

A limitation of the Church audit is the way it tends to underestimate
how the De La Salle Brothers became legitimated in Irish society. It pays
scant attention to how the De La Salle identity as a Church body was
socially reproduced in Irish society, how the order was historically appropriated and politically legitimated in Irish culture. For example, it makes no
mention of the high-level ecclesiastical co-operation of Irish bishops and
co-operation from the political establishment. Cultural elites facilitated
the order's development and rubber-stamped its identity onto the social
imaginary of nineteenth- and twentieth-century Ireland (Towey 1980).
These methods of social reproduction are crucial for understanding how
normative connotations and logics were historically configured, embedded
in Ireland's evolving history. Accounting for this Ireland's history in a more

critical way gives a more grounded picture of how self-understandings were shaped and moulded in historical times and how theological power was naturalized in the social imagination.

Ireland's former president Mary McAleese (2018) recently revealed how her younger brother was 'sadistically' abused as a child by a paedophile priest. Father Malachy Finnegan had served as president of a Catholic College, St Colman's College in Newry Northern Ireland (Armstrong and Donnelly 2018). Her revelation followed on from a BBC *Spotlight* episode, 'Buried Secrets', describing the activities of Fr Finnegan, who raped and abused children over four decades. Some of these abuses were actually known to the Catholic Church for a considerable time period beforehand and there was a considerable time lapse before complaints were passed on to civil authorities (*This Week* 2018). These new revelations led to the recent resignation of the local bishop, when it emerged that Bishop John McAreavey had jointly concelebrated mass with Fr Finnegan in 2000, despite a bar on him saying mass in public (*This Week* 2018). The bishop had also officiated at the requiem mass on the death of Fr Finnegan in 2002. These revelations angered parishioners and the victims of his crimes, 'Between 1994 and 2016, 12 allegations of abuse were made against him' (Armstrong and Donnelly 2018). Speaking on *The Sean O'Rourke Show* on RTÉ Radio One, McAleese said:

> My youngest brother, my baby brother, was seriously, physically sadistically abused by Malachy Finnegan. My mother, almost 90 years of age, had to discover that from an article in the Belfast Telegraph three weeks ago. Four of my five brothers went to that school. (Armstrong and Donnelly 2018)

McAleese added

> that her brother is going to turn 50 next year and they only found out about the ordeal he suffered throughout his childhood in recent months .... It went on all of the years he was there, it was known, and as he pointed out, so many people in the school would have had to have known, who could have done something about it. We know the very first complaints about Malachy Finnegan go back to the 1970s, not the 1990s, which means there is a body information that was available to people who could have done something ... What frightens me is that we only find this out all these decades later, I'm the oldest of nine children and I always said my brothers

could tell me anything but he didn't because the culture of silence was so oppressive and these children were so frightened. There are huge questions to be answered by all the people who were involved at a senior level in that school and in the diocese about what they knew and when they knew it ...

He's not the only one, there are legions of silent sufferers who carry it through their lives and it remains unresolved and causes so much suffering. The sad thing is that here we are, 20 years after the new guidelines were introduced, all of the secrets were supposed to be out, but here we are, there's a mountain of them and a mountain of hurt. (McAleese 2018, cited by Armstrong and Donnelly, *Irish Independent*)

While the allegations relate to the North, Taoiseach Leo Varadkar says he will consider backing calls by Mary McAleese for a public inquiry into the handling of complaints (*Breaking News* 2018). What is particularly striking about Ireland's history is how virtuous it is to silent and how this arbitrary virtue eats away at the fabric of people's lives. The idea of resistance/resilience is often touted as enabling transformative change. In Ireland's case, that idea is turned on its head. Resistance becomes concealment as an arid defence of the status quo. In my own life, this inverse dynamic has been so corrosive and toxic to assertiveness. When you open up, you think it right and proper to close down and take back. It is extremely wearing to carry around that kind of self-doubt for your worth as a human being. I have often felt like I was going nowhere without purpose and not being able to anchor my achievements into the pocketbook of self-esteem. Social change has extended me better insight about a part of my personality where the deeper manifolds of positive self-worth potentials are still not in sync. I do not want to feel shame about this restlessness and I want to use my restless energy to transform the imprint of bad information that inscribed low self-confidence to begin with.

The next section highlights the De La Salle Order's significant global financial reserves. Ireland's financial services centre (IFSC) was chosen for the launch of a world financial fund for this order. With this kind of skilful financial acumen on display, it is so inexcusable how the De La Salle Order have behaved. It is worth repeating how the De La Salle Order were one of five religious orders in Ireland who were censured for their child safeguarding practices, while acknowledging that current safeguards within the De La Salle Order have improved.

CHAPTER 21

The De La Salle Order and Other Catholic Religious Orders: Global Investment Strategies

The De La Salle Order are the original founders of CBIS Global. This investment scheme was setup in the USA in 1981. Recently, in 2009, CBIS Global launched a key arm of its operations through the IFSC (Irish Financial Services Centre) in Dublin. The president of CBIS Global in 2009 was De La Salle Brother, Louis DeThomasis. At the launch of the investment fund, it was announced 'BNY Mellon Asset Servicing, part of Bank of New York Mellon Corporation, as one of the largest fund administrators in the IFSC in Dublin, would help run the Irish Fund ... A spokesman for CBIS declined to say how much it would try to raise through the Irish-based fund' (Carswell 2009).

On its launch, the investment fund managed assets of over $3 billion (Carswell 2009). The main purpose of the fund is to assist Catholic organizations: 'in pursuing its investment objectives, and each Fund shall adhere to the principles of ethical and socially responsible investing' (Carswell 2009). The De La Salle Brothers achieves its aims and objectives through the mechanisms of the European Equity Fund, World Bond Fund and World Equity Fund. The US Core Equity Index Fund is soon to be launched (CBIS 2015). The fund in Dublin is regulated by the Central Bank in Ireland. Its legal advisors for Ireland are Arthur Cox Solicitors, a leading law firm. In the US, Bloomberg (2016) offers a descriptor for CBIS Global:

> The fund is co-managed by AXA Rosenberg Investment Management Limited and Degroof Fund Management Company S.A. It invests in the public equity markets of Europe. The fund invests in the stocks of companies operating across diversified sectors. It invests in the stocks of companies with a market capitalization greater than €65 million. The fund focuses on factors like relative earnings strength and valuation discrepancies within industry groups to create its portfolio.

As of 31 March 2017 CBIS Global in its own approved statement say the global asset management fund

> manages $6.9 billion for Catholic organizations worldwide, including dioceses, schools, hospitals and religious institutes. Specializing in Catholic Responsible Investing, CBIS combines research-driven stock screening with active ownership to help Catholic organizations align their investments with Catholic beliefs. CBIS is a Registered Investment Advisor owned by the De La Salle Christian Brothers in the US and the Centre of the Institute in Rome with offices in New York, Chicago, San Francisco and Rome. (Cision Newsletter 25 May 2017)

I read a book recently by the chairman of CBIS Global, Bro. Louis DeThomasis (2012). It is entitled *Flying in the Face of Tradition: Listening to the Lived Experience of the Faithful*. From 1984 to 2005, Bro. Louis served as president and Professor of Interdisciplinary Studies at St Mary's University of Minnesota. In his book, Bro. Louis is sharply critical of how Catholic leadership have mishandled crisis after crisis. Now based in Rome, Bro. Louis takes aim at how the official Church have responded to clerical child sexual abuse. That said, Bro. Louis never specifically alludes to the reputational damage to the De La Salle Brothers as reported in international inquiry findings on clerical abuses. These reports highlight how the brothers seriously mishandled and covered up sexual abuse cases. Furthermore, Bro. Louis makes no reference to the order's lack of pastoral response to victims and their litigious strategies in the courts. However, Bro. Louis (2012) offers a generic apology. Now in the eighth decade of his life, Bro. DeThomasis says:

> I know that I am as guilty as anyone of many of the sins decried in this book. I too have been insensitive, close-minded, arrogant, self-centred, too-quick-to-defend-the-indefensible and overly protective of myself and my fellow church-members. For this I am sorry. And for this reason I offer this book as a small token of atonement.

The Irish arm of the De La Salle Brothers have not been precise in recording minor sexual violations and have been critiqued for poor implementation of best practice guidelines (NBSCCC 2017). The 2017 audit of this order in Ireland highlighted how other Church bodies in Ireland have produced guidelines for best practice in child protection since 1996. In contrast, they expressed their dismay at the De La Salle Order: 'It is incomprehensibly late for a large religious congregation involved in the provision of schools to produce its first written policy and procedures in 2011' (NBSCCC 2017: 11). In the epilogue of his book, Bro. Louis' (2012) solution is to stress how the founder of the order, St John Baptist de La Salle, can serve as inspiration for the crisis of faith arising from the Church mishandling of child sexual abuses. With respect, Bro. Louis' weightless solutions are not appropriate, particularly, coming from a senior brother who has demonstrated such a high level of acumen for financial investment in his strategic management of the De La Salle global fund portfolio. In my view, the De La Salle Brothers are choosing to downplay the significance of the moral injury of children and its implications for adult health. This approach is not acceptable. The recently reported findings from the Australian Royal Commission (2017) capture the societal cover up of sexual abuse and neglect of young children:

> For many survivors talking about past events required them to revisit traumatic experiences which have seriously compromised their lives. Many spoke of having their innocence stolen, their childhood lost, their education and prospective career taken from them and their personal relationships damaged. For many, sexual abuse is a trauma they can never escape. It can affect every aspect of their lives. We also witnessed extraordinary personal determination and resilience among victims and survivors. We saw many survivors who, with professional help and the support of others, have taken significant steps towards recovery. (p. 2)

In my direct experience of the De La Salle Brothers, they want to be seen as victims, suggesting that they are being obstructed in their mission in education (Dept of Education 2011). From my vantage point and that of many others, the De La Salle Brothers seem to want to forget how many children were humiliated, beaten and abused in their care. And those who cannot forget such psychotic levels of violence and sexual abuses are to be pitied in weightless apologies. The Brothers view adult survivors with suspicion, as if the bearers are overly invested in suffer mongering at the expense of the noble aims of the De La Salle Order. To be sure, I acknowledge that the order have made a positive contribution to education in Ireland. That said, the manner they have dealt with the matters raised is inexcusable and indefensible. The Archdiocese of Dublin and the Diocese of Ardagh and

Clonmacnoise and the state should be more proactive in challenging this order on their legacy. The duty of De La Salle Order was to ensure young people got off to a better start in life. Instead, the behaviours of some of its brothers subjected already damaged young persons to further ill treatment. This historic pattern is sickening, cruel and unjust.

In 2017, the De La Salle Order still contest responsibility and fight abuse claimants with its superior clout of systemic resources in the Irish High Court. Meanwhile, abuse claimants get sicker and can die younger, without support, redress and reparation. Marmot (2015a), referring to social injustices as inequality, says, 'A causal thread runs through these stages of the life course from early childhood, through adulthood to older age and to inequalities in health' (p. 2442). The De La Salle Order should squarely confront how it created facilitative structures for some of its members to harm a not negligible number of children.

A further example of the subsequent wealth generated by Catholic religious orders who set up in Dublin under John Charles McQuaid's reign as Archbishop of Dublin is the recent sale of the Notre Dame School in Churchtown, Dublin, which was founded in 1953 by the Notre Dame des Missions Sisters and approved by the Dublin Archdiocese (Notre Dame School, n.d.). The order ceased its function as a Catholic private fee-paying school for girls in 2002 and had the approval of the Department of Education and Science since 1953 (Notre Dame School, n.d.). This religious order of nuns was originally founded in Lyons, France, on Christmas Day 1861 by Euphrasie Barbier (Vocations Ireland). Back then, the order's concerns was for 'the poorest and most abandoned in her day, especially the education of children and women.' In relation to recent disposal of assets, formerly the site of the Notre Dame Catholic School, Irish Life Investment Managers are reported to have paid '€100 million for a property scheme formerly owned by the Notre Dame School' (Hancock 2018; *The Irish Times* 2018). A further example of the historical wealth is given by Cooney (1999):

> In 1945, John Charles McQuaid became a Lord Archbishop in lifestyle as well as in ecclesiastical title. Shortly after celebrating his fiftieth birthday, McQuaid moved into a palatial residence in South Co. Dublin. Ashurst, a magnificent 100-year-old Victorian-Gothic mansion was situated on 12 acres of farm and woodland off Military Road in the exclusive Ballybrack-Killiney district. With a spectacular view of Killiney

Bay and the Wicklow Mountains, the mansion contained entrance and hallway reception rooms, 13 bedrooms and a well-cultivated garden. A gatehouse guarded the entrance, while the house was screened from public view and was reached via a long tree-lined drive. His chaplain-secretaries stayed with him, while his driver lived in the guesthouse. An order of nuns ran the household.

In memory of his French spiritual mentor, the late Pere Lamy, Archbishop McQuaid changed Ashurst's name to Notre Dame des Bois – Our Lady of the Woodlands ... A mansion of such proportions might seem contrary to McQuaid's priestly vow of poverty but it fitted his perception of his special status as Primate of a Catholic nation. Its acquisition was a signal of the dwindling propertied Protestant class that Catholics were taking possession of the best land as well as the most senior posts in the professions. (p. 204–5)

A recent book study on Irish poverty from 1920 to 1940 by Lindsey Earner-Byrne (2017) entitled *Letters of the Catholic Poor* examines letters written to the Catholic Archbishop of Dublin, Dr Edward Joseph Byrne (1921–1940), prior to Dr McQuaid's tenure. The book extends significant insight into the lives of very poor people, and the dire situations they faced in the early days of the new Irish state and the role Catholic clerics had in 'vetting and vouching' for the reality of their poverty status. Earner-Byrne (2017) introduces her study:

On letter-paper, copybook page, the backs of envelopes, postcards, and bill paper; in ink, pencil and crayon, the unemployed, widowed, under-paid, in debt, temporarily 'embarrassed' and dispossessed composed their poverty. In immaculate script or poorly formed letters, in fluid prose or sub-literate stuttering, these people have left one of the few traces in history of the experience of poverty .... Their letters articulate the hard edge of rage, the debilitating reality of impotence, the humiliation of need, the sour taste of failure, the unflagging spirit of hope, the tenacious sense of fight, the stirrings of entitlement, along with love and a sense of responsibility. They are also acts of testimony describing in highly personal ways the realities of living in appalling conditions, of having to beg, of losing the chief breadwinner and of being exposed to physical and sexual exploitation.

These realities were in stark contrast to lives of senior Church figures in Ireland and its increasing ability to develop its inheritance fortunes, a pattern that is not dissimilar to the 'scions of great wealth and the ability of rich family dynasties to retain control over corporations and to access sophisticated financial advice that makes fortunes last' (Korom, Lutter and Beckert 2017: 75). It is relatively easy to see how the tentacles of this religious ethos capital is borderless and further interconnected to powerful social/financial/legal capital from Dublin, France, Rome, Germany, UK, the US, Australia and elsewhere. In understanding a lack of social critique of these arrangements, the ideas of Slaby and Choudhury (2018) may help explain the inertia:

> Openly politicized forms of critique are no longer much in evidence in social studies of neuroscience) or more broadly, and may not currently seem very workable. Prevalent, for example, in science studies and cultural studies are approaches that appear to trade in critical engagement for an aestheticisation of scientific practices, stopping short of penetrating into manifestly pathological developments. One reason for this maybe increasing professionalization and differentiation of various meta-scientific approaches over the past 40 or so years: are practitioners no longer 'allowed' to operate on a broader/holistic level of social understanding that transcends clearly circumscribed local expertise? It is likely that certain intellectual as well as political and economic developments support some of this academic quietism. (p. 349)

Translating this critique to current patterns of increased social-economic inequality in Ireland, Lynch, Cantillon and O'Connell and Crean (2016) focus on:

> The extraordinary boom period of the Irish economy from the late 1990s to 2008 was followed by a period of intense recession. Mean annual equivalized disposable income per individual fell to € 20,681 in 2013, and deprivation rates across all households more than doubled from 13.7 per cent in 2008 to over 30 per cent in 2013. These economic and labour market changes have had a stark impact on the standard of living across the Irish population (Keane et al. 2015). (p. 254)

Apart from profound levels of migration out of Ireland from 2009 to 2015 the level of economic inequality in Ireland must be understood in historical context. Lynch, Cantillon and O'Connell and Crean (2016) offer the following insight on skewed distribution of resources as deepening class inequality in Ireland and its historical precursors:

> Since the 1970s, the top 10 per cent (those with incomes over €200,000 involving 18,741 tax cases) have had a rising share of gross income, while the share of the remaining 90 per cent has fallen (O'Connor and Staunton 2015: 30–1). Measures of market incomes – that is, incomes accrued before the impact of taxation or social

> transfers are calculated – show that Ireland is one of the most class-divided, unequal
> countries in gross income terms across the Organisation for Economic Co-operation
> and Development (OECD).
>
> Ireland relies heavily on social transfers to reduce inequality. Consequently, cuts
> to welfare provisions, increases in indirect taxes that are universal in character, and
> reduced spending on public services have a greater impact on inequality in Ireland
> than in comparator countries where market income inequalities are not so substantial
> in the first instance. (p. 254)

In relation to my own case, there was a chance for this 'esteemed' De La Salle order to reveal its heart. Instead, it has opted for a self-preservation route of denial and minimalist responses for the most significant challenge it has had to confront in its history, that is, the sexual exploitation and psychotic levels of violence inflicted on young children. This says a great deal about the moral intentionality of the De La Salle Order. It is more than shocking how this order still have charge of schools as a foregrounded religious ethos right to schools in Ireland. As the order approaches its tricentennial, the De La Salle order ought to take a long hard look at itself.

Regarding the Vatican and the Irish Church hierarchy, Andrew Madden (2018) believes apologies ring 'hollow':

> In December 2009, Catholic bishops in Ireland did acknowledge the finding that the
> sexual abuse of children had been covered up in the Archdiocese of Dublin, saying
> that they were shamed by the extent of it and that it reflected a culture of cover-
> up that existed throughout the Catholic church in Ireland. Within days, cover-up
> became 'mismanagement' and mismanagement became 'failure of leadership' and
> such dishonest spin has continued to this very day. (Madden 2018)

Anticipating Pope Francis' visit to Ireland in 2018, Andrew says 'it is most likely that Pope Francis will come to Ireland and apologize, again, while refusing, again, to acknowledge the Catholic church's concealment of these crimes. Empty words of no value whatsoever' (Madden 2018).

Finally, regarding the De La Salle Brothers when they defended their Vocations Director as an esteemed member of their order, this inferred that I was the one with a credibility deficit (Fricker 2017). In light of the recent audits of the De La Salle Order in Ireland and Australia, I think on the balance of probability, it is fair to suggest this order are hardly credible providers of legal testimony. Yet, the De La Salle Order are the ones with a wealth of resources, which ensured I could not even get off the ground to be heard. This order claims to speak for the voiceless, the marginalized and oppressed. My book suggests differently.

I am choosing to give voice, to not remain silent, and to speak up against oppressive knowledge and practices. It requires cognitive effort and persistence for grasping the 'complex interplay of sociocultural, political and ideological factors' (Tileaga 2015). It is much easier to silence people when they are not used of the practices of self-confidence or have high social status. It can be so difficult to stand up against unfair treatment. I do not trust that practices of authority are necessarily good. 'Vested group interests provide a causal explanation for the endurance of ideologies even when the evidence clearly refutes them' (Mills 2017: 104). Yet, emotions are like irritants, pushing us forward to transform and change. I believe negative influences on social cognition are often pervasive in normative social policies and mainstream knowledge. Capturing this, Volpp (2017) says:

> Citizenship is 'Janus-faced', simultaneously projecting the warm embrace of inclusion while excluding those who are outside the borders of belonging. Janus, the Roman god of doors and gates, was portrayed as having two faces, gazing in opposite directions. One face of citizenship welcomes 'we the people' within the circle of membership; the other face refuses admission to those outside. (p. 153–4)

The next section evaluates the role of the Dublin Archdiocese as it relates to my story.

CHAPTER 22

The Current Role of the Dublin Archdiocese

The Dublin Archdiocese's pre-occupations in dealing with cases of child
sexual abuse, at least until the mid 1990s, were the maintenance of secrecy,
the avoidance of scandal, the protection of the reputation of the Church,
and the preservation of its assets. All other considerations, including the
welfare of children and justice for victims, were subordinated to these
priorities. The Archdiocese did not implement its own Canon Law Rules
and did its best to avoid any application of the Law of the State. (The
Murphy Report 2009)

In my case, the Dublin Archdiocese ought to have been much more proactive at a formal senior level in confronting the De La Salle Order. Since the
court hearing in 2012, the Dublin Archbishop, Dr Diarmuid Martin has
never once informed me of his efforts to confront the De La Salle legacy
within his Archdiocese. Dr Martin as Archbishop has enjoyed a bird's eye
view for how the De La Salle Brothers have simply not dealt with mine
and others' abuse complaints in a humane and just way. Over a decade, Dr
Martin was also aware how the De La Salle Order takes a heavy handed
legalistic approach against abuse claimants in the Irish court system. Despite
the general social perception that Dr Martin is an independent mind,
capable of incisive critique and provocative intervention, I believe the
Archbishop should have proactively confronted the De La Salle Brothers
on its historic legacy in Irish education.

My critique is in a context where Dr Martin has shown an appreciation for how early adversity/trauma is damaging to human potential. The
Archbishop makes the connection that early adversity is a corrosive thread
to wellbeing. His sermons and speeches consistently address how the lack of
early interventions ultimately costs the state more in adult health inequities.

In this, Dr Martin shows courage in critiquing government policy. He is showing systemic awareness of how children are social persons and that they deserve a social contract to maximize their potential. There is nothing weightless about how he understands the development of human beings from a social justice perspective.

However, Dr Martin does not fulsomely apply the same hypothesis/ rationale when recognizing the harms of early sexual and physical violation to young children and its damaging impact on their adult lives. Dr Martin's diocesan solutions take the form of pastoral and therapeutic supports. His current positioning does not address the loss of economic opportunity and concrete health disparities for adult survivors of childhood sexual violations. Unlike, the Archdioceses of New York and Brooklyn, to my knowledge, the Dublin Archdiocese has no compensation scheme for adult survivors of Clerical Childhood Sexual Abuse (ABC News 2017).

To date, Dr Martin has been commended for implementing best practice procedures in the protection of children, and for his levels of co-operation with state authorities. That said, in my case, the Archbishop possessed reliable information that Bro. Bernard was not the esteemed figure which the De La Salle Order proclaimed him to be in the court system. Dr Martin is a former pupil of a De La Salle school. He went to the De La Salle School in Ballyfermot, Dublin. As Archbishop of Dublin, Dr Martin continues to extend visible legitimacy to the De La Salle Brothers on his Archdiocesan website.

On 18 December 2015, I received a letter from the Child Safeguarding and Protection Service at the Dublin Archdiocese. In the letter, the Child Protection Officer accepts my previous charge of weightless responses, stating 'we are no nearer to the accountability that you seek.' With reference to a proposed future pastoral meeting with the Archbishop of Dublin, the letter acknowledges 'there is no adequate response of the abuse of children, and what I am suggesting may seem wholly insignificant when set beside all that you have suffered, and continue to suffer' (CPO 2015). The letter offers the following rationale for such a meeting:

> It matters that you were abused. The particular circumstances of each abuse often serve to bring the evil that is done into sharp focus. In your case, the exploitation

of your vulnerability and the betrayal of your trust were unbelievably cruel. The damage that was done cannot be undone. It ought at least to be acknowledged. The De La Salle Order owed you that much. I thought that Bishop O'Reilly might be able to offer such acknowledgement. I am confident that Archbishop Martin would.

This offer of a pastoral meeting as an acknowledgement of minor sexual abuse did not feel like the right response to me, particularly in light of the recent audit on the De La Salle Brothers. As already outlined, the De La Salle Order owes its very existence in Dublin to the Archbishop of Dublin. The current Archbishop is treating this matter as a pastoral issue, when there are much greater issues for the Archdiocese to confront. That said, receiving the well worded and sincere apology from the Child Protection Office in the Dublin Archdiocese was therapeutic to me. I know it was issued with concern for my wellbeing. The Dublin Archdiocese have been the only Church body to have made such effort. No other religious body or civil institution has offered me a letter of apology in 2018. I do concur with aspects of the historian Crompton (2003) when he singled out Christianity for praise:

> How can we not be grateful for its works of compassion, its service to education, and its contribution to the world's treasury of great art, architecture, and music? We must recognize those church leaders who throughout the ages have worked for peace and the alleviation of human oppression. (p. 540)

Overall, the Irish bishops and leaders of religious orders make regular statements of sympathy towards sexual abuse claimants, where they seem to recognize the damaging impact of early trauma on child wellbeing. In the public domain, some religious leaders claim to have empathy for how persons go on to experience later life difficulties. In arriving at these conclusions, the bishops often cite scientific evidence which recognizes that mental health, and even biomedical issues of deteriorating health in adult functioning are strongly related to enduring experiences of early life abuses/traumas. Unfortunately, the Roman Catholic Church in Ireland are still not inclined to pay serious attention to the central message of scientific findings. Rather, their levels of recognition operate within pastoral solutions, therapy far downstream, often far too late for many survivors. Too many

persons have been left struggling in their day to day lives, opportunities
have been lost, relationships damaged and hope crushed. A report in 1996,
prepared for the Irish Bishops' Conference covers many of the themes that
have dominated the CSA research agenda:

> The negative impact of sexual abuse on children should never be underestimated or
> minimized. Such abuse has the potential to affect the child victim physically, emo-
> tionally, and spiritually, both in the short and long term ... The child's emotional
> well-being may also be affected, whereby feelings of guilt and shame are engendered
> in the child, leading to a loss of self-worth, to a development of a low self-esteem
> and to an impaired ability to trust. Awareness and acknowledgement, at an early
> stage, that a child has been abused allows for appropriate interventions to help the
> child victim deal with the abuse experience. If a child's abuse is not revealed and if
> appropriate help is not provided, the effects of that abuse can be long-lasting and can
> contribute to a variety of difficulties in adult life ... Even in adulthood, victims may
> feel stigmatized ... they may experience a deep sense of isolation ... (p. 12)

However welcome the above acknowledgements, the bishops choose to
remain silent about the broader impact of CSA and its relationship to
adult health patterns and economic inequities. They never seem to want
to calculate the concrete costs of damaging self-confidence and how this
can manifest as negative health outcomes across the lifespan. In a recent
research report from the ESRI (Economic and Social Research Institute),
Barrett, Kamiya and O'Sullivan (2014) have attempted to track how the
experience of sexual abuse on young lives increases the statistical risk of
adult negative impact. This research focused on male labour force participation and employment status '17% of CSA survivors were out of the labour
force as a result of being sick or permanently disabled. The corresponding
figure for men who had not experienced CSA was only 8%' (p. 2). This is
a significant disparity in how correlative outcomes are measured. A further finding in this ESRI research stated that 6 per cent of males between
the ages of fifty to sixty-four years had experienced CSA (n. 458). These
researchers offer a further significant finding of lower household incomes
for the CSA group and a greater statistical likelihood that abused males
were living alone (p. 2). 'Economic inequality is one of the most salient and
concrete expressions of social power. It entails inequality of control – over
resources, over people, over the purposes and goals of the community itself'

(Thompson 2018a, p. 201). As a critical theorist, Thompson says damaged lives are the epiphenomenon of 'hierarchical forms of social structure that are based on domination, control and subordination' (Thompson 2018). Benjamin (2017) says:

> The social recognition of trauma is not only healing for individuals, it promotes agency and gives weight to ethical considerations within the social discourse. Public acts of apology for injuries and restorative justice ... encourage the development of a civic consciousness that resists state terror, racism and denigration of the weak and vulnerable and advocates for facing painful truths .... The insights of psychoanalytic recognition theory should ultimately contribute to both awareness of interdependence and attachment to the social whole as well as the respect for the needs of unique and different individuals to be confirmed in their self-understanding. Recognition gives validation to victims that their injury matters; but also restores the connection to truth and the social bond with the larger Third that is inevitably denied during the exercise of violence. (p. 218)

However, a criticism of recognition theory is its practical failure to grapple with themes of power and how struggles for recognition downplay material inequality as an 'institutionalized social relation, not a psychological state or something symbolic. Misrecognition thus results in concrete material harms and injustices' (citing Nancy Fraser, Oksala 2017). Oksala (2017) analyses go beyond symbolic recognition registrars which may well re-enact a false consciousness and a false sense of security. I bring this critique to light because of the danger that recognition as social suffering is reified into reconciliation concepts that downplay how moral harm and exploitation objectifies cognition in an oppressive way (Thompson 2018). Axel Honneth's more recent work (2014) does ground the concept of recognition more substantively in social conditions, as a more multi-faceted conception of social freedom (Deranty 2016). In a further recent critique of Honneth's theory of recognition, Thompson (2018b) says the Frankfurt School tradition, as represented by Honneth, has 'broken with a more robust, more insightful and more radical project of understanding the mechanisms of social domination, the deformation of character and the perversions of cognitive and epistemic powers that explain the increasing acceptance of the prevailing social order and the integration and legitimacy of pathological forms of social life'.

Esteemed institutions in Ireland have had numerous opportunities to respond to the issues raised in this book in a just way. In the main, these hierarchical systems have simply refused to acknowledge how the historic structure played their role in blocking opportunity. These frames of thought in the social hierarchy also endorsed pathological and discriminating ideas which added insult to injury in a gay person's life. To have upheld and projected inherent pathology in legitimated exclusion of gay people certainly gave rise to undeserved pain and suffering.

To lend further power to empirical results and hypotheses, an award-winning research paper that won the 2010 Best Article Award elaborates on the long-term economic consequences of childhood physical, sexual abuse and neglect. Currie and Widom (2010) use a prospective cohort design of substantiated abuse claimants through the period from 1967 to 1971. The researchers assessed life outcomes of economic status and productivity at forty years of age in 2003–4 and longitudinally compared the results to controls comprising of non-abused and non-neglected children over the same time period (n. 807). Currie and Widom's (2010) results

> indicate that adults with documented histories of CSA and/or neglect have lower levels of education, employment, earnings, and fewer assets as adults ... There is a 14% gap between individuals with histories of abuse/neglect and controls, in the probability of employment in middle age, controlling for background characteristics ... and demonstrate that abused/neglected children experience large and enduring economic consequences. (p. 111)

These findings extend knowledge on the economic costs for adult survivors. Chu (2011), an Associate Professor of Psychiatry at Harvard Medical School, insists the damage is even greater for severe and chronic childhood abuse. His life work is the treatment of adults with trauma-related experiences: 'These persons cannot just simply go on with their lives; this kind of abuse cannot be forgotten, disregarded, or left behind, and it continues to have profound effects in almost every domain of their existence' (p. 18–19). Although scientific evidence is still not fully conclusive, Naess and Kirkengen's (2015) review of twenty-six studies on PubMed say, 'It has been shown that severe stress in childhood is harmful to later health' (p. 1356). Based on their recent analysis of twelve to fourteen new research studies, these medical and public health researchers offer the hypothesis that protective features of chromosomes (telomeres) may be damaged through early childhood stressors (p. 1356). These ongoing investigations are consistent with the way the health gradient is analysed by social epidemiologists tracking patterns of health inequality across the lifespan (Marmot 2015a).

As I get older, I have become more aware of the impact of early adversity on my health. I try to manage this situation by not aggravating my vulnerability with more stress. My current experience of my health status is largely the enacted relationship between biology (equilibrium) and the social markers of a stigmatic and traumatic culture (Ryan and Deci 2017; Marmot 2015; Shim et al. 2014; Wilkinson 2005). While I have been able to pursue an education up to doctoral level spanning two decades, my own health and employment and economic profile is significantly similar to the results from CSA research base, social epidemiology and the critical theory literature. While acknowledging the limitations of self-reports and its potential biases, the latest developmental science is in agreement on the following:

> In the last three decades, a growing number of studies have provided convincing evidence to conclude that adversity in childhood has a lasting influence on adult physical health, particularly chronic diseases associated with aging, like cardiovascular disease, diabetes, arthritis, and some cancers. This susceptibility to the chronic diseases of aging resulting from early adversity has been identified in diverse samples with a range of adverse risk factors, including socioeconomic disadvantage, maltreatment, and chaotic family environments. These findings suggest that these early stressful experiences leave a 'biological residue' manifesting in physical health problems in adulthood. (Ehrlich, Miller and Chen 2016: 1)

Since 2012, Dr Diarmuid Martin, has had a very advantaged position to know that the assertion that Bro. Bernard was a school principal in good standing is not remotely plausible. Both the Diocese of Ardagh and Clonmacnoise and the Archdiocese of Dublin are not acting with wholeheartedness by refusing to investigate Bro. Bernard's full tenure. Archbishop Martin knows that Bro. Bernard was a senior educationalist in the Dublin school system for a long number of years. It is even probable that Dr Martin may have met Bro. Doyle. Bro. Bernard was in charge of religious recruitment for his order in the Dublin region (Towey 1980). As a boy, the De La

Salle school in Ballyfermot which Dr Martin attended may have been part of Bro. Bernard's recruitment drive for junior religious vocations. It is largely incomprehensible to me, particularly in light of recent disclosures from the NBSCCC audit (2017) and the recent findings of Sir Anthony Hart's HIA Inquiry (2017) how the Dublin Archdiocese were not aware of the magnitude of problems facing the De La Salle Order in Dublin and elsewhere. Sangiovanni (2017) says these contexts 'so [risk] undermining one of the structural conditions for a flourishing life (p. 132) and undermines our sense of ourselves as self-presenters, as beings who need some degree of control over the terms in which we appear to others in public' (p. 135).

The Executive Director of Amnesty International in Ireland, Colm O'Gorman, and Irish abuse survivors Andrew Madden and Marie Collins have consistently expressed their deep frustrations with how the Church hierarchy have dealt with historic clerical abuses. Collins (2018) along with other survivors, met with Pope Francis on his papal visit to Dublin in 2018. She also contributed to the World Meeting of Families in Dublin. She acknowledged the Pope's words of contrition for devastating crimes committed by the clergy against children but said the Pope's words are out of sync with practice. For example, she says Church stances regarding statutes of limitations obstruct justice for survivors. Collins (2018) also says 'robust structures need to be in place to hold fully accountable those in leadership who protect a predator or those in the Vatican who would hinder safety measures, with strong sanctions for the guilty, dismissal from their post, removal of their titles and privileges and if necessary laicization.' To coincide with the papal mass in the Phoenix Park in August 2018, Colm O'Gorman organized an event 'Stand for Truth.' Colm told the crowd 'that he had been 13 years old, and deeply religious, when Pope John Paul II visited in 1979' – the last time a pope visited Ireland. 'A year and a half later I was raped by a Catholic priest' (cited by McKay 2018). O'Gorman, Andrew Madden and abuse survivor Mannix Flynn have long shared the view that the concealment of CCSA was systemic, extending all the way to the Vatican in Rome.

The next section describes how a majority ruling from the European Court found against the Irish government for its historic failures to protect children from harm in Irish education. As the section shows, it is remarkable how the moral tone in Ireland's repertories is consistently shown up as out of sync in its implementation of EU human rights laws.

CHAPTER 23

The State's Role in Education: Systemic Failures in Protecting Children

> Excellent and innovative education and training are the pivot around which personal fulfilment, a fair society and a successful nation should revolve. (Department of Education and Skills Strategy Statement 2016–19: 2)

Thus far, the analysis has largely taken aim at the systemic failures of the religious (non-state party) patrons. I have paid slightly less attention to the 'constitutional endorsement for the outsourcing of the State's duties in the field of primary education' (O'Mahony 2009: 315). It can be said the state failed in its positive duty of obligation to protect young persons from degrading treatment in national schools. O'Mahony (2009) describes the historical context of education in Ireland:

> So while the local National School itself is merely State funded, and not State owned or managed, there is little escaping the fact that the State uses its legislative power to compel the attendance of children at school. In addition, State policy over almost two centuries has resulted in a complete lack of freedom of choice and the de facto privatization of what might normally be considered the public education sector, with privately owned and managed denominational schools being the only type of school available in most instances. (p. 318)

Regarding the occurrences of childhood sexual abuses, and in reference to the Ryan Report, O'Mahony (2009: 319) says 'a significant degree of fault can be attributed to a systemic failure to prevent and detect sexual abuse in the Irish education system' (Ryan 2009: 451–9). The Commission of Investigation into the Catholic Archdiocese of Dublin (Ryan 2009) annexed a historical study which gave indication of the high incidences of child sexual abuse in Ireland:

> Professor Ferriter's report put the events before the Ryan Commission in their historical context. He described the Carrigan Report (1931) as a 'milestone' as regards the provision of compiled information about the rate of prosecution of sexual crime in Ireland. He also provided and analysed later prosecution statistics (1930s-1960s) drawn from criminal court archives. The police had been quite vigorous in its prosecution of paedophiles but the fact that most sexual crimes were not actually reported suggested that such crime was a serious problem throughout the 20th Century in Ireland. He went on to point out that the criminal court archives demonstrated a 'consistently high level of sexual crime directed against young boys and girls.' While most of those cases were not recorded in the media, he considered that the police had extensive contemporaneous knowledge of the existence of such crimes. (ECHR 2014, para. 82: 19)

Further retrospective evidence was outlined from Volume III of the Murphy Report (2009) with eighty-two reports of abuse from seventy witnesses in '73 primary and second-level schools: most concerned children leaving school prior to or during the 1970s and sexual abuse was reported by over half of the witnesses' (ECHR 2014, 80: 18–19). Ferriter (2012) adds that 'As early as 1975, complaints were made about sexual abuse at Trudder House in Wicklow, which accommodated traveller children' (p. 378). Referring to clerical sexual abuse of children, Ferriter (2012) cites the archivist work of Dr Catriona Crowe, who charges that Irish state agencies were slow to act when there was increased recognition of the prevalence of childhood abuses since '1975 at the latest' (p. 378). Regarding clerical abuses from the late 1970s 'priests with behavioural problems, including childhood sexual abuse, were being sent for assessment and treatment' (p. 378). Meehan (2013) traces a pattern of secrecy to the very heart of the Irish state's foundations 'where there was a conscious effort by both the Cumann na nGaedheal and Fianna Fáil governments to project an image of independent Ireland as a moral, virtuous nation' (p. 178). After the signing of the Anglo-Irish Treaty in 1921, Laffan (2016) says in his biographical assessment of W.T. Cosgrave that he exhibited a fervent alignment to his Catholic faith beliefs. As the first president of the Executive Council for Ireland, in seeking to 'impose his religious beliefs, Laffan says that

Cosgrave made one highly improbable and unworldly proposal: that an upper house should be added to the (unicameral) Dáil. This would take the form of a 'Theological Board' that would decide whether any legislation proposed by the Dáil would be 'contrary to Faith and Morals'. He also suggested that in return for a guarantee that the Dáil would not make laws at odds with Catholic teaching, the Pope might recognize it as a body entitled to legislate for Ireland.

While Cosgrave's proposal did not gain the traction it required, Ferriter (2004) traces 'such focus on moral panic … not only inhibited the development of strong social and labour movement but also facilitated the continued hiding of many of Ireland's social problems' (p. 324). More recently, arising from this history, the state has had to subsequently apologize to all victims of child sexual abuse in Ireland (Kilkelly 2012). Key reports into child sexual abuse in Ireland all point to systemic failures, involving cover up and incompetence by the religious authorities. These reports also highlight failures by the state authorities to implement protective policies in schools to prevent moral injury and harm to children in the school settings (ECHR 2014; Ryan 2009). In response, the state has vigorously contested historic cases in the courts, not accepting that its oversight function had failed in a positive duty of obligation for children in educational settings. The state largely succeeded in its defence arguments in both the Irish High Court and Supreme Court, against individual claimants of historic abuse in national school settings (O'Mahony and Kilkelly 2014). The state argued that vicarious state liability and negligence in child sexual abuse cases were ill founded. Furthermore, state defendants argued retrospective understanding of sexual violation as a common occurrence within the school system in the 1970s could not have been presupposed as a distinct risk to children during this time period.

A high-profile case in Ireland was that of Louise O'Keeffe. Having lost her case in the Irish court system, O'Keeffe eventually won her case in the European Court of Human Rights in 2014. Her central claim was that the state had not adequately protected her from inhuman and degrading treatment. Louise was nine years old when she was abused at Dunderrow National School in Co. Cork in 1973. O'Mahony (2018) says:

Louise was one of 21 girls abused by the school principal, Leo Hickey, on almost 400 occasions in the early 1970s. When a parent complained, Hickey resigned his post and took up another in a school in Ballincollig, where he taught for another twelve years. In February 2017, Hickey was convicted of fresh sex abuse charges in Ballincollig between November 1991 and June 1992. All of this occurred without so much as an eyebrow being raised in the Department of Education. (O'Mahony 2018)

The Strasburg majority EU judgement found in favour of O'Keeffe against Ireland in January 2014. The Grand Chamber: said 'that Ireland had violated her right to freedom from inhuman and degrading treatment and her right to an effective remedy, under Articles 3 and 13 of the Convention respectively' (O'Mahony and Kilkelly 2014: 320). Based on antecedent/concurrent knowledge of potential risks to children in the 1970s, the court found the state education system did not fulfil its obligations to minimize this risk (ECtHR 2014, Para. 169, p. 41). The EU ruling further stated:

The Court is therefore of the view that the mechanisms on which the Government relied did not provide any effective protective connection between the State authorities and primary school children and/or their parents and, indeed, this was consistent with the particular allocation of responsibilities in the National School model. (ECHR 2014, para. 165, p. 40)

The EU court further stated in 2014 that

It was, moreover, an obligation of acute importance in a primary education context. That obligation was not fulfilled when the Irish State, which must be considered to have been aware of the sexual abuse of children by adults through, *inter alia*, its prosecution of such crimes at a significant rate, nevertheless continued to entrust the management of the primary education of the vast majority of young Irish children to non-State actors (National Schools), without putting in place any mechanism of effective State control against the risks of such abuse occurring. On the contrary, potential complainants were directed away from the State authorities and towards the non-State denominational Managers (paragraph 163). The consequences in the present case were the failure by the non-State Manager to act on prior complaints of sexual abuse by LH, the applicant's later abuse by LH and, more broadly, the prolonged and serious sexual misconduct by LH against numerous other students in that same National School. (ECHR, 2014, para. 168, 41)

In a separate analysis on the case, the Child Law Clinic (2015) says that despite state and international knowledge of the potential risk of abuses and violations against children, this did not translate to implementing preventive policies in Irish schools. The Law Clinic says:

> No mechanisms whatsoever were designed to protect children against the risk of sexual abuse. The absence of such mechanisms created an environment that was conducive to the widespread incidence of sexual abuse, as documented in the Carrigan Report and Ryan Report. The systemic failure to implement a child protection framework, and not the failure to respond to a specific complaint, was the crux of the finding of a violation in O'Keeffe. (UCC 2015: 10)

In essence, highlighting state obligation to respond to the general risk of sexual abuses/crimes is of critical importance. In citing the EU judgement, UCC (2015) says the state had awareness of potential abuses, documented as 'a high level of sexual crime directed against young boys and girls' (p. 4). The lack of any social discourse and protective measures in schools extended a license to sexual abusers 'to operate with impunity for extended periods of time' (p. 4). The Irish state held a similar line on sexual norms consistent with the Catholic ethos. A moribund and repressive sociality tied the whole concept of sexuality to innocence/sin/purity ideals (Ferriter 2009). Kilkelly and O'Mahony (2015) say the Grand Chamber ruling

> makes the proactive and preventive nature of the State's obligation under Article 3 abundantly clear, referring to ensuring that individuals 'are not subjected to torture or inhuman or degrading treatment', and an obligation to 'provide effective protection' and to 'prevent ill-treatment'. Clearly, such an obligation goes much further than an obligation to investigate after the abuse has already occurred. (p. 8)

The advocacy and personal writings of Mannix Flynn (1983), Andrew Madden (2003), Colm O'Gorman (2009) and Louise O'Keeffe's ruling (O'Keeffe v. Ireland 2014) also highlight a consistent pattern of avoidance in tackling these issues. In their personal accounts, the writers experienced considerable resistance. Among others, their collective efforts extended a foregrounded awareness for the rape and molestation of minors in Irish history.

Despite the success of EU Grand Chamber in favour of O'Keeffe v Ireland (2014), the Irish government responses to date have not been in keeping with the spirit of the EU ruling. The State Claims Agency in 2016 maintained my own sexual abuse case did not fit their criteria and rejected my case for consideration. This agency is charged with implementing the state's interpretation of the ECHR Grand Chamber judgement (2014). RTÉ News (2016a) report on the government's submission to Strasbourg states that in '19 recent applications for compensation from the State in one particular category – 18 have been rejected'. UCC (2015) say the current interpretation by the Irish government is 'not supported by a holistic analysis of ECHR' judgement (p. 10). The state currently takes the position that violation of Article 3 needs proof of prior complaint and a prior case against the state, not just a prior case against the religious bodies alone. Claims not fitting these criteria are simply not considered. The *Irish Examiner* (2016) further reports that 'Out-of-court settlements of around €80,000 to adults who suffered sexual abuse at school is offered. Approximately 100 people had been pursuing legal actions against the Department of Education for abuse in day schools. Only seven/eight of them have so far been able to prove the existence of a prior complaint'.

In sum, when the EU court voted in favour of O'Keeffe vs Ireland (2014), the Grand Chamber ruled that the Irish state had an oversight responsibility to protect minors as it outsourced the function of education to the Church. The EU ruling deepens our understanding of Ireland's truncated view of its responsibility in the courts. Ireland has a long history of being taken to task for its stances on human rights violations. Formal declaration principles acknowledging social contract protections extend as far back as 1948 within the EU. Child protection issues came up for consideration from 1958 and were adopted by two International Human Rights Covenants in 1966. Judge Ziemle cites the general obligation in the 1958 Declaration of the Rights of the Child:

> The child shall enjoy special protection, and shall be given opportunities and facilities, by law and by other means, to enable him to develop physically, mentally, morally, spiritually and socially in a healthy and normal manner and in conditions of freedom and dignity. In the enactment of laws for this purpose, the best interests

of the child shall be the paramount consideration. (O'Keeffe vs Ireland 2014 Judge Ziemle Consenting Opinion p. 54)

This judge states that 'Ireland had ratified the Convention in 1973 and thus Article 3 was applicable'. Judge Ziemle added further context to the 1989 UN Convention on the Rights of the Child, reemphasizing the need to implement child protection policies. More generally, concurring with the majority opinion of the court, Judge Ziemele said the case was 'about the assessment of the State's compliance with its obligations over time' (p. 56). In a separate opinion, Judge Peter Charleton, while accepting that the sexual exploitation of a child is an exemplar of degrading and humiliating treatment, Charleton dissented from the majority opinion. He argued that the civil law had already established the criminality of child sexual abuse in Ireland and had not been negligent in its enactment of criminal law (O'Keeffe vs Ireland 2014: 66–80). That said, in a paper 'Responsibility and Redress: Theorizing Gender Justice in the Context of Catholic Clerical Child Sexual Abuse in Ireland and Australia', senior law lecturer, Dr Kate Gleeson (2016) says:

> The most fundamental of all conditions for making amends is the placing of responsibility on wrongdoers and others who share responsibility for wrongs. When responsibility for wrongs is not placed, or assumed by perpetrators and their enablers, victims of mass crimes may experience profound existential crises of 'normative abandonment' by state and society. This abandonment is, I argue, not soothed by a focus on individualistic justice at the expense of pursuing institutional accountability. The individualistic focus of the criminal law shapes the consciousness and reflexive understandings of self and society of entire communities, including and beyond survivors of abuse. Hence, in the context of systemic abuse, this focus makes for a truncation of the meaning making process of communities as they grapple with the nature and magnitude of institutional abuse. (p. 780–1)

As a young teen, I shouldered stigmatic ideas and was encouraged to think I was the problem, not dominant social oppression and predatory clerics. The Catholic patrons of my school were one of the transfer points for the moral devaluation of gay citizens. To this day, religion asserts its fundamental right to deny parity of esteem for LGBT persons. The Catholic Church still enjoys a foregrounded right to education, despite its discriminatory positions. It enjoys a strong vantage point to maintain its foregrounded social identity over so many institutional spheres of Irish life.

For me, the experience of childhood sexual abuse within the historical continuum of legally legitimated gay identity stigma added a significant level of insult to an already hurt teenager. As Axel Honneth (2008/1995) says, these intricate contexts of social experience 'can bring the identity of a person as a whole to a point of collapse' (p. 43). The words of the Investigative Spotlight Team at the *Boston Globe* (2016) further state that 'If there are any heroes in this squalid tale, they are the victims, who found their voice, who found the courage ... to step into the light, and say as one did, "This happened to me, and this is wrong"' (p. 12).

At a critical juncture for shaping autonomy, a key figure representing a macro-ethical structure, betrayed my vulnerable situation, setting me up for further victimization in early adolescent life. According to the religious criteria, I was imperfect and they were perfect. I was a misfit and inferior. Dominant narratives predicted dire and stigmatic consequences for a gay identified life. These pathological discourses explicitly inferred that I was the one who needed 'to get over' my innate sin/disorder. Church pathology was upheld in law and psychiatry. I was left carrying the weight of this stigma. I was the one deserving of shame while dominant players held public esteem. These thought insertions from the dominant realm were so wrong.

A significant portion of what has been written in this book has been brought to the previous attention of the Department of Education and the Dublin Archdiocese. A shortened version of my story was received by the Diocese of Ardagh and Clonmacnoise and the De La Salle Brothers. I was informed on 22 November 2017 by the Irish State Claims Agency that Mr Justice Iarfhlaith O'Neill, a retired High Court judge, has been appointed as an independent assessor, who will assess cases where an individual has had an application for an ex-gratia scheme declined by the State Claims Agency (Dept of Education 2017). I have forwarded an earlier draft of this book for the re-assessment of my claim. My case is still being considered, with an outcome expected at the end of September 2018. Many human rights groups in Ireland have made submissions to the Council of Europe regarding their disagreements with the interpretation of the Irish government on the EU ruling against Ireland in 2014 (e.g. Irish Human Rights and Equality Commission; Child Law Clinic UCC, plus a critique by the Ombudsman for Children, as cited by O'Mahony 2018). O'Mahony (2018) says, 'It is long past time for the State to acknowledge its failures in a meaningful way by providing redress to the victims in an inclusive manner. If this does not happen, then it is entirely possible that another Louise O'Keeffe will come along and the State will once more be shamed before the European Court of Human Rights.'

I have been outlining in various sections of this book how there is a growing recognition that early chronic adversity plays an important role in producing health disparities. Major, Dovidio and Link (2018) state in the Preface of the *Oxford Handbook of Stigma, Discrimination and Health*:

> Everyone has the right to health; however, circumstances deny some groups of people this right. As a consequence, group differences in physical health – health dispari-ties – are pervasive in the United States and globally. Health disparities are health differences that have their roots in inequitable economic, political, social, and psy-chological processes. Health disparities are multi-determined: They reflect the sys-tematic effects of differences in the economic and educational resources available to members of various groups; historical and contemporary discrimination; bias within the health care system; and the interactions among genetic, physiological, social, and environmental influences on health. Because they are shaped and mutually reinforced by culture, politics, economics, and social and personal biases, health disparities are persistent and in some cases expanding, despite significant technical and scientific advances in medical treatment.

When I read psychological literature, one can easily feel silenced and alien-ated by the way HIV, abuse, mental health disorders, trauma and self-harm are constructed. This is a profession I trained for and studied hard for. If devastation lies at the core of moral injury, then I would have no hesita-tion in saying that the dominant theories in the profession I trained for often struggle to do justice to how social ideologies harm human beings. As Freyenhagen (2013) says, 'Pessimism and optimism often come in a pair. In Adorno's case, his deep pessimism about the contemporary social world is coupled with a strong optimism about human potential. In fact, it is the latter which explains his negative views about the contemporary world and his demand that we should resist and change it' (p. 21).

To summarize, the critical argument advanced in this section, my story relates to a diminution of my social status to fairly contest the instances of oppression, exploitation and humiliation. It is uncontroversial to claim that 'stigma associated with unemployment, poverty, ... and social marginalization inhibits social interaction and can undermine opportunities for living a free and worthwhile life with others' (Ingram 2017).

While the last couple of decades in Ireland has certainly witnessed the de-monopolization of morals and ethics from the power of the Catholic Church, there is still a sense that certain ways of moral knowing are consistently reproduced in the structure of secular thought. This can be problematic for accountability and transparency. The power structure enacts particular notions of responsibility and neglects alternative modes of understanding. Susan Neiman (2009) says 'moral inquiry and political activism start where reasons are missing' (p. 4).

The next section critiques the types of knowledge that hold a dominant position in knowledge production in Ireland. There are significant gaps in grasping the impact of regional histories on different age-groups. Historians and psychologists need to converse. My own history was confronted with concepts to not accuse God for human suffering, to absorb external constraints and coercion and not speak ill of religious people. Eldridge (2003) says that 'the criteria for calling something what it is are there in practice before we are, and we cannot come to thought and linguistic practice without them. This fact has both positive and negative sides' (p. 3). When I reflect on the plight of elders, it is not to say I felt determined by this history. Rather, it is to recognize how this heritage was enacted in the structure of thought and I have struggled to articulate its meaning. 'If enlightenment is the courage to think for oneself, it is also the courage to assume responsibility for the world into which one is thrown' (Neiman 2002, p. 15). The book upends oppressive concepts for emancipatory aims.

CHAPTER 24

Foregrounding of Charitable/Religious Patronage in Mental Health: A Critique

Critical scholarship has a 'spotlight' duty to raise questions relating to social injustice. From my vantage point, this is not something that is taken seriously by the psychological/therapeutic disciplines. The primary reason for this relates to a fundamental disconnect in these professions that privilege certain epistemologies (ways of knowing) over others. For example, mindfulness concepts as presence of mind in psychotherapy have a strong resemblance to theological conceptions about training self-regulation to ameliorate the chances of the untrained ego succumbing to vices and disempowerment. These surveillance regimes caricature self-will/ego as innately unruly, requiring forms of micro-regulation to quieten an egotistical mind. The seductive appetite for this type of catchy discourse has intensified in recent times (Vogelmann 2018; Stenner 2015).

People who experienced multisite disempowerment through structural oppression and micro repression/stigma are more often not well captured in existing literature. Ireland does not have a good reputation for radical critique of the social order. For the purposes of this study, it is worth stating again how the precursors of political events in Ireland's nineteenth- and early twentieth-century history afforded a foregrounded place for Roman Catholicism in Ireland's constitution (Robinson 2012). This centralized privilege naturalized 'ought'-like prescriptions of right and wrong in Irish life and the social imaginary of Ireland (e.g. Duffy 2011; Ryan 2011). Any psychological theorization, particularly for older generations, that fails to incorporate an analysis of this historical trajectory is a socially lightweight theory (McNay 2014).

When psychological theory actively encourages mindful humility as a way of enduring social suffering, such ideas may only serve self-interests in maintaining the status quo rather than activate the possibility of social transformation. A significant proportion of counselling and social services in Ireland are positioned within religious patronage and charitable ethos. These systemic advantages have been accumulated over a long period of time in Irish history (Daly 2016; McCrea 2010/2009; O'Toole 1998; Inglis 1998; Towey 1980). In 1975, the year of our family trauma, the CDF in Rome spoke in highly negative terms, expressing a wish that gay persons might overcome their personal difficulties, arising from their inability to fit into society (CDF, 1975). Having soaked up demeaning religious tenets, I think not just of myself, but my mother, sister, brother and others. These stressful conditions amount to 'social inequities that penetrate everyday existence and are lived as embodied suffering' (McNay 2016: 58). Within this, there is much unexpressed loss and grief, beyond words, where a contextualist analysis of Irish history is lost. That said, analyses must try to unearth the weight of social suffering, as more active enactments in present-day human lives (Riggs 2015; McNay 2014; Lennon, Gonzalez and Jagger, 2012). The purpose of such analysis is balance. In an essay entitled 'Agency' McNay (2016) states that 'it is in these entangled issues of gender inequalities with emergent forms of social vulnerability and empowerment that one of the principal challenges for future feminist theory on agency lies' (p. 58). Personal narratives must take account of regional histories.

In my own case, I think of a young boy who was capable of expressing tenderness and care, who was emotionally shut down, within the transferences of proximate and structural violence and abuse. This is a boy who had always wanted to be embodied and proud. To end up taking on the weight of external conditions was mind-altering. These conditions did not protect 'the autonomy, judgement, creative imagination, and inviolability of the concrete individual in ways that society deems crucial' (Cohen 2002: 55).

Again, Ireland is a country that explicitly encouraged an outer persona, irrespective of the pain this caused. It encouraged ideas that any restlessness associated with this discourse related to the self, not the discourse itself. Human beings are designed to be complex creatures and not to be caught out by damaging social prophecies of shame in the social hierarchy. The redemptive self in my history encouraged me to fight the very core of self. Power over others is supposed to be 'productive, transformative, authoritative and compatible with dignity' (Lukes 2005: 109). In my young life, I was socially engineered to use my own power to terrorize myself. Dominant religious ideas on a generative life constructed gay desire and love as degenerate. For me, the recommendations from the social hierarchy were to distort my reflective capacities for making meaning of my life experiences. The force of this domination in my experience and for others was cruel and toxic.

In the book, I have explored the historical roots of how potent this was for human beings. People's emotive reactions and reasoned beliefs are not produced in a social vacuum. Sangiovanni (2017) says 'the wrongness of treating another as inferior is prior to an affirmation of the idea of treating another as an equal' (p. 3). Bernstein (2015) believes that

> Once we discover that the intrinsic worth of the human is dependent on the entire range of social practices – we simultaneously recognize that the fundamental pulse of the moral life turns on the recognition of moral injury as what should not be suffered by any being ... no being ... should suffer humiliation, degradation, devaluation, or devastation. (p. 313)

More recently, a mindedness for social progress was evident on the day my partner and myself went to Dublin Castle on 23 May 2015. We went there to celebrate the powerful Yes result for Ireland's referendum on marriage equality. On leaving the count, I spoke to a mother who had come into the city with her family. She had come into town especially for the referendum event. She said that the only other time she had marked a state occasion was 3 September 1975. Her own parents brought her into Dublin to attend the state funeral of Ireland's former President Eamon de Valera. On a day to mark marriage equality being extended to all Irish citizens, she said she felt it was important to bring her own young family into Dublin Castle. I thought of my mother, who had passed in 2014. On the day of marriage equality, I recognized how previous generations had been so aware of the extent of social stigma, how their moral knowing and responsiveness served to protect gay citizens. How social persons relate to themselves in their private thoughts is important. The social determinants of equality/freedom intimately shape the thoughts and feelings of psychological agents in time (O'Neill 2015).

The truncated lens of existing research is reductive, lending itself to fixed ideas that are not as open as they ought to be for alternative ways of conceptualizing human experience. In the writing of this book, I have grown. I have had to look outside the psychological disciplines for the development of a growth mindset. I want to believe that our professional knowledge can grow, in the same way we expect our clients to grow. We can mould new ideas together, by recognizing how the horizons of our self-beliefs were moulded in time. Ireland's history was prescriptive, authoritarian, fixed and close-minded. If our profession does not understand this history, how can we emancipate clients from congealed and oppressive self-beliefs? The pattern of the narratives in this book illustrates how psychological resistance was expressed as silence; an atmospheric demand to dissociate from pain and suffering. Such resistance is depleting over time. In the main, the socially engineered concept of *mea culpa* proved lethal for expanded autonomy. A normative demand to expect people to dissociate from being seen as a victim/survivor is literally identical with the self-abnegation concept of *mea culpa*, robbing people of a more expanded way of being-in-the-world. To foreground the seductive concept of *mea culpa* for taking responsibility was mind-altering, painful, hurtful and silencing.

Our more recent history illustrates we are open to transforming this history. We have the collective motivation and capacities to upend oppressive ideas. This collective effort unmasks the normative veil of ignorance and pain. Psychological disciplines must put in the effort to confront status quo concepts that proved oppressive to human potential. If we reinforce unrealistic and dominating ideas, we reward quietude, closing people down, rather than opening people up. A pattern of denial adds insult to injury. I have learned some tools for opening up the manifolds of historic denial; how growing up in this context certainly violated the trajectory of my own self-beliefs.

Conclusion

In the book, my challenge was to immerse personal experiences in critical historical thinking and psychosocial scholarship. My objective was to try and translate how the social/historical manifests in self-reflection. I hope a key strength of this work illustrates how an insider and outsider perspective deepens insight on how historic and changing social patterns constitutes and transforms human personalities. What can limit human reflection is our inability to see how we reproduce domination in our lived experiences. What is very striking about Ireland's socio-emotive development has been its distinct tendency to privilege innate moral/ethical discourses in the applied institutional domains of Irish life. As a negative experience, this deference in the institutional firewall generated by the powerful interface in Church/state regulation, meant that far too many people in Ireland were socialized to believe that socially induced suffering was a psychological problem (weakness of will).

As a young boy, religious vocation was conceived as a gift, what John Paul II spoke of as 'a precious adornment' on his trip to Ireland in 1979. Many people talk of the progress arising from Vatican II in the 1960s. However, in my youth, I was more familiar with the pious impulse of Vatican I (Howard 2017). I witnessed the mind-altering effects of these dogmas on others. I witnessed the psychotic and exalted episodes of moral puritanism where a woman thought she was the incarnation of the Blessed Virgin Mary. For myself, the thought-insertions of religious oppression made me fear that others could see through me. While critical of Christianity, my aim in this work is neither subversive nor vindicatory.

A key message from my own personal experience is to acknowledge the impact of social trauma and adversity. A congealed tension became normal. What was impressed on me from a young age was a 'virtuous' self-abnegation. A failure to comply with those normative prescriptions lent weight to the idea that any vulnerability I experienced was a self-imposed deficiency which I needed to overcome.

On his trip to Ireland in 2018, Pope Francis expressed his shame and begged for forgiveness for the repeated abuses and cover-ups in religious run institutions and schools in historic Ireland. Ireland is a very different country to the time when John Paul II visited Ireland in 1979. This was well exampled in the much lower turnout of our population to welcome Pope Francis in 2018 (McKay 2018). Many well-organized protest events were organized during the Pope's visit in 2018. In Dublin, Pope Francis visited the local church on Sean McDermott Street 'which venerates the bones of Matt Talbot, an alcoholic religious zealot who mortified his flesh by wrapping it in chains and died in the 1920s' (McKay 2018). Susan McKay said the Pope was not brought to 'see the now empty and last of the Magdalene laundries – institutions where girls and women were sent to atone for the "sin" of becoming pregnant while unmarried – which closed only in 1996' (McKay 2018). In this instance, the Roman Catholic Church in 2018 is still clinging to strange customs, whereby the religious self is encouraged to take on allegiance to sacrificial ideals as a model of self-restraint and responsibility. More than anything, it is these fundamentalist projections that capture the core of the *mea culpa* religious philosophy in Irish history. I am more than familiar with these deeply insincere and repressive ideas that concealed so much pain and suffering in my family history.

In the book, I have tried to capture lifespan development as situated in Ireland's history. Such analysis often involves a rigorous analysis of the social/historic determinants that make up the experiences of our citizens. Despite the exhaustive evidentiary audit trail, I was mostly treated with suspicion by the De La Salle Brothers. In truth, the ideology of this order, embedded in Ireland's norms, damaged my motivational capacity for self-confidence at a critical juncture in my self-development. The Brothers show little appreciation for the moral harm and rape of children. In my case, the De La Salle Brothers have done nothing of consequence to right this trauma. This is their privilege, arising from their place in the social hierarchy. This pattern ought to be a matter of public concern, when the order resists and discredits persons who come forward to report crimes. In Bernstein's essay on moral injury (2015), his social formulation of dignity resonates with experience:

> Human beings are the sorts of beings who can undergo devastation: they can be destroyed in their standing as a person; they have their dignity and self-respect destroyed. When one loses one's dignity, one also loses one's trust in the world. Dignity is the representation of self-respect, where self-respect is the stance of one who takes herself to be of intrinsic worth and acts accordingly. (p. 311)

Early traumas can shorten people's lives. I have tried to show this in the narrative trajectories of many of the souls in this book. These stories are not the stories of the innately afflicted or the personality disordered. The stories are about the psychosocial self in historical time. Our methods and our language are often 'too blunt' (Honneth, 2014/2011, p. 87) to capture these dynamics. For example, Shim et al. (2015), as part of a Group for the Advancement of Psychiatry (GAP) Prevention Committee, seems to accept that the social determinants of mental health are under-theorized: 'For a set of conditions that will affect a third or more of people at some point in their lives, this neglect is quite remarkable ... and shameful' (xiii).

Over the last two decades, I have been trying to bring about positive changes in my life circumstances. The change has involved a significant commitment to study. The process has been an isolating and challenging experience. Living on a low income, trying to fund my years of education, and not being able to contribute to my partner, important others and events have been significantly testing. Without my redundancy and help from philanthropy, I simply could not have afforded an education up to doctoral level. In writing about my experiences, I am aiming to transform experiences. When I reflect on where I am positioned now, I can appreciate the stability I have been able to cultivate in my life. I felt it was important to tell my story. I hope others might benefit from it. For the moment, I aim to apply myself to meaningful work that adds value. I am certainly more hopeful about living in a country like Ireland that places a value on equality/freedom (Rodgers 2018).

I consider myself very fortunate to be alive, to be in a very loving relationship, and to have good friends. I love you all and thanks especially to Paul for your special love for me and great patience. Paul and myself will tie the knot and marry each other in 2019.

Epilogue

In the writing of this book, I deepened my awareness on how my own self-beliefs were confronted by the informational array of foregrounded ideologies in Ireland's recent history. I felt I was pushing against the grain of enacted concepts to unearth deeper layers of meaning, woven into historic intentionality and empowered by social transformation. In this, I grasped, how the transactions of traumatic experience, situated in oppressive cultures, had yielded such a devastating blow to many members of my family, particularly how we reflected and absorbed what was happening to us. Any externalization of heightened distress was merely interpreted as idiosyncratic restlessness and irritation. Significantly, social hierarchies had the power to preordain mental distress as disorders of will formation, heightening shame and stigma. Furthermore, these multivalent force-fields cascaded to painful levels of internalized self-criticism, weakening and depleting selves over time. Beyond psychological tariffs, the transfers of historic and current values on intentionality are now more objectively tracked as biosocial imprints on lifespan epigenetic development. (e.g. allostatic stress measurement)

At the very least, in problem-solving the casual threads of disempowerment, the horizon of self-confidence can grow beyond limiting self-beliefs and mind-states. Because of how homogenous Ireland's culture was, and its current context of social transformation, this analytic task has been easier to achieve with rigor. This comes with a caveat. Given the rising trend of retrenchment populism, we see again how history repeats its paradoxical cycle of backward and forward movement. We have to be consistently aware of the power of the normative imagination and go against the grain of toxic ideas that morph our emotions, twist our ways of knowing, reducing our power to resist a multivalent tendency toward an arc of injustice. There is a lack of trust for what is knowledge with integrity or without it.

The study clearly illustrates how a person's capacity to respond was stretched by social trauma. In particular, my historical memory extends to the terrible pain in my mother's life, my eldest sister Yvonne, my brother Eamonn and those family members who carried enormous pain in a socio-historic context of silence, enacting shame and putting up a brave and smiley face in the face of toxic adversity. I have no problem accepting the transgenerational nature of trauma and how heightened sensitivities are a feature of lives.

As a child and teen, I took on the mantel of dissociation consistent with the normative penchant for secrecy. To cope with my chaotic early environs, I transitioned in early adolescence to abuse alcohol. I was not fully cognizant that altering reality through alcohol and religious concepts would backfire so badly. This is despite witnessing the family chaos these dynamics were causing. Words like harm-reduction never featured in my social context, other than remembering the heartfelt pleas/cries of my mother and others that this madness ought to stop. Traumatic atmospheres and the pattern of addiction altered our moods, narrowing our horizons for making meaning of terrible dynamics in our family history.

Desperate cultures are like corrosive undercurrents, impressing their power as force-fields, chipping away at significant aspects of personal, interpersonal and institutional cultures. Time and time again, institutional inquiries and reports on institutional failures consistently highlight brutish attitudes and behaviours toward those who highlight bad practices. Only the strongest, tenacious and steely whistle-blowers can withstand the blows of sinister and bullying leadership cultures. Many decent people have been crushed in these institutional settings, dying prematurely and they continue to suffer. My brother Eamonn had finely tuned antennae for institutional injustice. He did not retreat but suffered for what is now a well-documented institutional culture of not insignificant proportions in our historic legacy of obstructing others in revealing bad systemic practices. Like other siblings, he put up the good fight for others, who requested his help. Since my brother's Eamonn's untimely death, many people have commented on his warmth and empathy. I want the book study to reach the living souls, and impacted close others, and also, to help those who help them.

My concluding remarks will try to address the implications of the book study, particularly for those in the helping and research professions. As a mature learner, I want to stress how grateful I am for the opportunities extended to me in education. The critical impulse driving my work is re-envisioning narrative trajectories against the silencing power of status-quo pre-ordinances and worn practices that can keep people in an unhealthy state of ignorance. Corrupt power thrives in the micro-regulatory horizon of low self-confidence.

Firstly, it is no exaggeration to say that the reigning orthodoxy of the psychological professions I trained for is still largely embedded in ethical and moralizing concepts, that read like a continuation of old ways of hier-archical knowing to the exclusion of alternative knowledges. As a norma-tive impulse, in the context of Ireland's history, such resistance ought not surprise. It is still inexcusable from a leadership perspective that critical perspectives with normative resonance fail to lift the veil on unhealthy ignorance.

As previously stated, there is ample reason to believe that the way mindfulness concepts are consistently formulated within the informational array of modern theories, display little appetite for political/social/histori-cal horizons of lived experience. Is quieting the ego through mindfulness, a mere validation of the status quo? Micro-regulation in the lens of mind-fulness theory, reads like an agile tale of inner hero resilience. This picture is an impoverished formulation and is certainly not equipped for regional historical critical inquiry. With this significant gap, mindfulness places weight on the individual/interpersonal. In my view, this is the profession's slothfulness - our narrow and truncated attentional focus.

Secondly, Ireland has gone down a path of making history a non-man-datory subject. Such a move may be fuelled by lack of consumer/student appetite for a subject that is often unintelligible and cumbersome in the ways it is taught, a laziness that may be driven by an ideological position. Certainly, a narrowed focus on self-determination is driven by market forces, where historical scholarship may be viewed as a futile pattern of revisionism rather than a focus on imagined futures. Education is often at the mercy of populist dynamics which want to erase the past in protection of its inherited privileges and religious ethos rights.

In the book, we saw numerous examples of how key players in edu-cation even coercively tried to erase the egregious horrors when children were brutalized and harmed in religious run institutions. As some of these survivors age, some may still be confronted by invasive and repetitive questioning on basic mobility issues related to ageing. As ageing persons, these survivors of institutional abuse can spend years mired in a demeaning system the continues to repeat the theme of early trauma on fragile existences. Such lifespan patterns of pronounced inequality are inexcusable. I worry for my eldest sister Yvonne in the US in this regard. Closer to home, the age of austerity and mass migration out of Ireland, following the world financial crash made this situation much worse, and has had the severest impact on members of our societies, not well positioned to withstand the amputation of key services in Ireland. The last couple of years is seeing reinvestment in recruiting for these key services.

I want to thank Drs. Martin Milton, C. Fred Alford and Stephanie N. Arel for picking up the key themes on the situated nature of trauma. These authors recognise that theory as currently foregrounded is certainly complicit by not digging down on multifaceted nature of experiences. Professor Milton also focuses on the theme of gay men in history and unravels the misunderstandings, where misunderstood constituencies can end up colonized into silence by toxic social arrangements and ideas. My book interrogates the quietude. I do not want to recreate this pathology of reasoning in Ireland's history for gay men's identities. These issues I next address in my final remarks.

In earlier sections of this work, I highlighted how easy it was to pathologize gay male identities, where normative atmospheres, as created by toxic social hierarchies, purposively used demeaning concepts, even distorting the idea of a young gay male as a victim of sexual exploitation. Beyond individual incidences of distortion of information, my childhood experience of sexual exploitation was anchored in oppressive ideologies that specifically tried to leverage homosexuality as a pathological discourse, leaning toward a strong tendency of false narratives and suspicion. This negation in the social structure was severe and intensely felt. In terms of developmental psychology, the concrete operational thought pattern of childhood, can lead the child to cognitively conflate that the adult predator is gay. I was confronted by a clerical predator who was the symbolic signifier of self-abnegation as a supreme sacrificial/normative ideal. As the arbiter of norms, this enacted a licence for crimes as his inalienable right. In this scenario, I as a gay boy, easily enacted religious thought to transcend bad situations. This was natural through the social engineering of thought insertions in Ireland's history. The predator, coming into my national school, was my knight in shining armour. I was the handpicked angel for the resplendent splendour of an empire.

In absorbing the seeds of religious vocation and direct grooming, I felt small with little control. I learned inordinate blame/stress in earlier trauma. As a gay boy, I had absorbed the toxic atmosphere of the unspeakable religious stigma. After imbibing all this badness, I was set up to think I was the problematic one, if and when I chose to activate rather than overcome my will. As a young child and teenager, this whole twisted terrain was intense, embedded in the foregrounded and proximate invitation to take on the mantle of shame and guilt and acquiesce and roll over to the preordained socially engineered ideology of Mea Culpa – 'Through My fault, Through My fault, Through My Most Grievous Fault.'

Within my reviewer's interpretations, they capture the traumatizing and terrifying impulse that I and others were confronted with as children and its longitudinal implications for wellbeing. The book is about lifting a lid on the congealed master strokes of dominating ideas from repressive histories and the transforming impact of progress for un-concealment.

The image on the book captures the historic legacy. Thanks to the Production team @Peter Lang for cover design.

Bibliography

AA (2002). *Alcoholics Anonymous Big Book*, 4th revised edn, USA.

AAMC (2014). *Implementing Curricular and Institutional Climate Changes to Improve Health Care for Individuals Who are LGBT, Gender Nonconforming, or Born with DSD A Resource for Medical Educators*, 1st edn, 2014. Edited by Hollenbach, A.D., Eckstrand, K.L., Dreger, A. Association of American Medical Colleges.

Aarte Scholte, J. (2016). Why Global Redistribution is Needed. In Aarte Scholte, J., Fioramonti, L., Nhema, A.G. (ed.), *Global Justice Structural Redistribution in the Global Economy*. London: Rowman and Littlefield International.

ABC News (2017). 6 new settlements totaling $1.8M announced involving NY priest child sex abuse. Available from <http://abc7ny.com/2566562/> [Accessed 26 October 17].

Adoption Rights Alliance (2015). History and Heritage. Available from <http://www.adoptionrightsalliance.com/spg.htm> [Accessed 6 November 2015].

Affidavit communication (2009). Letter to Bro. Pius Mc Carthy, 22 October 2009.

Alcoff, L.M. (2017). Philosophy and Philosophical Practice. In Kid, I.J., Medina, J., Pohlhaus, G., Jnr (eds), *The Routledge Handbook of Epistemic Injustice*. London: Routledge.

Alkon, A. Wolff, B., and Thomas Boyce, W. (2012), Poverty, Stress, and Autonomic Reactivity. In King, R. and Maholmes (eds), *The Oxford Handbook of Poverty and Child Development*. Oxford: Oxford University Press.

Allen, A. (2016). *The End of Progress: Decolonizing the Normative Foundations of Critical Theory*. New York: Columbia University Press.

Allen, A., and Mendieta, E. (eds) (2018). *From Alienation to Forms of Life: The Critical Theory of Rahel Jaeggi*. University Park, PA: Penn State University Press.

Allen, J., and Allen, M. (2015). The social determinants of health, empowerment, and participation. In Clift, S. and Camic, P.M. (eds), *Oxford Textbook of Creative Arts, Health, and Wellbeing International Perspectives on Practice, Policy and Research*. Oxford: Oxford University Press.

Allen, J., Balfour, R., Bell, R., Marmot, M. (2014). Social Determinants of Mental Health. *International Review of Psychiatry*, August 2014; 26(4): 392–407.

Anderson, E. (2011). *The Imperative of Integration*. Princeton, NJ: Princeton University Press.

Armstrong, K., and Donnelly, M. (2018). Mary McAleese: My youngest brother was 'physically, sadistically abused' by paedophile priest. *Irish Independent*. Available from <https://www.independent.ie/irish-news/politics/mary-mcaleese-my-youngest-brother-was-physically-sadistically-abused-by-paedophile-priest-36695368.html> [Accessed 13 March 2018].

Arnett-Jensen, L. (2015). Cultural-Developmental Scholarship for a Global World: An Introduction. In Arnett-Jensen (ed.), *The Oxford Handbook of Human Development and Culture: An Interdisciplinary Perspective*, Oxford: Oxford University Press.

Attitude (2017). Chechen Authorities 'Summon Parents to Prison Camps to Kill their Gay Sons'. Available from <http://attitude.co.uk/chechen-authorities-summoning-parents-to-prison-camps-to-kill-their-gay-sons/> [Accessed 5 May 2017].

Australian Royal Commission (2017). Royal Commission into Institutional Responses to Child Sexual Abuse Final Report Preface and Executive Summary. Available from <https://www.childabuseroyalcommission.gov.au/final-report> [Accessed 20 December 2017].

Baggett, J. (2009). James Hardiman, Samuel Ferguson, James Clarence Mangan and the Politics of Translation. In Quintelli-Neary, M. (ed.), *Visions of the Irish Dream*. Cambridge: Cambridge University Press.

Bardon, S. (2018). State Apologizes for Criminalising Gay men in the past. *The Irish Times*. 20 June.

Barrett, A., Kamiya, Y., & O'Sullivan, V. (2014). The Long-Term Impact of Childhood Sexual Abuse on Incomes and Labour Force Status. <http://www.esri.ie/UserFiles/publications/RB20140301/RB20140301.pdf>. Also referenced as: Childhood Sexual Abuse and later life economic consequences. *Journal of Behavioural and Experimental Economics*. p. 1–26.

BBC (2005). On this Day 'Pope calls for Peace in Ireland'. Available from <http://news.bbc.co.uk/onthisday/hi/dates/stories/september/29/newsid_3926000/3926755.stm> [Accessed 8 January 2016].

BBC (2014). Rubane House: Sex abuse inquiry 'best forgotten' said senior cleric Available from <http://www.bbc.com/news/uk-northern-ireland-29430974> [Accessed 9 January 2016].

Beatty, A. (2016). *Masculinity and Power in Irish Nationalism 1884–1938*. London: Palgrave MacMillan.

Bejan, T.M. (2017). *Mere Civility: Disagreement and the limits of Toleration*. Cambridge, MA: Harvard University Press.

Benjamin, J. (2017). *Beyond Doer and Done to: Recognition Theory, Intersubjectivity and the Third*. Abingdon: Taylor and Francis. Kindle Edition.

Bernard, D. (1970). *Wine and Gold*. Available from <http://delasallecollege.com/galleries/wine-and-gold/wine-and-gold-1970/>. Image 24 of 57. [Accessed 6 November 2015].

Bernstein, J.M. (2015). *Torture and Dignity: An Essay on Moral Injury*. Chicago: Cambridge University Press Chicago.

Biancalana, P. (2009). The Roman Catholic Church, the National Schools and the Role of the Christian Brothers. In Quintelli-Neary, M. (ed.), *Visions of the Irish Dream*. Cambridge: Cambridge University Press.

Blanshard, P. (1954). *The Irish and Catholic Power: An American Interpretation*. Boston, MA: Beacon Press.

Bloomberg (2016). Company Overview of CBIS Global Funds plc – European Equity Fund. Available from <http://www.bloomberg.com/research/stocks/private/snapshot.asp?privcapId=58049896> [Accessed 10 August 2016].

Boland, R. (2018). Ann Lovett: Death of a 'strong, kick-ass girl'. *The Irish Times*. Available from <https://www.irishtimes.com/life-and-style/people/ann-lovett-death-of-a-strong-kick-ass-girl-1.3429792> [Accessed 11 May 2018].

Boland, R. (2018a). I was Ann Lovett's boyfriend. *The Irish Times*. Available from <https://www.irishtimes.com/life-and-style/people/i-was-ann-lovett-s-boyfriend-1.3484311> [Accessed 11 May 2018].

Boston Globe (2016). Betrayal: The Crisis in the Catholic Church The Findings of the Investigation that inspired *Spotlight*. The Investigative Staff of the *Boston Globe*. UK.

BRA (2015). De La Salle Brothers had a sex-abuser to recruit new Brothers. Available from <http://www.brokenrites.org.au/drupal/node/30> [Accessed 8 March 2016].

Brady, M.S., and Fricker, M. (eds) (2016). *The Epistemic Life of Groups Essays in the Epistemology of Collectives*. Oxford: Oxford University Press.

Brady, S. (2008). The impact of sexual abuse on sexual identity formation in gay men. *Journal of Child Sexual Abuse*, 17, 359–376.

Breaking News (2018). Latest: Taoiseach to consider McAleese call for inquiry into church's handling of Fr Finnegan allegations. Available from <https://www.breakingnews.ie/ireland/latest-taoiseach-to-consider-mcaleese-call-for-inquiry-into-churchs-handling-of-fr-finnegan-allegations-832098.html> [Accessed 13 March 2018].

Bromet, E., Karam, E., Koenen, K., Stein, D. (2018). *Trauma and Posttraumatic Stress Disorder: Global Perspectives from the WHO World Mental Health Surveys*. Cambridge: Cambridge University Press.

Brown, J., Cohen, P., Johnson, J.G., and Smailes, E.M. (1999). Childhood abuse and neglect: Specificity and effects on adolescent and young adult depression and suicidality. *Journal of the American Academy of Child and Adolescent Psychiatry* 38, 1490–6.

Browne, N. (1986). *Against the Tide*. Dublin: Gill and MacMillan.

Bryer, J.B., Nelson, B.A., Miller, J.B., and Krol, P.A. (1987). Childhood Sexual Abuse and Physical Abuse as Factors in Adult Psychiatric Illness. *American Journal of Psychiatry* 144, 1426–30.

Buchanan, R. (2016). The Murder that Created The Dublin Pride Parade. Available from <http://theoutmost.com/opinion/murder-created-dublin-pride/?platform=hootsuite> [Accessed 22 June 2016].

Butler, J. (2004). *Precarious life*. London: Verso.

Butler, J. (2018). Précis of Senses of the Subject. *Philosophy and Phenomenological Research* Vol. XCVI, No. 1, January 2018.

Caplan, R. (2016). Childhood Schizophrenia. In Cicchetti, D. (ed.), *Developmental Psychopathology Volume 3, Maladaptation and Psychopathology*. London: Wiley.

Carastathis, G.S., Cohen, L., Kaczmarek, E., & Chang, P. (2017). Rejected by Family for Being Gay or Lesbian: Portrayals, Perceptions and Resilience. *Journal of Homosexuality*, 64(3), 289–320.

Carswell, S. (2009). De La Salle Brothers launch investment fund in Dublin. *The Irish Times*, Finance Section, 10 June.

Carswell, S. (2018). Declan Flynn 'queer-bashing' murder 'still very raw' 36 years on. *The Irish Times*. Available from <https://www.irishtimes.com/news/social-affairs/declan-flynn-queer-bashing-murder-still-very-raw-36-years-on-1.3548395#.Wzb_POSiGXg.twitter> [Accessed 2 July 2018].

Caulfield, P. (2014). Hymns and screams: Abuse at St Gilbert's approved school revealed. Available from <http://www.bbc.com/news/uk-england-hereford-worcester-30231750> [Accessed 9 December 2015].

CBIS (2015). Interim Report and Unaudited Condensed Financial Statements for the Period Ended 30 June 2015. Available from <https://cbisonline.com/eu/wp-content/uploads/sites/3/2013/04/CBIS-Global-Semi-Annual-Report-6-30-2015.pdf> [Accessed 16 December 2015].

CDF (Congregation for the Doctrine of the Faith) (1975). Persona Humana – Declaration on Certain Questions Concerning Sexual Ethics (Section 8). Vatican City. Available from <http://www.vatican.va/roman_curia/congregations/cfaith/documents/rc_con_cfaith_doc_19751229_persona-humana_en.html> [Accessed 6 November 2015].

CDF (1986). Letter to the Bishops of the Catholic Church on the Pastoral Care of Homosexual Persons. Available from <http://www.vatican.va/roman_curia/congregations/cfaith/documents/rc_con_cfaith_doc_19861001_homosexual-persons_en.html> [Accessed 6 November 2015].

CDF (1992). Some Considerations Concerning The Response to Legislative Proposals on Non-Discrimination of Homosexual Persons. Available from <http://www.vatican.va/roman_curia/congregations/cfaith/documents/rc_con_cfaith_doc_20030731_homosexual-unions_en.html> [Accessed 6 November 2015].

Cision Newsletter (2017). Christian Brothers Investment Services Appoints Jeffrey McCroy as CEO: Reaffirms long-term commitment to Catholic Responsible Investing. Available from <https://www.prnewswire.com/news-releases/christian-brothers-investment-services-appoints-jeffrey-mccroy-as-ceo-300464143.html> [Accessed 12 May 2017].

Chandler, D., and Reid, J. (2016). *The Neoliberal Subject Resilience, Adaptation and Vulnerability*. London: Rowman and Littlefield International.

Christman, J. (2018). Decentered Social Selves: Interrogating Alienation in Conversation with Rahel Jaeggi. In Allen, A., and Mendieta, E. (eds). *From Alienation to Forms of Life: The Critical Theory of Rahel Jaeggi*. University Park, PA: Pennsylvania State University Press.

Chu, J.A. (2011). *Rebuilding Shattered Lives*, 2nd edn. Hoboken, NJ: John Wiley & Sons.

Clark, D.B., Lesnick, L., and Hegedus, A.M. (1997). Trauma and other adverse life events in Adolescents with Alcohol Abuse and Dependence. *Journal of the American Academy of Child and Adolescent Psychiatry* 36, 1744–51.

Clarke, V., Ellis, S.J., Peel, E., Riggs, D.W. (2010). *Lesbian, Gay, Bisexual, Trans & Queer Psychology*. Cambridge: Cambridge University Press.

Cohen, J. (2002). *Regulating Intimacy*. Princeton, NJ: Princeton University Press.

Coldrey, B. (1988). *Faith and Fatherland: Christian Brothers and the Development of Irish Nationalism, 1838–1921*. Dublin: Macmillan Press.

Coldrey, B. (1993). *The Scheme: The Christian Brothers and Childcare in Western Australia*. Argyle-Pacific Publishing.

Collins, M. (2018). Text of presentation – Safeguarding Panel at World Meeting of Families 24AUG201. Available from <http://www.mariecollins.net/talks.html> [Accessed 30 August 2018].

Congdon, M. (2017). What's Wrong with Epistemic Injustice? Harm, Vice, Objectification, misrecognition. In Kidd, J.I., Medina, J., and Pohlhaus Jnr, G. (eds), *The Routledge Handbook of Epistemic Injustice*. London: Routledge.

Cooke, M. (2006). *Re-Presenting the Good Society*. Harvard, MA: MIT Press.

Cooney, J. (1999). *John Charles McQuaid Ruler of Ireland*. Dublin: O'Brien Press.

Corbett, K. (2009). *Boyhoods: Rethinking Masculinities*. London: Yale University Press.

Corless, C. (2017). Standing Ovation for Local Historian on the Late Late Show. Available from <https://www.youtube.com/watch?v=VTqIhIf5KQE> [Accessed 22 March 2017].

Cote, J.E., and Levine, C.G. (2016). *Identity Formation, Youth, and Development: A Simplified Approach*. London: Psychology Press.

CPO (2015). Dublin Archdiocese Letter Correspondence. 18 December.

CPO (2016). Two letter communications. 14 January and 14 March.

Crary, D. (2013). Foes of Russia's Anti-Gay Laws Consider New Tactics. <http://www.nydailynews.com/news/world/groups-protest-russian-anti-gay-laws-article-1.1520015> [Accessed 2 November 2016].

Crompton, L. (2003). *Homosexuality & Civilization*. London, Harvard University Press.

Croome, R. (2014). Victims of anti-gay laws deserve an apology. Available from <http://www.abc.net.au/news/2014-01-14/croome-victims-of-anti-gay-laws-deserve-an-apology/5197904>.

Crowell, S.E. Derbidge, C.M., and Beachaine, T.P. (2014). Developmental Approaches to Understanding Suicidal and Self-Injurious Behaviors. In Nock, M.K (ed.), *The Oxford Handbook of Suicide and Self-Injury*. Oxford: Oxford University Press.

Currie, J., and Widom, C.S. (2010). Long-Term Consequences of Child Abuse and Neglect on Adult Economic Well-Being. *Child Maltreat* 15(2), 111–20.

Daly, C. (2018). Foreword in Redmond, Paul Jude (2018), *The Adoption Machine: The Dark History of Ireland's Mother & Baby Homes and the Inside Story of How 'Tuam 800' Became a Global Scandal*. Dublin: Merrion Press. Kindle Edition.

Daly, C.B. (1979). *Irish Press*, 14 May, cited by Towey, J., *Irish De La Salle Brothers in Christian Education*, Dublin: De La Salle Provincialate, p. 595.

Daly, C.B. (1998). *Steps on My Pilgrim Journey*. Dublin: Veritas.

Daly, E. (2012). *Religion, Law and the Irish State*. Dublin: Clarus Press.

Daly, E., and Hickey, T. (2015). *The Political Theory of the Irish Constitution*. Manchester: Manchester University Press.

Daly, M.E. (2016). *Sixties Ireland: Reshaping the Economy, State and Society, 1957–1973*. Cambridge: Cambridge University Press.

D'Arcy, B. (2015). *And Catch the Heart off Guard*. Dublin: Columba Press.

Das, V. (2007). *Life and Words: Violence and the Descent into the Ordinary*. London: University of California Press.

Davis-Siegel, J., Gottman, M., and Siegel, D.J. (2015). Mindfulness and Self-Regulation: A Medical Approach to the Mind and Mental Health. In Ostafin, B.D. Robinson, M.D., Meier, B.P (eds), *Handbook of Mindfulness and Self-Regulation*. London: Springer.

Department of Education (2011). Irish Minister meets Religious Orders on Redress Contributions. Available from <http://s3.documentcloud.org/documents/443207/minutes-of-meeting-between-minister-for.pdf> [Accessed 16 December 2015].

Department of Education and Skills (2016). Action Plan for Education 2016–19 Available from <http://www.education.ie/en/Publications/Corporate-Reports/Strategy-Statement/Department-of-Education-and-Skills-Strategy-State ment-2016-2019.pdf> [Accessed 16 September 2016].

Department of Education and Skills (2017). Available from <https://www.education.ie/en/The-Department/Management-Organisation/Residential-Institutions-Redress-Unit.html> [Accessed 22 November 2017].

Deranty, J.P. (2016). Between Honneth and Ranciere: Problems and Potentials of a Contemporary Critical Theory of Society. In Genel, K., and Deranty, J.P. (eds), *Recognition or Disagreement*. New York: Columbia University Press.

DeThomasis, L. (2012). *Flying in the Face of Tradition: Listening to the Lived Experience of the Faithful*. Chicago: ACTA Publications.

Dillon, M. (2002). Catholicism, Politics and Culture in the Republic of Ireland. In Jelen, T.G., and Wilcox, C. (eds), *Religion and Politics in Comparative Perspective: The One, The Few, and The Many*. Cambridge: Cambridge University Press.

Disch, L., & Hawkesworth, M. (2016). *Oxford Handbook of Feminist Theory*, Oxford: Oxford University Press.

Dolan, L. (1983). Kieran Seeks Rights for Gays. *Cork Examiner*, 3 August.

Dorcey, M. (1995). Interview in O'Carroll, I., and Collins, E. (eds), *Lesbian and Gay Visions of Ireland: Towards the Twenty-First Century*. London: Cassell Press.

Doyle, J. (2011). Cardinal Cullen and the System of National Education in Ireland. In Keogh, D. & McDonnell, A. (eds), *Cardinal Cullen and his World*. Dublin: Four Courts Press.

Duberman, M. (2018). *Has the Gay Movement Failed?* Berkeley: University of California Press.

Dubowitz, H., Black, M., Harrington, D., and Verschoore, A. (1993). A follow up study of behavioural problems associated with Child Sexual Abuse. *Child Abuse and Neglect* 17, 743–54.

Duffy, M. (2011). *Voices from the Hinterland: Lesbian Women's Experience of Irish Health Care*. Lap Lambert Academic Publishing.

Duffy, N. (2018). Ireland's former President Mary McAleese to march at Pride 'with my gay son and his wonderful husband'. *Pink News*. Available from <https://www.pinknews.co.uk/2018/06/18/irelands-president-mary-mcaleese-gay-son-pride/> [Accessed 20 June 2018].

Earner-Byrne, L. (2013) *Mother and Child: Maternity and Child Welfare in Dublin, 1922–60*. Manchester, Manchester University Press; Reprint edition.

Earner-Byrne, L. (2017). *Letters of the Catholic Poor: Poverty in Independent Ireland 1920–40*. Cambridge: Cambridge University Press.

ECHR (2014). CASE OF O'KEEFFE v. IRELAND (Application no. 35810/09) Grand Chamber Judgement. Available from <https://www.dfa.ie/media/dfa/alldfawebsitemedia/ourrolesandpolicies/internationallaw/O'keeffe-v-ireland.pdf> [Accessed 23 June 2016].

Eckenrode, J., Laird, M., and Doris, J. (1993). School Performance and Disciplinary Problems among Abused and Neglected Children. *Developmental Psychology* 29, 53–62.

Egan, O. (2016). *Queer Republic of Cork Cork's Lesbian, Gay, Bisexual & Transgender Communities 1970s-1990s.* Onstream Publishers.

Ehrlich, K.B., Miller, G.E., Chen, E. (2016). Childhood Adversity and Adult Physical Health. In Cicchetti D. (ed.), *Developmental Psychopathology, Volume 4, Risk, Resilience, and Intervention*, 3rd edn. London: Wiley.

Eile magazine (2018). Historic Apology to LGBT People from Taoiseach Leo Varadkar and Seanad. *Eile*. Available from <https://eile.ie/2018/06/20/historic-apology-to-lgbt-people-from-taoiseach-leo-varadkar-and-seanad/> [Accessed 20 June 2018].

Eldridge, R. (2003). Introduction: Between Acknowledgement and Avoidance. In Eldridge, R. (ed.), *Stanley Cavell*. Cambridge: Cambridge University Press.

Eribon, D. (2004). *Insult and the Making of the Gay Self* (Series Q). Translated by Michael Lucey. Durham, NC: Duke University Press.

Fagan, S. (1997). *Does Morality Change*. Dublin: The Liturgical Press.

Fanning, B. (2014). Noël Browne, Against the Tide (1986). In Fanning, B., and Garvin, T. (eds), *The Books that Define Ireland*. Dublin: Merrion Press.

Fanning, B., and Garvin, T. (2014). *The Books that Define Ireland*. Dublin: Merrion Press.

Feiring, C., Taska, L., and Lewis, M. (1999). A process model for understanding adaptation to sexual abuse: the role of shame in defining stigmatization. *Child Abuse and Neglect* 17, 743–54.

Fergusson, D.M., Horwood, I.J., and Lynskey, M.T. (1996). Childhood Sexual Abuse and Psychiatric Disorder in Young Adulthood: II. Psychiatric outcomes of childhood sexual abuse. *Journal of the American Academy of Child and Adolescent Psychiatry*, 35, 1365–74.

Ferriter, D. (2004). *The Transformation of Ireland 1900–2000*. London: Profile Books.

Ferriter, D. (2009). *Occasions of Sin: Sex and Society in Modern Ireland*. London: Profile Books.

Ferriter, D. (2012). *Ambiguous Republic Ireland in the 1970s*. London: Profile Books.

Ferriter, D. (2014). DeValera's Ireland 1922–58. In Jackson, A. (ed.), *The Oxford Handbook of Modern Irish History*. Oxford: Oxford University Press.

Ferriter, D. (2017). How OECD reports came to replace the papal encyclicals. *The Irish Times*. Available from <https://www.irishtimes.com/culture/books/diarmaid-ferriter-how-oecd-reports-came-to-replace-the-papal-encyclicals-1.3149566> [Accessed 20 December 2017].

Finkelhor, D., Hotaling, G., Lewis, I.A., and Smith, C. (1990). Sexual Abuse in a National Survey of Adult Men and Women: Prevalence, Characteristics and Risk Factors. *Child Abuse and Neglect*, 17, 743–54.

Flannery, T. (2013). *A Question of Conscience*. Dublin: Londubh Books.

Flynn, M. (1983). *Nothing To Say*. Dublin: Ward River Press.

Fonagy, P., and Allison, E. (2015). A Scientific Theory of Homosexuality For Psychoanalysis. In Lemma, A., and Lynch, P.E. (eds), *Sexualities: Contemporary Psychoanalytic Perspectives*. London: Routledge.

Fonagy, P., and Higgitt, A. (2007). The Development of Prejudice: An Attachment Theory Hypothesis Explaining its Ubiquity. In Mahfouz, A., Twemlow, S., Scharff., D.E., and Aronson, J. (eds), *The Future of Prejudice: Psychoanalysis and the Prevention of Prejudice*. Lanham, MD: Rowman and Littlefield.

Frankowski, B.L. (2004). Sexual Orientation and Adolescents. *Pediatrics* 113; 1827–32.

Frawley-O'Dea, M.G. (2007). *Perversion of Power Sexual Abuse in the Catholic Church*. Nashville, TN: Vanderbilt University Press.

Frawley-O'Dea, M.G. (2007a). Preface: From the Bayou to Boston: History of a Scandal. In Frawley-O'Dea, M.G., and Goldner, V. (eds), *Predatory Priests, Silenced Victims The Sexual Abuse Crisis and The Catholic Church*. London: Analytic Press.

Freyenhagen, F. (2013). *Adorno's Practical Philosophy: Living less Wrongly*. Cambridge: Cambridge University Press.

Fricker, M. (2017). Evolving Concepts of Epistemic Injustice. In Kidd, I.J., Medina, J., Pohlhaus, G. (eds), *The Routledge Handbook of Epistemic Injustice*. London: Routledge.

Friedrich, W.N., Urquiza, A.J., and Beilke, R.L. (1986). Behaviour Problems in Sexually Abused Young Children. *Journal of Paediatric Psychology*, 11, 47–7.

Fuchs, T. (2018). *Ecology of the Brain: The phenomenology and biology of the embodied mind*. Oxford: Oxford University Press.

Fuller, L. (2002). *Irish Catholicism since 1950*. Dublin: Gill and Macmillan.

Gallagher, C. (2016). Gay Community recalls dark days before decriminalization. *The Irish Times*. Available from <http://www.irishtimes.com/news/social-affairs/gay-community-recalls-dark-days-before-decriminalisation-1.2886652> [Accessed 30 November 2016].

Gallagher, S. (2017). *Enactivist Interventions: Rethinking the Mind*. Oxford: Oxford University Press.

Gartland, F. (2014). Church said Ann Lovett's Death was due to her 'immaturity'. *The Irish Times*. Available from <https://www.irishtimes.com/news/politics/church-said-ann-lovett-s-death-was-due-to-her-immaturity-1.2041461> [Accessed 11 May 2018].

Gartner, R. B. (2001). *Betrayed as Boys*. New York: Guilford Press.

Gartner, R. B. (2005). *Beyond Betrayal*. Hoboken, NJ: John Wiley & Sons.

Garvin, T. (1986). Nationalist Revolutionaries. In *Ireland 1858–1928: Patriots, Priests and the Roots of the Irish Revolution*, reprint edn 2005. Dublin: Gill and Macmillan.

Garvin, T. (2004). *Preventing the Future: Why was Ireland so poor for so long?* Dublin: Gill Books.

Gately, S. (2014). American-born nuncio sees new enthusiasm among young Irish Catholics. Available from <http://catholicphilly.com/2014/06/news/world-news/american-born-nuncio-sees-new-enthusiasm-among-young-irish-catholics/> [Accessed 21 December 2017].

Gleeson, K. (2016). Responsibility and Redress: Theorizing Gender Justice in the Context of Catholic Clerical Child Sexual Abuse in Ireland and Australia. In Thematic: Responsibility and Redress in *UNSWLJ*, 39, 779.

Goldblatt, M.J. (2014). Psychodynamics of Suicide. In Nock, M.E. (ed.), *The Oxford Handbook of Suicide and Self-Injury*. Oxford: Oxford University Press.

Goode, H., McGee, H., and O'Boyle, C. (2003). *Time to Listen: Confronting Child Sexual Abuse by Catholic Clergy in Ireland*. Dublin: Liffey Press.

Gordon, M. (1990). Males and Females as Victims of Childhood Sexual Abuse: An Examination of the Gender Effect. *Journal of Family Violence*, 5, 321–32.

Gries, L.T., Goh, D.S., Cavanagh, J. (1996). Factors associated with disclosure during child sexual abuse assessment. *Journal of Childhood Sexual Abuse*, 5, 1–19.

Grilo, C.M., Sanislow, C., Fehon, D.C., Martino, S., and McGlashan, T.H. (1999). Psychological and Behavioural Functioning in Adolescent Psychiatric Inpatients who Report Histories of Childhood Abuse. *American Journal of Psychiatry*, 156, 538–43.

The Guardian (2013). As a Gay Parent I must flee Russia or lose my children. Available from <https://www.theguardian.com/commentisfree/2013/aug/11/anti-gay-laws-russia> [Accessed 2 November 2017].

Hammack, P. L. (2018). Social Psychology and Social Justice: Critical Principles and Perspectives for the Twenty-First Century. In Hammack P.L. (ed.), *The Oxford Handbook of Social Psychology and Social Justice*. Oxford: Oxford University Press.

Hammack, P.L., Forst, D.M., Meyer, I.H., Pletta, D.R. (2017). Gay Men's Health and Identity: Social Change and the Life Course. *Archives of Sexual Behavior*. 5 June.

Han, S.C., Gallagher, M.W., Franz, M.R., Chen, M.S., Cabral, F.M., and Marx, B.P. (2013). Childhood Sexual Abuse, Alcohol Use and PTSD Symptoms as Predictors of Adult Sexual Assault Among Lesbians and Gay Men. *Journal of Interpersonal Violence* 28(1), 2505–20.

Hancock, C. (2018). Investor buys entire apartment scheme for rental. *The Irish Times*, 12 May.

Harper, K. (2013). *From Shame to Sin: The Christian Transformation of Sexual Morality in Late Antiquity*. Cambridge, MA, Harvard University Press.

Harter, S. (2017) Developmental and Prosocial Dimensions of Hypo-Egoic Phenomena. In Brown, K.W., and Leary, M.R. (eds), *The Oxford Handbook of Hypo-Egoic Phenomena*. London: Oxford University Press.

Haslanger, S. (2017). Objectivity, epistemic objectification, and oppression. In Kidd, I.J., Medina, J. Pohlhaus, G. (eds), *The Routledge Handbook of Epistemic Injustice*. London: Routledge.

Heilbron, N., Franklin, J.C., Guerry, J.D., Prinstein, M.J. (2014). Social and Ecological Approaches to Understanding Suicidal Behaviours and Non-suicidal Self-Injury. In Nock, M.K. (ed.), *The Oxford Handbook of Suicide and Self-Injury*. Oxford: Oxford University Press.

Herman, J.L. (1992). Complex PTSD: A Syndrome in Survivors of Prolonged and Repeated Trauma. *Journal of Traumatic Stress*, 5, 377–91.

Hewitt, P.L., Flett, G.L., and Mikail, S.F. (2017). *Perfectionism: A Relational Approach to Conceptualization, Assessment and Treatment*. London, Guildford Press.

HIA Inquiry (2017). Chapter 11, Module 3, De La Salle Boys Home Rubane House. Available from <https://www.hiainquiry.org/> [Accessed 9 April 2017].

Hibbard, R.A., Ingersoll, G.M., and Orr, D.P. (1990). Behavioural Risk, Emotional Risk/Child Abuse Among Adolescents in Nonclinical Setting. *Paediatrics* 86, 896–901.

Hogan, G. (2012). *The Origins of the Irish Constitution 1928–1941*. Dublin: Royal Irish Academy.

Holohan, C. (2011). *In Plain Sight: Responding to the Ferns, Ryan, Murphy and Cloyne Reports*. Dublin: Amnesty International Ireland.

Honneth, A. (1995). *The Struggle for Recognition: The Moral Grammar of Social Conflicts*. Cambridge, UK: Polity Press.

Honneth, A. (2001). Invisibility: On the Epistemology of 'Recognition' from Recognition by Axel Honneth and Avishia Margalit. *Aristotelian Society Supplementary Volume* 75 (1): 111–26.

Honneth, A. (2008/1995). Personal Identity and Disrespect. In Seidman, S., and Alexander J.C. (eds), *The New Social Theory Reader*, 2nd edn. London: Routledge.

Honneth, A. (2009). *Pathologies of Reason: On the Legacy of Critical Theory*. Cambridge: Cambridge University Press.

Honneth, A. (2012). *The I in We: Studies in the Theory of Recognition*. London: Polity Press.

Honneth, A. (2012a). Foreword in O'Neill, S., Smith, N.H. (eds), *Recognition Theory as Social Research: Investigating the Dynamics of Social Conflict*. Basingstoke: Palgrave McMillan.

Honneth, A. (2014). *Freedom's Right The Social Foundations of Democratic Life*. London: Polity Press.

Howard, T.A. (2017). *The Pope and the Professor: Pius IX, Ignaz von Döllinger, and the Quandary of the Modern Age*. Oxford: Oxford University Press.

Hug, C. (1999). *The Politics of Sexual Morality in Ireland*. London: Palgrave Macmillan.

Hulatt, O. (2016). *Adorno's Theory of Philosophical Truth*. New York: Columbia University Press.

Humphreys, J. (2014). Change in 'archaic' rule on religious teaching sought: Rule 68 decrees 'religious spirit should inform and vivify whole work of school'. *The Irish Times*, 24 September. Available from <http://www.irishtimes.com/news/education/change-in-archaic-rule-on-religious-teaching-sought-1.1939144> [Accessed 9 December 2015].

Humphreys, J. (2018). Catholic Church teaching on homosexuality 'evil', McAleese says. *The Irish Times*. Available from <https://www.irishtimes.com/news/social-affairs/catholic-church-teaching-on-homosexuality-evil-mcaleese-says-1.3548765#.WziX20Wtq-B.facebook> [Accessed 2 July 2018].

Independent News Desk (2001). A special Malahide Visit – St Therese of Lisieux. *The Irish Independent*. Available from <https://www.independent.ie/regionals/fingalindependent/news/a-special-malahide-visit-st-therese-of-lisieux-27781284.html> [Accessed 10 January 2018].

Independent News Desk (2017). Varadkar and Zappone among LGBT award nominees. *The Irish Independent*. Available from <http://www.independent.ie/entertainment/going-out/varadkar-and-zappone-among-lgbt-award-nominees-36205189.html> [Accessed 10 October 2017].

Inglis, T. (1998). *Moral Monopoly: Rise and Fall of the Catholic Church in Modern Ireland*. 2nd rev. edn. Dublin: Dublin University Press.

Inglis, T. (2005). Origins and Legacies of Irish Prudery: Sexuality and Social Control in Modern Ireland. *Eire-Ireland*, Vol. 40:3–4 Fall Winter, pp. 9–37.

Inglis, T. (2012). *Making Love: A Memoir*. Dublin: New Island Books.

Ingram, D. (2017). Critical Theory and Global Development. In Thompson M.J. (ed.), *The Palgrave Handbook of Critical Theory, Political Philosophy and Public Purpose*. London: Palgrave.

Institute of Medicine (2011). *The Health of Lesbian, Gay, Bisexual and Transgender People: Building a Foundation for Better Understanding*. Washington, DC: The National Academic Press.

IPH (2016). Improving Health and Wellbeing Outcomes in the Early Years: Institute of Public Health in Ireland partnered with the Centre for Effective Services. Available from <http://www.publichealth.ie/document/iph-report/improving-health-and-wellbeing-outcomes-early-years> [Accessed 28 July 2016].

Irish Catholic Bishops' Advisory Committee (1996). *Child Sexual Abuse: Framework for a Church Response*. Dublin: Veritas Publications.

Irish Examiner (2016). Abuse redress scheme claims. Available from <http://www.irishexaminer.com/ireland/abuse-redress-scheme-claims-408130.html> [Accessed 7 July 2016].

Isay, R. A. (2009). *Being Homosexual: Gay Men and Their Development*, revised and updated. New York: Vintage.

Jackson, A. (2014). *The Oxford Handbook of Modern Irish History*. Oxford: Oxford University Press.

Jackson Nakazawa, D. (2016). *Childhood Disrupted*. London: Atria Books.

Jaeggi, R. (2018). 'Resistance to the Perpetual Danger of Relapse': Moral Progress and Social Change. In Allen, A., and Mendieta, E. (eds), *From Alienation to Forms of Life: The Critical Theory of Rahel Jaeggi*. University Park: Pennsylvania State University Press.

Jaspal R., Carriere, K.R., Moghaddam, F.M. (2015). Bridging Micro, Meso, and Macro Processes in Social Psychology. In Valsiner, J., Marsico, G. Chaudhary, N., Sato, T., Dazzani, V. (eds), *Psychology as the Science of Human Being: The Yokohama Manifesto*. London: Springer.

Jaspal, R., and Breakwell, G.M. (eds) (2014). *Identity Process Theory*. Cambridge: Cambridge University Press.

Johnson, J.G., Cohen, P., Gould, M.S., Kasen, S., Brown, J., and Brook, J.S. (2002). Childhood Adversities, interpersonal difficulties, and risk for suicide attempts during late adolescence and early adulthood. *Archives of General Psychiatry*, 59, 741–9.

Juster, R.P., et al. (2016). Social inequalities and the road to allostatic load: from vulnerability to resilience. In Cicchetti, D. (ed.), *Developmental Psychopathology: Volume 3: Maladaptation and Psychopathology*. London: Wiley.

Juster, R.P, Vencill, J.A., and Johnson J. P. (2017). Impact of Stress and Strain on Current LGBT Health Disparities. In Eckstrand, K.L., & Potter, J. (eds), *Trauma, Resilience, and Health Promotion in LGBT Patients*. New York: Springer International Publishing.

Keating, A. (2015). Censorship: The Cornerstone of Catholic Ireland. *Journal of Church and State* 57 (2) p. 289–309.

Kelly, B.D. (2014). *Ada English: Patriot and Psychiatrist*. Dublin: Irish Academic Press.

Kelly, B.D. (2015). *Dignity, Mental Health and Human Rights Coercion and the Law*. London: Routledge.

Kelly, B.D. (2016). Homosexuality and Irish psychiatry: medicine, law and the changing face of Ireland: Perspective Piece. In *Irish Journal of Psychological Medicine*, College of Psychiatrists.

Kelly, B.D. (2016a). *Mental Illness, Human Rights and the Law*. London: RC Psych Publications.

Kelly, B.D. (2016b). *Hearing Voices: The History of Psychiatry in Ireland*. Dublin: Irish Academic Press.

Kennedy, F. (2001). *Cottage to Crèche: Family Change in Ireland*. Dublin: Institute of Public Adminstration.

Kennedy, F. (2011). *Frank Duff: A Life Story*. London, Continuum.

Keogh, D., & McDonnell, A. (2011). *Cardinal Cullen and his World Dublin*. Dublin: Four Courts Press.

Keohane, K., Petersen, A., and van den Bergh, B. (2017). Introduction to a Series. In *Late Modern Subjectivity and its Discontents: Anxiety, Depression and Alzheimer's Disease*. London: Routledge.

Kerrigan, G. (1998). *Another Country: Growing Up in the '50s Ireland*. Dublin: Gill and MacMillan.

Kerrigan, G. (2018). When Victims Sue, the Bullying has to End. *Sunday Independent*, 6 May.

Kidd, I.J., Medina, J., Pohlhaus, G. (eds) (2017). *The Routledge Handbook of Epistemic Injustice*. London: Routledge.

Kilkelly, U. (2012). Learning lessons from the past: Legal issues arising from Ireland's child abuse reports. *Irish Journal of Applied Social Studies*, 12(1), 2.

Kilkelly, U., and O'Mahony, C. (2015). Submission to the Committee of Ministers of the Council of Europe under Rule 9(2) of the Rules of the Committee of Ministers for the Supervision of the execution of judgements in relation to O'Keeffe v Ireland, Application No. 35810/09, 28 January 2014 (Grand Chamber). Child Law Clinic, School of Law, University College Cork. 22 April.

King, N. (2000). Childhood Sexual Trauma in Gay Men: Social Context and the Imprinted Arousal Pattern. In Cassese, J. (ed.), *Gay Men and Childhood Sexual Trauma: Integrating the Shattered Self*. New York: Harrington Park Press.

Kirkengen, A. L., et al. (2016). Medicine's perception of reality – a split picture: critical reflections on apparent anomalies within the biomedical theory of science. *Journal of Evaluation in Clinical Practice*, 22 (2015) 496–501.

Kirmayer, L., and Gold, I. (2012). Re-Socializing Psychiatry: Critical Neuroscience and the Limits of Reductionism. In Choudury, S., and Slaby, J. (eds), *Critical Neuroscience: A Handbook of Social and Cultural Contexts of Neuroscience*. London: Blackwell Publishing.

Kitcher, P. (2011). *The Ethical Project*. Cambridge, MA: Harvard University Press.

Klein, M. (1921). The Development of a Child: The Influence of Sexual Enlightenment and Relaxation of Authority on the Intellectual Development of a Child. In *Love, Guilt and Reparation and Other Works (1921–1945)*. London: Vintage.

Knauer, N.J. (2010). *Gay and Lesbian Elders: History, Law, and Identity Politics in the United States*. London: Routledge.

Knauer, N.J. (2013). Identity/Time. In *Laws*, 2, 362–375; doi:10.3390/laws2030362.

Knaus C. (2017). 4444 victims: extent of abuse in Catholic Church in Australia Revealed. *The Guardian*. Available from <https://www.theguardian.com/australia-news/2017/feb/06/4444-victims-extent-of-abuse-in-catholic-church-in-australia-revealed> [Accessed 9 April 2017].

Kohut, H. (1971). *The Analysis of the Self: A Systematic Approach to the Psychoanalytic Treatment of Narcissistic Personality Disorders*. Chicago: Chicago University Press.

Koopman, C. (2013). *Genealogy as Critique Foucault and the Problems of Modernity*. Bloomington: Indiana University Press.

Korom, P., Lutter, M., and Beckert, J. (2017). The Enduring Importance of Family Wealth: Evidence from the Forbes 400 1982 to 2013. In *Social Science Research*, Vol. 65, July 2017, pp. 75–95.

Kreide, R. (2016). Between Morality and Law: In defence of a political conception of human rights. In *Journal of International Political Theory*, Vol. 12(1), 10–25.

Lacey, B. (2008). *Homosexuality in Irish History: Terrible Queer Creatures*. Dublin: Wordwell.

Laffan, M. (2016). *Judging W.T. Cosgrave*. Dublin: Royal Irish Academy. Kindle Edition.

Laitinen, A., and Sarkela, A. (2018). Four Conceptions of Social Pathology. In *European Journal of Social Theory*, XX(X).

Lamb, S., and Edgar-Smith, S. (1994). Aspects of Disclosure: Mediators of Outcome of childhood sexual abuse. *Journal of Interpersonal Violence*, 9, 307–26.

Lanius, R.A., Vermetten, E., and Pain, C. (2010). *The Impact of Early Life Trauma on Health and Disease: The Hidden Epidemic*. Cambridge: Cambridge University Press.

Larkin, E. (1997). *The Historical Dimensions of Irish Catholicism*. Washington, DC: Catholic University of America Press.

Larkin, E. (2011). Paul Cullen: The Great Ultramontane. In Keogh, D., & McDonnell, A. (eds), *Cardinal Paul Cullen and His World*. Dublin: Four Courts Press.

LaSalle (2016). Who We Are. Available from <http://www.lasalle.org/en/who-are-we/> [Accessed 6 April 2017].

Lennon, K., Gonzalez-Arnal, S., and Jagger, G. (2012). *Embodied Selves*. New York: Palgrave MacMillan.

LeVay, S. (1996). *Queer Science: The Use and Abuse of Research into Homosexuality*. Cambridge, MA: MIT Press.

Lew, M. (2000). Foreword: The State of the Art: Working with Gay Male Survivors of Sexual Trauma. In Cassese, J. (ed.), *Gay Men and Childhood Sexual Trauma: Integrating the Shattered Self*. New York: Harrington Park Press.

Lisak, D.L., and Luster, L. (1994). Educational, Occupational and Relationship Histories of men who were sexually and or physically abused as children. *Journal of Traumatic Stress*, 4, 507–23.

Lisdahl, K.M., Shollenbarger, S., Sagar, K.A., Gruber, S.A. (2018). The Neurocognitive Impact of Alcohol and Marijuana Use on the Developing Adolescent and Young Adult Brain. In Monti, P.M., Colby, S.M., and O'Leary-Tevyaw, T. (eds), *Brief Interventions for Adolescent Alcohol and Substance Abuse*. London: Guilford Publications.

Little, J. (2018). Five religious orders criticised for 'significant' child safeguarding weaknesses. Available from <https://www.rte.ie/news/ireland/2018/0220/942147-child-abuse-catholic-church/> [Accessed 13 March 2018].

Livingston, T. (2010). Anti-Sectarian, Queer, Client-Centredness: A Re-Iteration of Respect in Therapy. In Moon, L. (ed.), *Counselling Ideologies: Queer Challenges to Heteronormativity*. London: Ashgate.

London, B., and Rosenthal, L. (2013). The Social Stigma of Identity – and Status-Based Rejection Sensitivity. In DeWall, C.N. (ed.), *The Oxford Handbook of Social Exclusion*. Oxford: Oxford University Press.

Longford Leader (1976). Longford Family Lived in Fear: Youth Cleared of Father's Manslaughter. 12 November, front page.

Longford Leader (1984). Front Page Statement from Granard Town Commissioners with a note of support from local TD Albert Reynolds in the Aftermath of Ann Lovett, 17 February.

Lord, M. (2018). Dáil Sketch Lesbian Minister has soft kiss for gay Taoiseach. *The Irish Times*. 20 June.

Lucas, J.W., Ho, H.Y., and Kerns, K. (2018). Power, Status and Stigma: Their Implications for Health. In Major, B., Dovidio, J.E., and Link, B.G. (eds), *The Oxford Handbook of Stigma, Discrimination and Health*. Oxford: Oxford University Press.

Lucey, A., Roche, B., Smyth, P., McMahon, A. (2018). Kerry Babies: Compensation issue should be dealt with quickly. *The Irish Times*. Available from <https://

www.irishtimes.com/news/ireland/irish-news/kerry-babies-compensation-issue-should-be-dealt-with-quickly-1.3358640> [Accessed 7 February 2018].

Lukes, S. (2005). *Power: A Radical View*. 2nd edn. London: Palgrave.

Lynch, D.L., Stern, A.E., Oates, K., and O'Toole, B.I. (1993). Who participates in child sexual abuse research? *Journal of Child Psychology and Psychiatry* 34, 935–4.

Lynch, K., Cantillon, S., and Crean, M. (2016). Inequality. In Roche, W.K., O'Connell, P.J. and Prothero, A. (eds), *Austerity and Recovery in Ireland: Europe's Poster Child and the Great Recession*. Oxford: Oxford University Press.

McAdams, D. (2015). *The Art and Science of Personality Development*. London: Guildford.

McCafferty, N. (1985/2010). *A Woman to Blame: The Kerry Babies Case*. Cork: Attic Press.

McCafferty, N. (2018). The Legal Crucifixion of Joanne Hayes. *Sunday Business Post*. 21 January.

McCarthy, P. (2011). De La Salle: Character Reference for Bro. Bernard.

McCrea, R. (2009). The Recognition of Religion within the Constitutional and Political Order of the European Union. In LSE 'Europe in Question' Discussion Paper Series, London, LSE. Available from <http://www.lse.ac.uk/europeanInstitute/LEQS/LEQSPaper10.pdf> [Accessed 7 November 2015].

McCrea, R. (2010). *Religion and the Public Order of the European Union Studies in European Law*. Oxford: Oxford University Press.

McDDD (2006). Medico Legal Psychiatric Report.

MacDonald, S. (2016). Two newly announced Cardinals have links with Ireland. Available from <https://www.catholicireland.net/two-newly-announced-cardinals-links-ireland/> [Accessed 31 March 2017].

MacDonald, S. (2018). Vatican blocks McAleese from giving keynote speech 'over views on gay rights'. *The Irish Independent*. Available from <https://www.independent.ie/irish-news/vatican-blocks-mcaleese-from-giving-keynote-speech-over-views-on-gay-rights-36558790.html> [Accessed 5 February 2018].

McGahern, J. (1965/1983). *The Dark*. London: Faber and Faber.

McGahern, J. (2005). *Memoir*. London: Faber and Faber.

McGarry, F. (2014). Southern Ireland 1922–32. In Jackson, A. (ed.), *The Oxford Handbook of Modern Irish History*. Oxford: Oxford University Press.

McGarry, P. (2018). Mary McAleese: Baptised Children 'Infant Conscripts'. *The Irish Times*. Available from <https://www.irishtimes.com/news/social-affairs/religion-and-beliefs/mary-mcaleese-baptised-children-infant-conscripts-1.3540624?mode=sample&auth-failed=1&pw-origin=https%3A%2F%2Fwww.irishtimes.

com%2Fnews%2Fsocial-affairs%2Freligion-and-beliefs%2Fmary-mcaleese-
baptised-children-infant-conscripts-1.3540624#.Wy4HocDjjcU.facebook>
[Accessed 2 July 2018].

McGee, E. (1984). Editorial Comment: Ann Lovett's Decision. *Longford Leader*,
Friday, 10 February.

McGrath, M. (2016). Half of LGBT survivors of sexual violence wait over 10 years to
report the crime. *The Irish Independent*. Available from <http://www.independ
ent.ie/irish-news/half-of-lgbt-survivors-of-sexual-violence-wait-over-10-years-
to-report-the-crime-report-34873439.html> [Accessed 11 July 2016].

MacGreil, M. (1977). *Prejudice and Tolerance in Ireland*. Dublin: CIR.

McKay, S. (2018). Opinion: No, the Church Does Not Love Ireland. *The New York
Times*. Available from <https://www.nytimes.com/2018/08/27/opinion/pope-
visit-ireland.html> [Accessed 27 August 2018].

McKechnie, J.L. (sup.) (1971). *Webster's New 20th Century Dictionary of the English
Language*, 2nd edn. Cleveland, OH: World.

MacLellan, A. (2018). Preventing Tuberculosis in Twentieth-Century Ireland: BCG
Vaccination for Infants and Children. In Hatfield, M., Kruse, J., and Nic Con-
gail, R. (eds), *Historical Perspectives on Parenthood and Children in Ireland*.
Dublin: Arlen House.

McNay, L. (2012). Suffering, Silence and Social Weightlessness: Honneth and Bourdieu
on Embodiment and Power. In Gonzalez-Arnal, S., Jagger, G., Lennon, K.,
Embodied Selves. New York: Palgrave MacMillan.

McNay, L. (2014). *The Misguided Search for the Political*. London: Polity Press.

McNay, L. (2016). Agency. In Disch, L., and Hawkesworth, M. (eds), *The Oxford
Handbook of Feminist Theory*. Oxford: Oxford University Press.

Madden, A. (2003). *Altar Boy: A Story of Life after Abuse*. Dublin: Penguin.

Madden, A. (2018). As a Survivor of Abuse, the Apologies are Still Hollow: Papal
Visit Comment, *The Times*, 23 August. Available from <https://www.thetimes.
co.uk/edition/ireland/as-a-survivor-of-abuse-the-apologies-are-still-hollow-
vp3ppf9qo> [Accessed 26 August 2018].

Major, B., Dovidio, J.E., and Link, B.G. (2018). Preface in Major, B., Dovidio, J.E., and
Link, B.G. (eds), *The Oxford Handbook of Stigma, Discrimination and Health*.
Oxford: Oxford University Press.

Manning, F. (2015). De La Salle Order Correspondence. 7 October.

Marmot, M. (2015). *The Health Gap: The Challenge of an Unequal World*. London:
Bloomsbury Publishing.

Marmot, M. (2015a). The Health Gap: The Challenge of an Unequal World: Viewpoint, *The Lancet* 386: 2442–4. Published online, 10 September.

Martinez, A.G., and Hinshaw, S.P. (2016). Mental Health Stigma: Theory, Developmental Issues, and Research Priorities. In Cicchetti, D. (ed.), *Developmental Psychopathology*, 3rd edn, Volume Four: *Risk, Resilience and Intervention*. London: Wiley.

Marx, B.P., Heidt, J.M., and Gold, S.D. (2005). Perceived Uncontrollability and Unpredictability, Self-Regulation and Sexual Revictimization. *Review of General Psychology* Vol. 9, No. 1, 67–90.

Medina, J. (2017). Varieties of Hermeneutical Injustice. In Kidd, J., Medina, J. and Pohlhaus Jr, G. (eds), *The Routledge Handbook of Epistemic Injustice*. London: Routledge.

Meehan, C. (2010). *The Cosgrave Party: A History of Cumann na nGaedheal. 1923–33*. Dublin: Royal Irish Academy.

Meehan, C. (2013). *A Just Society for Ireland? 1964–87*. London: Palgrave Macmillan.

Merriman, D. (2014). *From Ireland to Alabama*. Available from <https://www.youtube.com/watch?v=7getuixVblI#t=123> [Accessed 7 November 2015].

Messler-Davies, J., and Frawley, M.G. (1994). *Treating the Adult Survivor of Childhood Sexual Abuse: A Psychoanalytic Perspective*. New York: Basic Books.

Meyer, I.H. (2007). Prejudice and Discrimination as Social Stressors. In Meyer, I. H., and Northridge, M. E. (eds), *The Health of Sexual Minorities*. London: Springer.

Miller, J.A., and Plants, N. (2014). *Sobering Wisdom Philosophical Explorations of Twelve Step Spirituality*. Charlottesville: University of Virginia Press.

Mills, C.W. (2017). Ideology. In Kidd, J., Medina, J. and Pohlhaus Jr, G. (eds), *The Routledge Handbook of Epistemic Injustice*. London: Routledge.

Monti, P.M., Colby, S.M., and O'Leary-Tevyaw, T. (2018). *Brief Interventions for Adolescent Alcohol and Substance Abuse*. London Guilford Publications.

Mukherjee, S. (2016). *The Gene: An Intimate History*. London: Bodley Head, Penguin.

Mullally, U. (2014). *In the Name of Love: The Movement for Marriage Equality in Ireland: An Oral History*. Dublin: The History Press Ireland. Kindle Edition.

Mullally, U. (2017). Preventative HIV drug must be made available. *The Irish Times*. Available from <https://www.irishtimes.com/opinion/una-mullally-preventative-hiv-drug-must-be-made-available-1.3264837> [Accessed 24 October 2017].

Murphy Report (2009). Commission of Investigation: Report into the Catholic Archdiocese of Dublin. Available from <http://www.dacoi.ie> [Accessed 11 March 2016].

Murray, P., and Feeney, M. (2017). *Church, State and Social Science in Ireland*. Manchester: Manchester University Press.

Naess, A. B., & Kirkengen, A. L. (2015). Is childhood stress associated with shorter telomeres?. 135(15), 1356–60. Available from <http://europepmc.org/abstract/med/26315236> [Accessed 12 April 2018].

Najavits, L.M. (2002). *Seeking Safety: A Treatment Manual for PTSD and Substance Abuse*. London: Guildford Press.

NBSCCC (2017). Overview Report and Review of Child Safeguarding Practice in the Institute of the Brothers of the Christian Schools undertaken by the NBSCCCI. 5 April. Available from <https://www.safeguarding.ie/news/253-overview-report-on-the-publication-of-the-final-four-review-reports> [Accessed 9 April 2017].

Neiman, S. (2002). *Evil in Modern Thought: An Alternative History of Philosophy*. Princeton, NJ: Princetown University Press.

Neiman, S. (2009). *Moral Clarity: A Guide for Grown-Up Idealists*. London: Bodley Head.

Neuberg, S.L., and Kenrick, A.C. (2018). Discriminating Ecologies: A Life History Approach to Stigma and Health. In Major, B., Dovidio, J.F. and Link, B.G. (eds), *The Oxford Handbook of Stigma, Discrimination and Health*. Oxford: Oxford University Press.

The New York Times (2017). The Lost Children of Tuam. Available from <https://www.nytimes.com/interactive/2017/10/28/world/europe/tuam-ireland-babies-children.html> [Accessed 28 October 2017].

Norris, D. (1998). The Development of the Gay Movement in Ireland: A Personal and Political Memoir. Chapter for a book published in Holland, sent to Kennedy, F. (2001), *Cottage to Crèche: Family Change in Ireland*. Dublin: Institute of Public Administration.

Norris, D. (2012). *A Kick Against The Pricks: The Autobiography*. Dublin: Transworld.

Norris, D. (2018). A Generation of Young Men Released from Shame. *The Irish Times*. 20 June.

Notre Dame School (n.d.). Our History. Available from <http://notredame.ie/content/our-history> [Accessed 12 May 2018].

Nussbaum, M. (2001). *Upheavals of Thought: The Intelligence of Emotions*. Cambridge: Cambridge University Press.

O'Callaghan, M. (2018). Murder of Declan Flynn in 1982. *Today with Miriam O'Callaghan*. Available from <https://www.rte.ie/radio/utils/radioplayer/rteradioweb.html#!rii=b9_21393973_15036_04-07-2018> [Accessed 21 August 2018].

O'Connor, P. (1998). *Emerging Voices: Women in Contemporary Irish Society*. Dublin: Institute of Public Administration.

O'Donoghue, W.T., and Ferguson, K.E. (2016). Historical and Philosophical Dimensions of Contemporary Cognitive-Behavioural Therapy. In Maguth Nezu, C., and Nezu, A.M. (eds), *Oxford Handbook of Cognitive and Behavioural Therapies*, Oxford: Oxford University Press.

Oettingen, G., and Gollwitzer, P.M. (2015). *Self-Regulation in Adolescence* (The Jacobs Foundation Series on Adolescence). Cambridge: Cambridge University Press.

O'Gorman, C. (2009). *Beyond Belief: Abused by his priest, betrayed by his church, the story of the boy who sued the pope*. London: Hodder and Stoughton.

O'Gorman, C. (2011). Preface. In Holohan, C., *In Plain Sight: Responding to the Ferns, Ryan, Murphy and Cloyne Reports*. Dublin: Amnesty International Ireland.

Ogden, P., Minton, K., Pain, C. (2006). *Trauma and the Body: A Sensorimotor Approach to Psychotherapy*. London: Norton Publishers.

O'Halloran, M., and O'Regan, M. (2018). Some of the State's founding members were gay, says Varadkar. *The Irish Times*, 20 June.

Oksala, J. (2017). Feminism, Capitalism, and the Social Regulation of Sexuality. In Bargu, B., and Bottici, C. (eds), *Feminism, Capitalism, and Critique Essays in Honor of Nancy Fraser*. New York: Palgrave MacMillan.

O'Keeffe, A. (2018). Silence is broken as Ann Lovett's boyfriend speaks. *Sunday Independent*, 6 May.

O'Keeffe vs Ireland (2014). Application No. 35810/09, 28 January 2014 (Grand Chamber).

Olson, K. (2016). *Imagined Sovereignties: The Power of the People and other Myths of the Modern Age*. Cambridge: Cambridge University Press.

O'Mahony, C. (2009). State liability for Abuse in Primary Schools: Systemic Failure and O'Keeffe v. Hickey. *Irish Educational Studies*, Vol. 28, No. 3, September 2009.

O'Mahony, C. (2018). Official Ireland remains in denial about its child abuse legacy. Available from <https://www.rte.ie/eile/brainstorm/2018/0213/940369-official-ireland-remains-in-denial-about-its-child-abuse-legacy/> [Accessed 15 February 2018].

O'Mahony, C., and Kilkelly, U. (2014). O'Keeffe v Ireland and The Duty of the State to Identify and Prevent Child Abuse. *Journal of Social Welfare & Family Law*, Vol. 36, No. 3, 320–329.

O'Neill, R. (2014). *Woman in the Making: Panti's Memoir*. Dublin: Hachette Books.

O'Neill, R. (2014a). Panti's Noble Call at the Abbey Theatre. Available from <https://www.youtube.com/watch?v=WXayhUzWnlo> [Accessed 7 November 2015].

O'Neill, R. (2015). 'All the Little Things', Panti | TEDxDublin. Available from <https://www.youtube.com/watch?v=hIhsvi8lrqY> [Accessed 1 December 2015].

O'Neill, S. (2010). Struggles against injustice: contemporary critical theory and political violence. *Journal of Global Ethics*, Vol. 6, No. 2, August 2010, 127–139.

O'Regan, M. (2014). Taoiseach says Same-Sex Marriage to be held in Spring. *The Irish Times*. Available from <http://www.irishtimes.com/news/politics/oireachtas/taoiseach-says-same-sex-marriage-referendum-to-be-held-in-spring-1.1851674> [Accessed 7 November 2015].

O'Toole, F. (1998). *The lie of the land: Irish Identities*. Dublin: New Island Books.

O'Toole, F. (2015). Opposition to social housing is matter of ideology not economics. *The Irish Times*. Available from <https://www.irishtimes.com/opinion/fintan-o-toole-opposition-to-social-housing-is-matter-of-ideology-not-economics-1.2397695#.WfQzSt72kyo.facebook> [Accessed 28 October 2017].

O'Toole, F. (2017). Ireland is still defined by the Church's mindset. *The Irish Times*. Available from <http://www.irishtimes.com/opinion/fintan-o-toole-ireland-is-still-defined-by-the-church-s-mindset-1.3008295> [Accessed 22 March 2017].

Ó Tuathaigh, G. (2018). Introduction: Ireland 1880–2016: Negotiating Sovereignty and Freedom. In Bartlett, T. (ed.), *The Cambridge History of Ireland Volume IV 1880 to the Present*. Cambridge: Cambridge University Press.

Park, A., Bryson, C., Clery, E., Curtis, J., and Phillips, M. (eds) (2013). British Social Attitudes: the 30th Report, London: Nat Center Social Research. Available from <http://www.bsa.natcen.ac.uk/media/38723/bsa30_full_report_final.pdf> [Accessed 7 November 2015].

Peakman, J. (ed.) (2011). *A Cultural History of Sexuality in the Enlightenment*. Oxford: Berg Publishers.

Perez, C., & Widom, C. (1994). Childhood Victimization and long-term intellectual and academic outcomes. *Child Abuse and Neglect* 18, 617–33.

Phelan, S. (2017). 'Big Seven' Irish law firms earned €720m last year: Huge earnings revealed in report on elite firms across Europe, writes Legal Affairs Editor Shane Phelan. *The Irish Independent*. Available from <https://www.independent.ie/irish-news/big-seven-irish-law-firms-earned-720m-last-year-36238417.html> [Accessed 23 October 2017].

Philpott, G. (1999) in Hug, C., *The Politics of Sexual Morality in Ireland*. London: MacMillan.

Pickard, H., & Ahmed, S.H. (2015). How do you know you have a drug problem? The role of knowledge of negative consequences in explaining drug choice in humans and rats. In Heather, N., and Segal, G. (eds), *Addiction and Choice: Rethinking the Relationship*. London: Oxford University Press.

Pippin, R.B. (2015). *Interanimations: Receiving Modern German Philosophy*. Chicago: Chicago University Press.

Pope Benedict XVI (2010). Pastoral Letter of the Holy Father Pope Benedict XVI to the Catholics of Ireland, 19 March.

Privilege, J. (2009). *Michael Logue and the Catholic Church in Ireland, 1879–1925*. Manchester: Manchester University Press.

PSI (2015). *Guidelines for Good Practice with Lesbian, Gay and Bisexual Clients*. Dublin: The Psychological Society of Ireland.

Putman, F.W. (1997). *Dissociation in Children and Adolescents: A Developmental Perspective*. New York: Guilford Press.

Pynoos, R.S., Steinberg, A.M., and Aronson, L. (1997). A Developmental Model of Childhood Traumatic Stress. In Cicchetti, D., and Cohen, D.J. (eds), *Developmental Psychopathology*, Vol. 2, *Risk Disorder and Adaptation*. New York: John Wiley.

Pynoos, R.S., Steinberg, A.M., and Wraith, R. (1997). Traumatic Experiences: The Early Organization of Memory in School-Age Children and Adolescents. In Appelbaum, P., Elin, P.M., and Uyehara, L. (eds), *Trauma and Memory: Clinical and Legal Controversies* (pp. 272–88). New York: Oxford University Press.

Rabbitte, P. (2018). When Theocracy, not Democracy, Ruled Ireland. *Sunday Business Post*, Kerry Babies (p. 7), 21 January.

Raftery, M., & O'Sullivan, E. (1999). *Suffer the Little Children: The Inside Story of Ireland's Industrial Schools*. Dublin: New Island Books.

Redmond, P. (2015). Screaming Rooms and Banished Babies: The sad history of where I was born. Available from <http://www.thejournal.ie/castlepollard-mother-and-baby-home-2040421-Apr2015/> [Accessed 12 January 2016].

Renault, E. (2017). *Sociology, Psychology, Politics*. London: Rowman and Littlefield.

Rensmann, L. (2017). Critical Theory of Human Rights. In Thompson, M.J. (ed.), *The Palgrave Handbook of Critical Theory, Political Philosophy and Public Purpose*. London: Palgrave.

Riggs, D. W. (2015). Gay Men. In Richards, C., and Barker, M. (eds), *The Palgrave Handbook of the Psychology of Sexuality and Gender*. London: Palgrave.

Road to Equality Exhibition (2016a). The Early Years: 1970s and 1980s Activism. Sponsored by Dublin City Council, LGBT Federation and Dialogue and Diversity.

Road to Equality Exhibition (2016b). Crisis in the Community: HIV and AIDS. Sponsored by DCC, National LGBT Federation & Dialogue & Diversity.

Roberts, J., and Hawton, K. (1990). Child Abuse and Attempted Suicide. *British Journal of Psychiatry*, 137, 319–23.

Robinson, M. (2012). *Everybody Matters: A Memoir*. London: Houghton & Stoughton.

Robson, C. (1995). Anatomy of a Campaign. In O'Carroll, I., and Collins, E. (eds), *Lesbian and Gay Visions of Ireland: Towards the Twenty-First Century*. London: Cassell Press.

Rochat, P. (2009). *Others in Mind: Social Origins of Self-Consciousness*. Cambridge: Cambridge University Press.

Rochat, P. (2013). The Gaze of Others. In Banaji, M.R., and Gelman, S.A. (eds), *Navigating the Social World: What Infants, Children, and Other Species Can Teach Us*. Oxford: Oxford Oxford University Press.

Rochat, P. (2014). *Origins of Possession: Owning and Sharing in Development*. Cambridge: Cambridge University Press.

Rodgers, G. (2018). *Being Gay in Ireland: Resisting Stigma in the Evolving Present.* Lanham, MD: Lexington Books.

Rodley (2014). Catholic belief system in Ireland and human rights abuses from child abuse to Symphysiotomy. Available from <https://www.youtube.com/watch?v=XwK-XVBw6ec> [Accessed 16 December 2015].

Rohsenow, D.J., Corbett, R., and Devine, D. (1988). Molested as Children: A hidden contribution to Substance Abuse? *Journal of Substance Abuse Treatment*, 5, 13–18.

Rose, K. (1994). *Diverse Communities: The Evolution of Lesbian and Gay Politics in Ireland.* Cork: Cork University Press.

Rose, N., and Abi-Rached, J.M. (2013). *Neuro: The New Brain Sciences and the Management of the Mind.* Princeton, NJ: Princetown University Press.

Rosenberg, H.J., Jankowski, M.K., Sengupta, A., Wolfe, R.S., Wolford, G.L., and Rosenberg, S.D. (2005). Single and Multiple Suicide Attempts and Associated Health Risk Factors in New Hampshire Adolescents. *Suicide and Life-Threatening Behaviour*, 35, 547–57.

RTÉ News (2016). Taoiseach says Pope will visit Ireland in 2018. Available from <https://www.rte.ie/news/2016/1128/834873-pope-kenny-church-vatican/> [Accessed 31 March 2017].

RTÉ News (2016a). Government Accused of Denying Abuse Victims Justice. Available from <http://www.rte.ie/news/2016/0729/805719-abuse/> [Accessed 29 July 2016].

RTÉ News (2018). McAleese says Pope Francis has not acknowledged her letter <https://www.rte.ie/news/ireland/2018/0312/946776-mary-mcaleese-catholic-church/> [Accessed 12 March 2018].

Ryan, P. (2011). *Asking Angela Macnamara: An Intimate History of Irish Lives.* Dublin: Irish Academic Press.

Ryan, R.M., and Deci, E. (2017). *Self-Determination Theory: Basic Psychological Needs in Motivation, Development and Wellness.* London: Guildford Press.

Ryan, S. (2009). Commission to Inquire into Child Abuse Report. Dublin.

St Augustine (1992). *The Confessions*, trans. H. Hadwick. New York: Oxford University Press.

Salverda, W., Nolan, B., and Smeeding, T.M. (2009). *The Oxford Handbook of Economic Inequality.* Oxford: Oxford University Press.

Sanderson, C. (2006). *Counselling Adult Survivors of Child Sexual Abuse*, 3rd edn. London: JKP Publishers.

Sangiovanni, A. (2017). *Humanity without Dignity Moral Equality, Respect, and Human Rights.* Cambridge, MA: Harvard University Press.

Savin-Williams, R. C. (1998). *'And then I became gay': Young men's stories.* London: Routledge.

Schaffer, H.R. (2004). *Introducing Child Psychology*. Oxford: Blackwell Publishing.

Schmidt, J., Bro. (2012). *Walking the Little Way of Therese of Lisieux: Discovering the Path of Love*. Frederick, MD: The Word Among Us Press. Kindle Edition.

Schmidt, J., Bro. (2013). Walking the Little Way of Thérèse of Lisieux, Part 1. Available from <https://www.youtube.com/watch?v=wsH7VWGH_8w&t=5s> [Accessed 10 January 2018].

Schwartz, H. L. (2000). *Dialogues with Forgotten Voices*. London: Basic Books.

Scottish Bishops' General Assembly (2009). 'For Such is the Kingdom of Heaven – Creating a Church where all may safely live'. Joint Report of the Mission and Discipleship Council and the Safeguarding Committee/Forgiveness Working Group.

Siggins, L. (2016). Zappone backs dig at Tuam Mother and Baby home burial site. *The Irish Times*. Available from <http://www.irishtimes.com/news/ireland/irish-news/zappone-backs-dig-at-tuam-mother-and-baby-home-burial-site-1.2812440> [Accessed 22 March 2017].

Singer, M. (1996). A dose of drugs, a touch of violence, a case of AIDS: Conceptualizing the SAVA syndemic. *Free Inquiry in Creative Sociology* 24(2), 99–110.

Shahar, G. (2015). *Erosion: The Psychopathology of Self-Criticism*. Oxford: Oxford University Press.

Shannonside Radio (2015). Bishop of Ardagh and Clonmacnoise apologises for alleged abuse of former Ballymahon priest. Available from <http://www.shannonside.ie/news/bishop-of-ardagh-and-clonmacnoise-apologises-for-alleged-abuse-of-former-ballymahon-priest/> [Accessed 16 December 2015].

Shim, R.S., Compton, M.T. (eds) (2015). The Social Determinants of Mental Health: From Evidence to Policy. In *The Social Determinants of Mental Health*. Washington, DC: American Psychiatric Publishing.

Shim, R.S., Koplan, C., Frederick, J.P., Langheim, M.D., Manseau, M.W., Powers, R.A., Compton, M.T. (2014). The Social Determinants of Mental Health: An Overview and Call to Action. *Psychiatric Annals*. 2014; 44(1):22–6, <https://doi.org/10.3928/00485713-20140108-04>.

Shneidman, E. (1985). *Definition of Suicide*. Chichester: Wiley Publishers.

Slaby, J., and Choudhury, S. (2018). Proposal for a Critical Neuroscience. In Meloni, M., Cromby, J., Fitzgerald, D., and Lloyd, S. (eds), *The Palgrave Handbook of Biology and Society*. London: Palgrave.

Smith. N.H., and O'Neill, S. (2012). Introduction: A Recognition-Theoretical Research Program for the Social Sciences. In O'Neill, S., Smith, N.H. (eds), *Recognition Theory as Social Research: Investigating the Dynamics of Social Conflict*. Basingstoke: Palgrave McMillan.

Spiegel, J. (2003). *Sexual Abuse of Males*. London: Routledge.

Stahl, T. (2017). Collective Responsibility for Oppression. In *Social Theory and Practice*, Vol. 43. No. 3 (July 2017).

Staines, M. (2018). Health Minister launches impassioned call for repeal of the Eighth Amendment. Available from <http://www.newstalk.com/Health-Minister-launches-impassioned-call-for-repeal-of-the-Eighth-Amendment> [Accessed 9 April 2018].

Stepien, A. (2017). *Shame, Masculinity and Desire of Belonging: Reading Contemporary Male Writers*. Oxford: Peter Lang.

Stenner, P. (2015). A Transdisciplinary Psychosocial Approach. In Martin, J., Sugarman, J., and Slaney, K.L. (eds), *The Wiley Handbook of Theoretical and Philosophical Psychology: Methods, Approaches, and New Directions for Social Sciences* (p. 308). London: Wiley.

Stringer, R. (2014). *Knowing Victims: Feminism, Agency and Victim Politics in Neoliberal Times*. London: Routledge.

Sugarman, J. (2015). History Ontology. In Martin, J., Sugarman, J., and Slaney, K.L. (eds), *The Wiley Handbook of Theoretical and Philosophical Psychology: Methods, Approaches, and New Directions for Social Sciences*. London: Wiley.

Sunday Business Post (2018). Generation Yes. 27–8 May 2018. Michael Brennan and Hugh O'Connell.

Sweeney, E. (2010). *Down, Down, Deeper and Down: Ireland in the 70s and 80s*. Dublin: Gill and Macmillan

Talbot, W.J. (2005). *Which Rights Should be Universal*. Oxford: Oxford University Press.

Tatchell, P. (1972). Aversion Therapy 'is like a visit to the dentist'. *Gay News*, No. 11. Available from <http://www.petertatchell.net/lgbt_rights/psychiatry/dentist.htm> [Accessed 9 July 2017].

Teicher, M.H., et al. (2010). Neurobiology of childhood trauma and adversity. In Lanius, R.A., Vermetten, E., Pain, C. (eds), *The Impact of Early Life Trauma on Health and Disease: The Hidden Epidemic*. Cambridge: Cambridge University Press.

The Telegraph (2010). Cardinal Cahal Daly (Obituary). Available from <http://www.telegraph.co.uk/news/obituaries/religion-obituaries/6921746/Cardinal-Cahal-Daly.html> [Accessed 16 December 2015].

Terr, L. (1990). *Too Scared To Cry*. New York: Basic Books.

Terry, K.J., et al. (2011). The Causes and Context of Sexual Abuse of Minors by Catholic Priests in the United States, 1950–2010. Available from <http://www.bishop-accountability.org/reports/2011_05_18_John_Jay_Causes_and_Context_Report.pdf> [Accessed 4 August 2016].

Teunis, N., and Herdt, G. (2007). *Sexual Inequalities and Social Justice*. Berkeley: University of California Press.

Tighe-Mooney, S. (2018). *What About Me? Women and the Catholic Church*. Cork: Mercier Press.

Tileaga, C. (2015). *The Nature of Prejudice: Society, Discrimination & Moral Exclusion*. London: Routledge.

Tileaga, C. (2018). Extending the Social Psychology of Racism: A Framework for Critical Analysis. In Hammack, P.L., *The Oxford Handbook of Social Psychology and Social Justice*. Oxford: Oxford University Press.

This Week (2018). Seán Faloon Child abuse victim, Seán Faloon on why he backs Mary McAleese's call for Pope Francis to visit Newry. Available from <http://www.rte.ie/radio/utils/radioplayer/rteradioweb.html#!rii=b9%5F21331317%5F72%5F11%2D03%2D2018%5F> [Accessed 13 March 2018].

Thompson, J. (2018). 'Better Together': RISN reaches out to Longford survivors of institutional abuse. *Longford Leader*. Available from <https://www.longfordleader.ie/news/local-news/293298/better-together-risn-reaches-out-to-longford-survivors-of-institutional-abuse.html#.WmrmCCYTyw8.facebook> [Accessed 26 January 2018].

Thompson, M.J. (2013). *The Domestication of Critical Theory*. London: Rowman and Littlefield.

Thompson, M.J. (2013a). Alienation as Atrophied Moral Cognition and its Implications for Political Behavior. *Journal for the Theory of Social Behaviour* 43, 3.

Thompson, M.J. (2017). Introduction: What Is Critical Theory? In Thompson, M.J. (ed.), *The Palgrave Handbook of Critical Theory, Political Philosophy/Public Purpose*. London: Palgrave.

Thompson, M.J. (2018). Hierarchy, Social Pathology and the Failure of Recognition Theory. In the *European Journal of Social Theory* XX(X).

Thompson, M.J. (2018a). The Political Dimensions of Economic Division: Republicanism, Social Justice and the Evaluation of Economic Inequality. Available from <https://www.academia.edu/17068465/The_Political_Dimensions_of_Economic_Division_Republicanism_Social_Justice_and_the_Evaluation_of_Economic_Inequality> [Accessed 25 August 17].

Thompson, M. J. (2018b). The Failure of the Recognition Paradigm in Critical Theory. In Schmitz, V. (ed.), *Axel Honneth and the Critical Theory of Recognition, Political Philosophy and Public Purpose*. London: Palgrave MacMillan.

Thompson, M. J. (forthcoming). Reification, Values and Norms: Toward a Critical Theory of Consciousness. In G. Smulewicz-Zucker (ed.), *Confronting Reification: The Revitalization of a Concept in Late Capitalism*. Leiden: Brill Publishing.

Toews, J. (2004). *Becoming Historical*. Cambridge: Cambridge University Press.

Towey, J. (1980). *Irish De La Salle Brothers in Christian Education*. Dublin: De La Salle Provincialate.

Tyrrell, P. (2006). *Founded on Fear*. Dublin: Irish Academic Press.

UCC Child Law Clinic (2015). Child Law Clinic helps secure landmark Human Rights Judgment. Available from <https://www.ucc.ie/en/childlawclinic/news/louiseokeeffejudgment/fullstory-417668-en.html>. Accessed 30 April 2016.

Van der Kolk, B.A., McFarlane, A.C., and Weisaeth, L. (eds) (1996). *Traumatic Stress*. New York: Guilford Press.

Vatican (1979). Holy Mass for the Youth of Ireland: Homily of his Holiness John Paul II. Available from <http://w2.vatican.va/content/john-paul-ii/en/homilies/1979/documents/hf_jp-ii_hom_19790930_irlanda-galway-giovani.html> [Accessed 8 January 2015].

Vatican Information Service (2011). Pope Benedict XVI on St. Therese of Lisieux and the Little Way. Available from <http://www.catholic.org/news/saints/story.php?id=40962> [Accessed 10 January 2018].

Vazquez-Arroyo, A. (2016). *Political Responsibility: Responding to Predicaments of Power*. New York: Columbia University Press.

Vocations Ireland. Notre Dame des Missions (Our Lady of the Missions). Available from <http://www.vocationsireland.com/notre-dame-des-missions/> [Accessed 12 May 2018].

Vogelmann, F. (2018). *The Spell of Responsibility: Labour, Criminality, Philosophy*. Trans. Steuer, D. London: Rowman and Littlefield International.

Volpp, L. (2017). Feminist, Sexual and Queer Citizenship. In Shachar, A, Baubock, R., Bloemraad, I, Vink, M. (eds), *The Oxford Handbook of Citizenship* (Oxford Handbooks in Law). Oxford: Oxford University Press

Wall, T. (2013). *The Boy from Glin Industrial School*. Amazon EU Media, Kindle Edition.

Walsh, D. (2017). Mental health services in Ireland, 1959–2010. In Prior, P.M. (ed.), *Asylums, Mental Health Care and the Irish: 1800–2010*. Dublin: Irish Academic Press.

Walsh, J. (2015). Remembering Pope John Paul II's 1979 visit to Ireland. *Irish Central News*. Available from <http://www.irishcentral.com/news/remembering-pope-john-paul-ii-1979-visit-to-ireland-62563642-237662091.html> [Accessed 16 December 2015].

Walsh, W. (2016). *No Crusader Blackrock*. Dublin: Columbia Press.

Warner, S. (2009). *Understanding the Effects of Child Sexual Abuse: Feminist Revolutions in Theory, Research and Practice*. London: Routledge.

Widom, C.S., Weller, B.L., Cottler, L.B. (1999). Childhood Victimisation and Drug Abuse: A Comparison of Prospective and Retrospective. *Journal of Consulting and Clinical Psychology* 62, 1167–76.

Whitlock, J., and Selekman, M.D. (2014). Non-Suicidal Self-Injury Across the Lifespan. In Nock, M.K. (ed.), *The Oxford Handbook of Suicide and Self-Injury*. Oxford: Oxford University Press.

WHO (2013). Mental Health Action Plan 2013–20. World Health Organization.

Wilkinson, R.G. (2005). *The Impact of Inequality: How to Make Sick Societies Healthier*. London: Routledge.

Wilson, E.O. (2017). *The Origins of Creativity*. London: Allen Lane Publishing.

WPA (2016). WPA Position Statement on Gender Identity and Same-Sex Orientation, Attraction, and Behaviours, WPA. Available from <http://www.wpanet. org/detail.php?section_id=7&content_id=1807> [Accessed 24 March 2016].

Zappone, K. (2017). Remarks by Minister for Children and Youth Affairs, Dr. Katherine Zappone Dáil Statements on the Announcement by the Commission of Investigation confirming human remains on the Site of the former Tuam Mother and Baby Home. Available from <https://www.dcya.gov.ie/viewdoc. asp?DocID=4155> [Accessed 22 March 2017].

De La Salle Brothers Australia: Alan's Story

In an article from *Broken Rites Australia*, entitled 'The De La Salle Brothers had a sex abuser to recruit new Brothers,' 'Alan's Story' is cited in full:

My father died, from an illness, in 1941, when I was seven, and my mother had to go to work to support my two young sisters – the younger sister had just been born. My baby sister was put into foster care, and a very devout Catholic aunt of mine arranged for me to be put into the 'care' of the De La Salle Brothers as a boarder at St Bede's for a year. My aunt said that the saintly Brothers could be trusted to look after me well.

I was delivered to St Bede's (about 20 kilometres away from my family's house) after dark on the first Sunday night in February 1942. This was two days before classes began. Aged 7, I was due to start Grade 3, which was the youngest grade at St Bede's. I was one of the youngest boys in the school and possibly the youngest boarder.

When I arrived, it was already past bed-time. The first (and only) adult I encountered there on that evening was Brother Fintan. He was not to be my class teacher but, as he was in charge of boarders, he took me to a small bedroom containing four beds. A couple of other young boys, who had arrived on the Sunday, like me, were already in bed in that room. Brother Fintan told me to get undressed and get into bed.

Still grieving over the death of my father (and grieving over the separation from my mother), I burst into tears. Brother Fintan ordered me to stop crying. While I was half undressed, he dragged me to a bathroom, where he clumsily interfered with my genitals, while I cried and struggled. I knew, even then, that he was breaking the rules that my Catholic parents had taught me. I now know that his action was a criminal offence, called an indecent assault. I also now realize that I was not the only boy whom he assaulted in this way.

Finally, giving up on me, he ordered me back to bed, while I was still sobbing. Just then, another Brother came to the bedroom and asked Brother Fintan why I was crying. Fintan replied that I was a naughty boy and had been punished. Fintan had a perverted idea of punishment.

Throughout the year, as a boarder, I was under Fintan's authority at all times outside the classroom, including an hour every evening while the primary-age boarders had to sit silently in a classroom until bedtime. Fintan never touched me again sexually but, throughout the year, he continued labelling me as naughty, as though it was I, not he, who was the offender. This prevented me from telling anybody about the sexual attack because any complaint would have resulted in me being punished for defaming a Brother.

I have learned that Brother Fintan was aged 36 when I encountered him – about the same age as my father. Fintan's role was to supervise me as a replacement for my deceased father. The contrast between the abusive Fintan and my loving father made me grieve for my father even more.

I was unable to tell anybody about Fintan's sexual attack. There was a prohibition on saying anything negative about the Brothers. Anyway, there was nobody to whom I could complain. When I went home for the Easter break and for the end-of-term holidays, I knew that I was not allowed to tell my mother. Anyway, she would not have believed that a Catholic religious Brother would do such a thing. Even if she did believe me, the news would hurt her and make her feel guilty for having agreed to send me to St Bede's. So, like most other young church-abuse victims, I remained silent – and feeling hurt. I was feeling hurt not only by Fintan's assault but also by the cover-up and by the gullibility of my relatives. I was also badly damaged and I had to make desperate efforts to survive. In fact, survival has been the main driving force in my life ever since then.

At the end of the year at St Bede's, when I was just eight, my mother had recovered sufficiently from her bereavement to take me back to our house in inner-Melbourne with my sisters. I then transferred to a local parish school to do Grade 4. But I have never recovered from the cruelty and hypocrisy that I encountered under Brother Fintan Dwyer, during my time of bereavement, at the age of seven. I felt hurt not only by the clumsy sexual attack but also by the whole year of neglect and emotional cruelty. The neglect and cruelty were more damaging than the sexual attack. I was also hurt by the cover-up and the hypocrisy.

After I returned to my mother, she forced me to keep going to Mass and Confession throughout my school years but (in order to evade this) I left school at 14 and left home at 16 and took jobs in the country, living in boarding houses. I was forced to raise myself. My experience of child-abuse at St Bede's (and the cover-up) left me cautious about trusting anybody ever again. I became a loner and my main instinct was survival.

In my late teens, I studied part-time on my own, and qualified for university entrance at age 21, gaining a government scholarship to study for a Bachelor of Arts degree. I then did post-graduate research, gaining higher degrees. Thereafter, I had a career as a fulltime academic and researcher in social studies. I achieved these things on my own, despite my Catholic upbringing, not because of it.

Later, when I had children of my own, the cruelty and neglect of 1942 became even clearer to me. When my children were in their teens, I told them about 1942 and the cover-up.

My mother was always hurt by the fact that I steered clear of the Catholic Church and that I sent my children to government schools. In 1980, when I was 45, I finally told my mother, then aged 70, about the reality of 1942. She was devastated by the news and she felt guilty. She stopped attending the Catholic Church and changed to another denomination. She never went near a Catholic church again. The loss of her trust in the Catholic Church was a great upheaval for her. Later she developed dementia, so she had forgotten my story by the time she died.

But I will never forget. And I will never forgive the Catholic cover-up and hypocrisy.

BRA (2015). De La Salle Brothers had a sex-abuser to recruit new Brothers. Available from <http://www.brokenrites.org.au/drupal/node/30> [Accessed 8 March 2016].

Index